Wage Regula[illegible] in Pre-Industr[illegible] England

The control of wages is a perennial problem of modern government, and indeed one of the main economic issues of today. Four centuries ago our ancestors were also endeavouring, by provisions such as those in the Statute of Artificers of 1563, to control wages.

The two classic studies of this policy have long been difficult to obtain. Professor R. H. Tawney's discussion of 'The assessment of wages in England by the justices of the peace' was published in a German economic quarterly with a limited circulation in 1914, and Professor R. K. Kelsall's book, *Wage Regulation under the Statute of Artificers*, published in 1938, has been out of print for some time.

These two accounts are now brought together and prefaced by an introductory essay by Professor W. E. Minchinton, which sets the discussion of the question in the light of modern research.

£4.20 net
in UK only

ISBN 0 7153 4893 0

WAGE REGULATION
in Pre-Industrial England

WAGE REGULATION: ERRATUM SLIP

The following two lines should appear on p112 at the beginning of the final paragraph, following line 30:

Cases of accepting more than the assessed rates are even less common. The North Riding records (excluding the abnormal period of the early

Edited and introduced by
W. E. MINCHINTON

Comprising works by
R. H. TAWNEY and
R. KEITH KELSALL

WAGE REGULATION in Pre-Industrial England

DAVID & CHARLES : NEWTON ABBOT

ISBN 0 7153 4893 0

Set in 10/12pt Press Roman and printed in Great Britain by Redwood Press Limited, Trowbridge and London for David & Charles (Publishers) Limited South Devon House Newton Abbot Devon

CONTENTS

ACKNOWLEDGEMENTS

We wish to thank the following for permission to reproduce the material listed below:

Professor Tawney's literary executor and the editor for R.H. Tawney, 'The assessment of wages in England by the justices of the peace', *Vierteljahrschrift fur Sozial – und Wirtschaftsgeschichte,* XI (1914), 307-37 and 533-64.

Associated Book Publishers for R.K. Kelsall, *Wage regulation under the Statute of Artificers* (Methuen, 1938).

The editor for R.K. Kelsall, 'A century of wage assessment in Herefordshire', *English Historical Review,* LVII (1942), 115-119.

In reprinting Professor Kelsall's book, three changes have been made. First, because the notes are printed here as endnotes rather than footnotes some of the footnote material has been incorporated in the text in order that the endnotes shall only contain references and not discussion. Secondly, the list of wage assessments has been revised to include all assessments known to January 1970. Thanks are due to all the archivists and librarians who so readily co-operated in this revision. And, thirdly, the bibliography has also been extended to include more recent material. The compilation of the new list of assessments and the revision of the bibliography are the work of Celia M.King.

LIST OF ABBREVIATIONS

CR	County Records
EcHR	*Economic History Review*
EHR	*English History Review*
EJ	*Economic Journal*
HMC	*Historical Manuscripts Commission*
NRQSR	John C. Atkinson, ed. *North Riding Quarter Sessions Records, 1605-1786* (North Riding Record Society, old series, I-IX, 1884-1892)
QS	Quarter Sessions
VCH	*Victoria County History*
WRS	West Riding Sessions

WAGE REGULATION IN PRE-INDUSTRIAL ENGLAND

W. E. MINCHINTON

Introduction

Wage regulation in pre-industrial England

In the 1960s popular concern about the persistence of inflation led to pressure for the control of prices and incomes and the government attempted to regulate wage and salary increases and to control prices. Four centuries ago England faced somewhat similar problems – a price inflation of unprecedented proportions and a pressure for wage increases in the context of a disturbed international trading situation when, after the close of the Antwerp market, overseas sales became more difficult. Matters came to a head early in 1563. During a brief session in the spring of that year parliament passed fourteen statutes in a flurry of legislation to deal with the situation. Among these acts were a poor law, a navy act, a fish act, acts prohibiting the import of unnecessary articles, an act to encourage husbandry and an act to license middlemen, such as corn badgers and cattle drovers. But undoubtedly the major achievement of the session was the 'Act touching divers Orders for Artificers, Labourers, Servants of Husbandry, and Apprentices' which is known to us as the Statute of Artificers.[1] This Act (5 Eliz c 4)[2] became the main instrument of Elizabethan policy in the field of labour.

In considering the legislation of the 1563 parliament thirty years ago, Professor Fisher suggested that the Statute of Artificers might be considered as 'a classic example of the restrictive legislation which great depressions tend to produce'.[3] More recently he has discussed the enactments of 1563 in the context of the demographic history of the third quarter of the sixteenth century. 'It has never been easy', he has written, 'to reconcile these statutes with each other or with the commercial depression which obtained when they were under discussion. ... Yet a sudden fall in population would provide a reconciliation of a sort. A decline in the number of adults would not only make labour scarce and wages high but would also leave a larger number of dependents to be cared for by means of poor relief; the fall in the number of adults would depress the price of corn as well as raise the price of labour; and dearer labour might well encourage a switch from arable to pasture despite the sluggishness of wool and textile prices. At least, no student of the period', Professor Fisher concluded in characteristic vein, 'ought to be surprised or shocked by the suggestion that the famous Statute of Apprentices is as likely to have been the result of an epidemic of influenza as of a sudden outbreak of the intellectual malady known as "mercantilism" '.[4]

For contemporaries, as the preamble suggests, this statute, which drew heavily on precedent, was probably little more for the most part than a convenient summary and restatement of laws already on the statute book:

> So if the substance of the said laws as are meet to be continued shall be digested and reduced into one sole law and statute; and in the same an uniform order presented and limited concerning the wages and other orders for apprentices, servants and labourers, there is good hope that it will come to pass that the same law, being duly executed should banish idleness, advance husbandry and yield unto the hired person both in time of scarcity and in time of plenty a convenient proportion of wages.

Although it was enacted to deal with an emergency, this particular act had a much longer-run significance than the rest of the legislation of the 1563 parliament.

I The Statute of Artificers

This elaborate industrial code, which had five main parts and forty clauses,[5] was based on the medieval notion of the universal obligation to work.[6] Since agriculture provided the necessities of life, two sections were devoted to ensuring that there were sufficient able-bodied men to work on the land. One, by laying down that all 'artificers and persons as be meet to labour' should be obliged to work in the field at harvest time if needed, provided for a temporary augmentation of the labour supply. The other, attempting to ensure a sufficient permanent labour force for agriculture, ordained that all unmarried persons and all young poor who were not employed in certain occupations could be compelled to work for a farmer.[7] Thirdly, in an attempt to reduce the mobility of labour since men on the move were potentially a threat to the Tudor state, the act provided that workers in a wide range of occupations should be hired for periods of not less than one year. It also laid down methods of engagement, hours of labour and means of giving notice and provided that every person seeking employment had to produce a certificate from his last master. The final two provisions were more important. The act was concerned to regulate the course of industrial training by establishing nationally the principle of apprenticeship for at least seven years, a practice which had previously been subject to municipal or gild control. It also provided that superior callings such as those of clothier, goldsmith or merchant were to be confined as far as possible to the sons of the wealthier sections of the population.[8] By the same token the act attempted to raise the level of craftsmanship, to impose a brake on the occupational mobility of labour and to restrict the flow of labour into industry.[9]

Finally, the act dealt with the question of wage assessment. In the preamble the ground had been cleared by a provision for the repeal of previous statutes because they had fixed maximum rates which were now held to be too low and 'not answerable to the time respecting the advancement of prices of all things'. Then, in clause XI, it provided for the annual review each Easter or thereabouts of wages by justices of the peace in the counties and by mayors, bailiffs and other chief officers in cities and corporate towns taking into account 'the plenty or scarcity of the time'. Professor Tawney has suggested that because the agricultural wage labourers had many alternatives to working for wages there probably was a real labour shortage. While the extent to which agricultural labourers had other reliable sources of sustenance needs to be probed, a contributory factor in the situation must have been the temporary but sizeable drop in the population in the early 1560s.[10] The assessed wages were therefore to be maximum wages, ie the wages actually paid. The act also provided for penalties for breaches of these provisions. This new system of assessment in the localities by justices therefore provided a more flexible basis of wage determination than the older statutes of labourers which had attempted to fix a uniform rate for the whole country. But, it should be noted, wage assessment remained in the hands of the justices who were at the same time the magistrates, the police, the army recruiting officials, and the landlords.

In general the act was a conservative measure which attempted to slow down the pace of economic change. The major principles of apprenticeship and wage assessment which it reaffirmed were of some, albeit diminishing, significance for two centuries or more. But so complicated were some of its detailed provisions that they became almost immediately inoperative. The requirement, for example, which gave labourers virtually a twelve-hour day in summer while laying down that they should be at their work in winter, with provision for meal-times, 'from the springe of the daye in the morninge untill the nyght of the same daye' did not attract much attention while the provisions for compulsory harvest service were largely ignored.[11] Later, in 1694, the rules for training apprentices in the rural woollen industry were abolished since they had 'been found to be very inconvenient and a great prejudice to the clothing trade'.[12]

As far as the clauses relating to wage assessment are concerned, some doubt seems to have grown up in the later sixteenth century about the scope of the statute. Did the clauses cover 'all manner of artificers, workmen and workwomen' or only 'such as did work in husbandry'? A bill drafted to deal with this problem in 1593 did not become law[13] but in 1597 an act was passed which clearly laid down that the justices of the peace and the town authorities had power to assess the 'wages of any labourers, weavers, spinsters and workmen or workwomen whatsoever, either working by day, week, month, year or taking any work at any person or persons' hands whatsoever be done'.[14] This position was confirmed by a further act of 1604[15] which, in the context of difficult trading conditions in the domestic woollen textile industry leading to pressure to reduce costs, made two significant changes. It provided for the assessment of minimum (rather than maximum) wages for workers in the textile industry and it provided that 'no clothier being a justice of the peace ... shall be any rater of any wages for any weaver, tucker, spinster or other artisan that dependeth upon the making of cloth'. The act required the rates to be engrossed on parchment, signed and sealed by the justices making the rate, and to be kept by the custos rotulorum with the other county records. Apart from one or two minor changes in the reigns of Charles II and William III, the wage provisions of the 1563 act remained on the statute book until their repeal in 1813.

In later discussions of the three major aspects of the 1563 statute, the first, the control of the contract of service which involved restricting the mobility of all labour with a view to ensuring a sufficient supply of workers for agriculture and so bring about a situation of stable and regular employment, has been largely ignored, although the so-called piece-worker clause which enabled justices of the peace to punish by imprisonment craftsmen who left their work unfinished was enforced until the middle of the nineteenth century.[16] Rather, discussion has been concentrated on the two other aspects. On the second issue, that of apprenticeship, there have been several studies, notably those by O.J. Dunlop,[17] by T.K. Derry[18] and by Margaret Gay Davies.[19] The major assessments of the wage regulation aspect of the 1563 statute, an article by R.H. Tawney and a book by R.K. Kelsall, are printed below.[20]

II The debate about the statute

Towards the end of the nineteenth century Thorold Rogers initiated a debate on the 1563 act. For him the statute, the most powerful instrument devised for degrading and impoverishing the English labourer, was a deliberate conspiracy on the part of employers and landlords 'to cheat the English workman of his wages, to tie him to the soil, to deprive him of hope, and to degrade him into irremediable poverty'.[21] In the course of the discussion which ensued, three main points emerged. First, it became clear that wage regulation was by no means a unique phenomenon confined to sixteenth-century England but that similar policies had been adopted from time to time in France, Germany, Italy, the Netherlands and Spain.[22] Further, the statute itself was not an innovation for wage assessment had been carried on for many years before it was placed on the statute book. And, thirdly, on the basis of the forty-seven wage assessments then available, Cunningham recorded a decided dissent from Thorold Rogers' view that the clauses were used by the justices for the degredation of the English labourer and argued instead that they were practically a dead letter.[23] For his part, W.A.S. Hewins asserted that while the justices did from time to time attempt to enforce the wage regulation clauses, there was no continuous attempt to administer the law in this respect. Finally, he argued that far from leading to a reduction in income, the effect of the statute was to raise wages.[24]

The next contribution to the debate was made by the late Professor Tawney in the article printed below. After setting out the pedigree of the 1563 act, he discussed the extent of enforcement, distinguishing between the textile trades and the non-textile trades and attempted to gauge the effect of assessment on wages but confining his attention to the century and a half after the act was passed. At some points his language dates his article. He speaks, for example, of 'the great industry' and 'the distributive state', terms taken from the contemporary arguments about political, economic and social questions in which Tawney was interested.[25] Exactly why Tawney published this work in a German historical periodical is not known but it probably happened as a result of some time Tawney had spent in Germany. But it was a decision which resulted in the comparative neglect of this article which is not mentioned, for example, in the festschrift compiled in his honour.[26]

The intellectual roots of Tawney's interest were two-fold.[27] First, as reference to both the inaugural lecture to the Ratan Tata Foundation which he delivered in 1913[28] and to the introductions to the two studies on the chainmaking industry and the tailoring trades show,[29]

Tawney was emphasising at this time that the period of free wage-bargaining in England had been very short indeed. It only ran from 1824 when Parliament abolished the last working remnants of the old regime until 1909 when the Trades Boards Act was passed.[30] Compared with this brief interlude, regulation appeared to be the norm. In consequence, in describing how the current system of wage regulation operated, Tawney was led on to discuss how the previous system had functioned. The second intellectual stimulus for this investigation came from Tawney's abiding interest in the economics of labour broadly conceived. Earlier he had written an article on 'The economics of boy labour',[31] which suggests that he was interested in the apprenticeship as well as the wage regulation aspects of the 1563 act even though in the case of the article printed below he confined his discussion to the question of wage assessment. Further, in any discussion of his own position it ought to be remembered that Tawney considered himself rather as a social investigator than as an historian.

Some of the detailed ways in which subsequent research has affected the picture painted by Tawney are set out in the pages which follow. But more recent writing has also affected our view of the government of Tudor England[32] and of economic and social life in sixteenth-century England.[33] Tawney's remarks on shortages of labour in rural areas,[34] particularly considering the evidence from other material that the growing population was only with difficulty absorbed into employment, seem overdone. What shortages of labour there were tended to be highly localised and many towns had surpluses of labour.[35] Neither Winthrop's description of early seventeenth-century Massachusetts, where conditions were very different from England,[36] nor the rather unnatural conditions of England in the 1650s,[37] when some labourers may have been under arms thus creating an artificial shortage of labour, can be regarded as typical of the situation in England in the century after the passage of the Statute of Artificers. And, given the prevailing level of techniques, the existence of much surplus land in England available for colonisation by subsistence farmers seems doubtful. Sixteenth-century virgin land required heavy expenditure on drainage, manure and so on to bring it into cultivation effectively.[38]

Apart from Miss Putnam's discussion of the Northamptonshire wage assessments of 1560 and 1667[39] and Miss Waterman's article on Kent wage assessments in the eighteenth century,[40] discussion of matters relating to the Statute of Artificers virtually lapsed until the 1930s when there was a renewal of interest. In 1931 Lipson published a detailed discussion of wage regulation in his general account of the economic history of England in the age of mercantilism.[41] About the same time T.K. Derry was studying the apprenticeship provisions of the statute[42] and Miss Hindmarsh was investigating 'The assessment of wages by justices of the peace, 1563-1600'.[43] Concentrating on material relating to Sussex and other southern counties, Dr Hindmarsh came to the conclusion that the wage clauses were a genuine attempt to give the worker a living wage. Three years later, based largely on documentary evidence from the eastern and northern counties, Professor Kelsall, who was concerned not only with wage assessment but also with the closely allied parts of the Elizabethan labour code, published his book which is here reprinted. Subsequently yet more work has been done on the statute of 1563 and its enforcement, notably by Professor Bindoff[44] and Mrs Margaret Gay Davies.[45]

III Origins of the statute

Since Professor Tawney's article appeared in 1914, three main aspects have dominated discussion: the origins of the statute, the number of assessments, and the operation of the system of wage regulation.

As far as the origins of the statute are concerned, the line of descent from the Ordinance of 1349, the Statutes of Labourers of 1388 (12 Richard II c 3) and of 1390 (13 Richard II c 8), which imposed the responsibility of assessing wages on the justices of the peace, and subsequent legislation[46] and the gild and municipal regulations of the middle ages and the early sixteenth century, as set out by Professor Tawney,[47] still commands general acceptance in most respects.[48] Rather, attention has been concentrated on the years immediately preceding the passage of the 1563 act. Stemming from the predicament of the cloth industry as a result of the difficulties in the overseas markets, the economic unheavals of the 1540s and the 1550s led to a number of legislative attempts to control the growth of the rural woollen textile industry. By 1557 the provisions of successive cloth acts[49] had restricted entry into textile occupations by requiring a strict system of apprenticeship with the intention of checking the growth of rural industry by direct prohibition as well as by limitations on the size of the individual craft unit. Two years later the problem of wages led to adjustments being made locally in the statutory rates and to debate in Elizabeth's first Parliament.

It has been customary 'to regard both the statute of artificers and the economic and social measures which accompanied it in 1563, as the culmination of efforts made by Elizabeth's government from the beginning of her reign'.[50] But such an interpretation rests on the view set forward by Professor Knowles[51] that between 1559 and 1563 policy was shaped by Cecil. Certainly both Tawney and Kelsall accepted that the 'Considerations delivered to Parliament, 1559' were drafted by Cecil.[52] But Professor Bindoff holds that 'there is no proof that the "Considerations" owed more to Cecil than preservation among his papers ... nor is there anything to connect him with the bills introduced in 1559'.[53] 'Conservatively, even reactionarily paternalistic in outlook, and wide-ranging in its scope', Bindoff goes on to argue, 'the "Considerations" give the impression of being an aggregate of similar, but different, opinions, and one is tempted to ascribe them, not to a single person, but to a group addressing its mind collectively to the problems concerned'.[54] He further suggests that a committee of which Sir Thomas Smith and Richard Goodrich were members were the authors of this statement.

During the 1559 session of parliament a number of bills dealing with economic matters were laid before the Commons, including two dealing with the questions of labourers and apprentices but neither got beyond a second reading. To what extent such intended legislation was related to the 'Considerations' is not clear, but the government's failure to secure such legislation faced it with alternative lines of policy. 'It could either attempt to enforce such statutory controls as it had, even though they were out of date, or it could forego controls until a new Parliament enabled it to revise them'. A third alternative was to oscillate between these two possible courses of action; and this was the course, it has been suggested, which the government appears to have followed.[55]

The discovery in the 1920s of the Northamptonshire assessment of 1560 – the first shire assessment, so far as is known, for more than a century – led Miss Putnam to conclude that, having early in Elizabeth's reign failed to secure legislation, 'Cecil was persuading the Privy Council to command the county justices of the peace to assess wages without regard to the statutory limits, and was thus anticipating the Statute of Artificers'.[56] Professor Bindoff agrees that this wage assessment may have owed something to him although, he adds, 'the only hint of influence from above is a mention not of Cecil but of Chief Justice Catlin'.[57] The wage rates assessed by the Northamptonshire justices were uniformly somewhat higher than the maximum rates authorised by the act of 1515 but do not appear to have been enforced, partly perhaps because the increases fell short of the rise in prices since 1515 and partly perhaps because it was hoped that the reform of the currency was the more appropriate remedial action for the prevailing situation.

In the following years, 1561 and 1562, there was further action on a local basis. Proclamations were issued which required justices to take steps to enforce legislation relating to a number of matters including the regulation of service, apprenticeship and wages. On the basis of a document annexed to a letter from William Tyldesley, a justice of the peace in Buckinghamshire,[58] it has been argued that the Buckinghamshire justices issued a wage assessment for agricultural labour and rural craftsmen as well as orders dealing with the other matters noted above in 1561.[59] This document is, however, open to another interpretation. Could it not be a draft assessment devised by Tyldesley which was sent to Cecil as a suggestion?[60]

But the economic position of the country did not improve and problems remained which had to be tackled by parliament which was summoned in November 1562 and which met in January 1563. Of the bills presented to that parliament, a well-established view was that Cecil was the author of the artificers' bill. This attribution was, however, rejected by Conyers Read who held that there was no evidence at all for this belief,[61] while Professor Bindoff has gone further and argued that Bacon rather than Cecil ought to be given the credit of authorship of the bill. He also attaches great importance to the changes which he has argued the bill underwent in the course of its passage through parliament. But neither of these points has won unanimous support. As Dr Penry Williams has pointed out,[62] William Cecil wrote on 27 February 1563 that 'there is also a very good law agreed upon for indifferent allowances for servants' wages in husbandry' and therefore may not have been so out of touch with the bill's progress as Bindoff suggests. And the nature of the changes made in the bill need to be more fully examined before a thoroughly convincing explanation can be put forward. Nevertheless, the point still stands that the Statute of Artificers was not a grand design which was the product of one mind but a less coherent affair, the patchwork creation of many hands.

IV Assessments and reissues

When Thorold Rogers wrote about wage regulation he was able to use only twelve assessments but in the following years W.A.S. Hewins reported that he had discovered 47 post-1563 assessments.[63] Two years later, in 1900, Miss McArthur further increased the total by four and was able to demonstrate that the long gap between 1568 and 1590 which Professor Hewins had argued existed could to some extent be filled by a series of assessments for London,[64] a city for which, according to Thorold Rogers, there were no wage assessments. By the time that Professor Tawney came to write his article he calculated that 'the number of distinct and complete assessments at present available for analysis is 73, and that when their reissues and references to other assessments are included the total number known with certainty to have been made is not less than 112'.[65] When his book was first published, Professor Kelsall listed 159 assessments and to these should be added the assessments for London which he did not include.[66] Since 1938 many further assessments have come to light. Altogether these now total over one thousand four hundred. All the information about assessments now available has been brought together in the revised Appendix A which includes, in order that as full a picture of the situation as possible can be obtained, not only all assessments and reassessments but all reissues as well.[67] Much more is therefore known about the number of assessments made by justices of the peace and chief officers in cities and towns than when Tawney and Kelsall wrote. What is now required is for historians to make use of this information.

In the following table the availability of assessments by counties and boroughs is set out, comparing the information available when Tawney wrote with that available today.

TABLE I ASSESSMENTS BY COUNTIES AND BOROUGHS

County or borough	1914	1970	County or borough	1914	1970
Bedfordshire	-	4	Kent	1	57
Buckinghamshire	4	32	Lancashire	1	3
Cambridgeshire	-	41	Lincolnshire	6	6
Cheshire	1	-	Holland	-	5
Derbyshire	3	4	Kesteven	-	3
Devonshire	3	34	Lindsey	-	1
Dorset	-	30	Middlesex	2	100
Co Durham	-	9	Norfolk	1	21
Essex	3	50	Northamptonshire	2	66
Gloucestershire	4	8	Northumberland	-	1
Hampshire	-	5	Nottinghamshire	2	18
Herefordshire	-	10	Oxfordshire	-	14
Hertfordshire	1	51	Rutland	2	1

Shropshire	7	33	Warwickshire	10	36
Somerset	10	40	Westmorland	-	1
Staffordshire	-	34	Wiltshire	88	85
Suffolk	2	73	Worcestershire	1	7
Sussex	-	62	Yorkshire East Riding	1	7
East Sussex	-	33	North Riding	3	6
West Sussex	-	16	West Riding	7	129
Caernarvonshire	-	1	Merionethshire	-	1
Cardiganshire	1	2	Monmouthshire	-	1
Arundel	-	1	Liverpool	-	3
Barnstaple	-	1	London	15	20
Bath	-	13	Maidstone	-	8
Blackburn	-	1	Manchester	-	1
Bury St Edmunds	-	3	New Romney and Lydd	-	1
Canterbury	-	10	New Sarum (Salisbury)	2	1
Chester	6	9	Norwich	-	64
Colchester	1	1	Portsmouth	-	1
Doncaster	-	1	Reading	1	-
Exeter	-	6	Rochester	-	1
Faversham	-	1	Sandwich	1	-
Higham Ferrers	-	1	Shrewsbury	-	4
Hull	1	4	Southampton	1	2
Ipswich	-	20	St Albans	1	3
Kendal	-	1	Tenterden	-	45
Lancaster	1	-	Warwick	1	1
Leicester	1	35	Winchester	-	2
Lincoln	1	2	York	-	5

The second table, which again compares Tawney's information with the 1970 situation, sets out the availability of assessments by decade.

TABLE II ASSESSMENTS BY DECADE

Number of assessments, including reissues which can be dated

	1914	1970		1914	1970
1560-69	5	35	1660-69	3	80
1570-79	2	43	1670-79	3	85
1580-89	1	38	1680-89	7	88
1590-99	11	47	1690-99	1	93
1600-09	3	37	1700-09	6	88
1610-19	3	49	1710-19	5	71
1620-29	1	67	1720-29	3	79
1630-39	6	91	1730-39	10	70
1640-49	4	70	1740-49	-	61
1650-59	12	97	1750-59	1	55

1760-69	3	40	1790-99	-	10
1770-79	-	27	1800-09	-	10
1780-89	-	18	1810-12	-	3

Totals: 1914 = 90 1970 = 1452

Substantial though the increase in the availability of assessments has been, it is now clear that the 1970 figures do not represent the final situation. It is likely that further assiduous research in borough and county record offices will reveal the existence of more assessments.[68]

V The debate since 1938

All that can be done further within the space of this introduction is to touch briefly on some of the questions which may be raised about wage regulation under the Statute of Artificers and indicate what additional information has become available since Tawney and Kelsall wrote. The first question, about the extent to which wage assessments were made initially and reissued, is even less in doubt than when Professor Kelsall published his volume, for wage assessments continue to be discovered. Now only six English counties – Berkshire, Cheshire, Cornwall, Cumberland, Huntingdon and Leicestershire – are unrepresented while assessments are also known to survive for four Welsh counties, Caernarvon, Cardigan, Merioneth and Monmouth. Although more assessments have been found for the boroughs also, they continue to be less well-represented than the counties.

These additional assessments confirm Professor Kelsall's view of their astonishing variety in form and types of work covered. In the Merioneth wage assessment for 1601 the rates of artificers and labourers are said to be unusually detailed[69] while the Bedfordshire assessment for 1684 is stated to be a much fuller assessment than is usually found in the late seventeenth century.[70] The form of the Herefordshire assessment of 1732 is held to lend support to the view that assessments tended as a rule to become more rather than less detailed.[71] The range of occupations covered also varies. In the two wage assessments for Shrewsbury for 1628 and 1640 there is an almost complete absence of regulations for urban industrial trades, such as weaving.[72] In common with other county assessments, the Bedfordshire assessment of 1684 has a distinctly agricultural bias and there is in it no attempt to assess the wages for such domestic industries as spinning and weaving.[73]

In the light of the information set out in Appendix A, it is even clearer than it was in the late 1930s when Professor Kelsall wrote, that Hewins' view that the activity of the justices in rating wages was greatest during seven short periods – 1563-7, 1591-6, 1608-12, 1619-21, 1632-4, 1651-5 and 1682-8[74] – is too precise and does not accord with the facts.[75] The list printed below provides evidence of considerable administrative activity on the part of justices of the peace in the counties and chief officers in the cities and towns in making wage assessments. Indeed, it suggests that wages were assessed, in parts of the country, fairly regularly to the 1700s, less frequently until the 1760s and hardly at all after that. Moreover, it is now possible to improve on Professor Kelsall's statement that 'until the late eighteenth century there are few periods of more than a year or two for which evidence of assessment in some parts of England is lacking'.[76] Subsequent discoveries have filled the gaps and our list shows that assessments are now available for every year during which the statute was in force.

But justices were not always active in wage assessment. From time to time, therefore, in the late sixteenth and early seventeenth centuries, the Privy Council reminded JPs of their responsibilities in this direction. Later, during the Interregnum, the House of Commons enjoined the lord mayor of London and all the justices in the city in 1649 'forthwith to put into execution the several statutes of Eliz, cap 4 and I Jac, cap 6, made and enacted for the rating and settling of the wages of the several artificers within the limits aforesaid, for their better relief and subsistence in these dear times ... And that care be taken annually to do the same, if need require, according to the tenor of the said laws. And all justices of the peace in the several counties of this commonwealth and dominion of Wales are, in like manner, required to do the same'.[77] After the Restoration, there are other examples of attempts to induce justices to act. In 1661 the grand jury of Worcestershire stated that 'we desire that servants' wages may be rated according to the Statute, for we find the unreasonableness of servants' wages a great grievance'.[78]

Granted that wage assessments were made and reissued, was the procedure a formality or was the matter done after due consideration?[79] Where a wage assessment was simply reissued, there is commonly no evidence that this procedure was more than routine though Tawney argues it would certainly be wrong to assume that the frequent reissue of old assessments implied negligence.[80] Rather, as Kelsall argues,[81] the significance of a run of reissues cannot be judged in isolation but must be considered in relation to such factors as the movement of prices and the demand for labour. Clearly, on some occasions, as the Privy Council pointed out to the justices of Wiltshire in 1614, a formal reissue of the wage schedule without alteration year by year could defeat the purpose of the 1563 statute which enjoined justices to take into account 'the plenty or scarcity of the time'.[82] But reassessment presumes some consideration of the case. In addition to the examples mentioned by Tawney and Kelsall there is more recent discussion of this subject. In three out of four of the early seventeenth century assessments for Shrewsbury changes were made[83] while between 1666 and 1762 the assessed wages for Herefordshire were altered in some respect on twenty occasions.[84]

While assessments continued to be made in some places in the late seventeenth and early eighteenth centuries, there was not universal agreement that the system was satisfactory. In 1724 a parliamentary committee expressed doubts about it and recommended that 'some more effectual method be provided for obliging justices of the peace to assess the wages of servants and labourers mentioned in the statute of the fifth of Queen Elizabeth'.[85] So much obviously depended on the justices themselves whether wage assessments were made or not. In the West Riding of Yorkshire assessment apparently continued until 1732 'and from that time onwards all life slowly ebbed out of the system'.[86] Elsewhere it had come to an end earlier while in some places the practice of annual wage assessment still continued. As late as 1787 one writer commented that 'in some places, as I am informed, [the statute] now is carried into execution but ... has been in others totally neglected'.[87]

When reissue or reassessment took place, on what basis did the justices act? Under the statute the justices were enjoined to take account of changes in the price level[88] but the assessments have not so far been analysed systematically to establish what took place. Many wage assessments were not only prefaced by a conventional statement relating to the obligation to take account of price changes[89] but they are also concluded by tail-pieces which because they were not obligatory may contain, it has been suggested,[90] an element of truth. Thus the tail-piece of the 1563 Rutland assessment asserted that it was drawn 'upon consideration of the great pryses of lynnen, woolen, lether, corne, and other victuals' while the reason for the 1576 Canterbury assessment was 'onely the dearth of vitayles, cloth, and other necessaries, which at this present are so scarce and deare within the sayde Citie, that poore men are not able at reasonable prices to attayn theyr necessaries'.[91] Perhaps local variations are important here.[92] While a number of wage assessments seem to have been reissued without change when the general level of prices was rising, as for example the Kent assessment between 1563 and 1589,[93] in other counties changes were made. In the 1590s at Chester the justices raised the maximum rates payable to workers who received yearly wages and had to provide their own food in 1596 and 1597[94] and the 1607 rates for Hertfordshire were higher, some substantially, some marginally, than the previous assessment.[95] Further, despite the fact that it was said that prices in Shrewsbury were falling slightly in the 1630s rather than rising, the justices there increased all wages (except those of the mowers of grass and of grain and the woman reaper) in 1640.[96] On the basis of the Herefordshire assessments between 1666 and 1762,[97] however, Kelsall suggests that the cost of living was not a major consideration in the minds of the justices in the late seventeenth century but that they were more conscious both of short-run and of long-run changes in the labour market. Differing from Miss Hindmarsh, Professor Kelsall, holds, moreover, that the existence of a class of landless labourers was from the first envisaged and that the aim of the justices in increasing wage rates was to deter landless labourers from leaving their work to become squatters on the waste. At least one commentator raised the question whether the manipulation of wage rates, unaccompanied by other and more drastic action, would have been effective or could have been expected to have been effective in putting an end to squatting. Nor, indeed, he suggests, would a household's squatting on the waste necessarily prevent some, at least, of its members from hiring themselves as day-labourers.[98]

Wage rates could be stated as either yearly rates or daily rates. In most cases the daily rates applied to different workers from the yearly rates but in a few cases, as in the Chester assessments of the 1590s, both yearly and daily rates are to be found for the same category of worker. In such cases, who decided which rate should be paid? And how do the yearly and daily rates compare?[99] To the first question no adequate answer can be given. But a comparison of the daily rates with the yearly rates shows that the time taken by a daily worker to earn the same as a yearly worker in the same trade varied considerably from trade to trade. To quote just one year's comparison. It has been calculated that in 1593 the pewterer paid a daily wage could earn the yearly rate in 96 days; the linen weaver took 240 days. Do these differentials cast any light on the relative scarcity of day workers in particular trades? And do they also suggest, given the high levels of unemployment and under-employment, that it was more advantageous to be a yearly worker and be assured of a regular (if lower) income rather than to be in the more precarious position of the day worker? Or did such differentials happen inadvertently, the justices being conscious neither of the discrepancies between daily and yearly rates nor of the variations between trades? This again is a matter which deserves further investigation.

And what of apprentices? The commonly-held view has been that since an apprentice lived in, and in return for his service he received instruction, he was not paid wages. Yet the preamble to the 1563 act speaks of the wages of apprentices and many of the assessments contain rates for apprentices. The Hull assessment of 1570, for example, stated that 'a prentice ... of two yeres service and under shall have like wages as to common labourers'.[100] Is the solution to this conundrum, as put forward by Mr Woodward recently, that the wages laid down for apprentices were not in fact to be paid to them but were to be given to the master craftsmen for work done by their apprentices? 'This suggestion', Mr Woodward argues,

> is supported by the assessments. In most cases wages were assessed for the apprentices of craftsmen such as carpenters, masons, bricklayers or slaters who were not making and then retailing over the counter a finished good. Rather, they hired themselves out for particular jobs and would be paid for their labour, for the labour of their apprentices and journeyman, and for the cost of materials consumed. The apprentices of craftsmen such as tailors and shoemakers were not normally mentioned in the assessments, presumably because the value of the work done by such apprentices could be incorporated directly into the price of the suit of clothes or pair of shoes being produced'.[101]

To what extent were the wage schedules enforced?[102] Professor Kelsall goes into this question in some detail, dealing with the three offences in turn: giving higher wages, taking higher wages and refusing to work.[103] Subsequent work has cast a little further light on the extent of infringement. In his discussion of the role of the common informer in the enforcement of economic regulations, Professor Beresford has shown that the informer's main activity centred on the infringement of market regulations. Some informations were laid in Exchequer relating to breaches of the apprenticeship provisions of the 1563 statute but for the sample years Beresford has chosen he records no cases relating to the wage regulation clauses of the act.[104] More recently, Mrs Davies has noted that justices were asked to inquire of servants, both men and women for excessive wages in 1566,[105] while in 1601 in Devon the justices required the high constables to report cases of giving or taking excessive wages.[106] And, following the act of 1604 (1 James I c 6) which provided for the assessment of *minimum* wages in the woollen textile industry, presentments concerning some forty-three clothiers for not paying their weavers the assessed rates of wages were placed before the Wiltshire Quarter Sessions.[107] Further, a large number of cases were periodically brought to the Quarter Sessions in the North Riding in the early seventeenth century.[108] Was the level of activity here higher than elsewhere or would more investigation in other counties reveal a greater interest by justices of the peace elsewhere also? But the absence of cases may not mean, however, that the statute was completely without effect. We may not infer, Professor Kelsall has argued, 'that the justices' scales had no effect unless *for the same area and date* it can be shown that actual wages in excess of these scales were being paid'.[109] In addition, the justices frequently compelled persons to go into service and enforced the yearly contract on master and servant alike. Could it be that the justices' most important activity in relation to wages was compelling masters to pay their servants the yearly wages due to them?

And how were assessed wages related to actual wages? With some qualification, W.A.S. Hewins held that the rate of wages sanctioned by the justices was actually paid,[110] whereas both Thorold Rogers earlier and Tawney later were of the opinion that market wages were usually higher than the official maxima.[111] Kelsall's view was that assessed and market rates corresponded fairly closely until the middle of the seventeenth century and thereafter tended to diverge.[112] But more recent investigation of the situation in Chester, Durham, Kent and Lancashire has tended to support Tawney's view of divergence in the sixteenth century.[113] Certainly it is clear there were differences between localities and over time and no doubt the general presumption that market forces were more important than assessments in determining wage rates is true. A good example of local study is provided by Professor Willan's analysis of a Bedfordshire wage assessment for 1684. From a comparison of the assessed rates with various pieces of evidence about wages actually paid, Willan came to the conclusion that wage assessment in Bedfordshire was not taken seriously either by employers or their workpeople in the 1680s and that actual wages exceeded assessed rates.[114] But much more work needs to be done by local historians before a clear picture will emerge.

The decay in the system of wage regulation under the Elizabethan statute in the eighteenth century, as Kelsall argues below,[115] was due not to a shift in the attitude of the central government but to a fundamental change in the labour situation which, together with legal developments, made it easier for the propertied classes to restrict the wages of a class now denied some of its old opportunities of living idly. Enclosure and consequent diminution in 'by-employments' weakened the bargaining position of the individual wage-earner and made the legal assessment of maximum wages less necessary. And combination amongst wage-earners was to be met by other means than those provided by the statute of 1563. Moreover, times had changed since the middle of the sixteenth century. The political situation was more secure and the economic problems were less pressing. Prices were generally more stable, the rising corn production since the middle of the seventeenth century had largely banished fears of harvest failures with their accompaniment of famine and social disorders and there had been a broadening of employment opportunities which rendered largely superfluous attempts to keep down wages. Altogether the political, social and economic climate was less precarious and tense than it had been in the 1550s and 1560s. As a result, by the mid-eighteenth century the wage assessment system 'was moribund, but', as Sir John Clapham has written, 'it died harder than historians used to think – and the memory of it did not die'.[116]

In discussions of the sixteenth century it is now generally agreed that Tudor governments were more concerned to regulate industry in the name of public order than to establish any unified set of economic objectives. And local authorities, justices of the peace and petty constables largely concurred with the central government that the main aim should be to prevent social disorder by maintaining a stable, predominantly agricultural society. In such an ordered society the regulation of wages has its place. It seemed to provide a means to check the operation of market forces and to call a halt to the too rapid pace of industrial change. Hitherto historians have considered the operation of the system of wage regulation by the justices of the peace on the basis of fairly limited information. Over the years the volume of evidence available has grown considerably and there seems little doubt that more wage assessments will be found, particularly amongst borough records. Complementary work to collect together information about wage rates will then enable a more systematic investigation to be carried out. Even if substantial reservations have to be made about the effectiveness of the policy, nevertheless, properly handled the wage assessments made under the statute of 1563 can be induced to tell us more about the structure of the market for labour and other questions than they have so far revealed,[117] and to augment our as yet meagre knowledge of the life of the common man in early modern England. The re-publication of these two classical studies of wage regulation, together with a revised and expanded list of assessments, could encourage further investigation of this aspect of life and work in pre-industrial England.

Notes

1 This is the modern usage though in the past many historians have written of the 1563 act as the Statute of Apprentices. Recently Dr W.H. Chaloner has spoken of 'the Statute of Artificers (sometimes misnamed "of Apprentices")' in his *The skilled artisans during the industrial revolution, 1750-1850* (Historical Association, 1969), p 6 basing his objection on the fact that the 1563 act 'contains only a small proportion of clauses touching apprenticeship and as apprenticeship was only a stage in becoming an artificer, the part cannot be allowed to give its name to the whole' (letter from Dr Chaloner to the author, 26 November 1969).

2 The fullest outline of the provisions of the act, emphasising its character as uniform national legislation can be found in William Cunningham, *The growth of English industry and commerce in modern times, Part I. The mercantile system* (4th ed Cambridge UP, 1907), pp 27-44. The statute, together with related documents, is printed in Richard H. Tawney and Eileen Power, *Tudor economic documents* (Longmans, Green, 1924), I, 325-83 and a summary of the wage regulation sections is given below in Appendix B, pp 236-8. I am greatly indebted to Mr D.M. Woodward for his helpful comments on this introduction.

3 'Commercial trends and policy in sixteenth century England', *EcHR*, X (1940), 113, reprinted in Eleanora M. Carus-Wilson, ed *Essays in economic history*, I (Arnold, 1954), p 168.

4 F.J. Fisher, 'Influenza and inflation in Tudor England', *EcHR*, 2nd series, XVIII (1965), 128. Neither Professor J.D. Gould's criticism of Professor Fisher's thesis ('F.J. Fisher on influenza and inflation in Tudor England', *EcHR*, 2nd series, XXI (1968), 361-8) nor Professor Fisher's 'Rejoinder' (*EcHR*, 2nd series, XXI (1968), 368-70) are concerned with this particular point.

5 See below, pp 41-3.

6 For France, see Henri Hauser, *Ouvriers du temps passé (XVe - XVIe siécles* (Paris, 1906), pp 60-3.

7 ie all others under 30 and not having estates worth more than 40s per annum nor any goods worth £10. Altogether thirty occupations were named.

8 Similar limitations applied to entry to continental gilds such as the

Arti Maggiori in Florence, the Six Corps de Métiers in Paris and the Herrenzünfte in Basel (William J. Ashley, *An introduction to English economic history and theory, Part II. The end of the middle ages* (Longmans, Green, 1906), p 134.

9 'Untill a man growe unto the aige of xxiiijtie yeares, he (for the moste parte thoughe not allwayes) is wilde, withoute judgment, & not of sufficyent experience to governe himselfe, Nor (many tymes) growen unto the full or perfect knowledge of the arte or occupacion that he professeth, And therefore had more neede still to remayne under government, as a servaunt and learner, then to become a ruler, as a maister or instructor' (memorandum on the Statute of Artificers, 1573? printed in Tawney and Power, *Tudor economic documents,* I, 354). In suggesting that the object of this passage was as much social as economic, George M. Trevelyan altered the age of discretion to 23 *(English social history: a survey of six centuries, Chaucer to Queen Victoria* (Longmans, Green, 1942), pp 191-2).

10 See Fisher, 'Influenza and inflation', p 128.

11 See Thomas K. Derry, 'The enforcement of a seven years' apprenticeship under the Statute of Artificers', DPhil thesis, University of Oxford, 1931, pp 2-3. I am most grateful to Dr Derry for kindly lending me his copy of his thesis.

12 Eli Hechscher, *Mercantilism* (revised 2nd ed Allen & Unwin, 1955), I, 230.

13 See below, pp 72-3 and Ephraim Lipson, *Economic history of England, III. The age of mercantilism* (3rd ed Black, 1943), p 254. The draft bill is printed in Tawney and Power, *Tudor economic documents,* I, 371-6.

14 39 Elizabeth c 12 and continued by 43 Elizabeth c 9.

15 I James I c 6.

16 See Sidney and Beatrice Webb, *The history of trade unionism: revised edition extended to 1920* (Longmans, Green, 1926), pp 249-52 and Daphne Simon, 'Master and servant' in John Saville, ed *Democracy and the labour movement: essays in honour of Dona Torr* (Lawrence & Wishart, 1954), pp 195-7.

17 Olive Jocelyn Dunlop, *English apprenticeship and child labour: a history with a supplementary section on the modern problem of juvenile labour* by O. Jocelyn Dunlop and Richard D. Denman, MP (T. Fisher Unwin, 1912), On this book see Tawney's comments, p 40 below.

18 'The enforcement of a seven years' apprenticeship'.

19 *The enforcement of English apprenticeship: a study in applied mercantilism, 1563-1642* (Cambridge, Mass: Harvard UP, 1956). See

also Stella Kramer, *English craft gilds: studies in their progress and decline* (New York: Columbia UP, 1927).

20 The bibliography on pp 239-54 below provides a guide to other literature dealing with the statute.

21 *Six centuries of work and wages* (T. Fisher Unwin, 1884), pp 398-9. For Tawney's comments on Thorold Rogers' views see below, pp 39-41.

22 William A.S. Hewins, 'The regulation of wages by the justices of the peace', *EJ,* VIII (1898), 340.

23 'Dr Cunningham and his critics', *EJ,* IV (1894), 513-14.

24 Hewins' promised book on the state regulation of wages mentioned in his article (*EJ,* VIII (1898), 340) was never published.

25 See below pp 64-5, 68.

26 Frederick J. Fisher, ed *Essays in the economic and social history of Tudor and Stuart England* (Cambridge UP, 1961).

27 The substance of this paragraph derives from correspondence with Professor David Joslin to whom I am most grateful for invaluable help.

28 *Poverty as an industrial problem* by R.H. Tawney, director of the Ratan Tata Foundation, being an inaugural lecture delivered on October 22nd 1913 at the London School of Economics and Political Science (Ratan Tata Foundation, 1914).

29 *Studies in the minimum wage, No 1. The establishment of minimum rates in the chain-making industry under the Trade Boards Act of 1909* (Bell, 1909) and *Studies in the minimum wage, No 2. The establishment of minimum rates in the tailoring trade under the Trade Boards Act of 1909* (Bell, 1915).

30 By the 1880s the unions were pressing for 'fair wages' and 'by 1894 a hundred and fifty local authorities had adopted some kind of "Fair Wages" resolution. In 1890, and more explicitly still in 1893, successive Governments found it necessary to repudiate the old principle of buying in the cheapest market, in favour of the now widespread feeling that public authorities as large employers of labour, instead of ignoring the condition of their employees, should use their influence to maintain the Standard Rate of Wages and Standard Hours of Labour recognised and in practice obtained by the Trade Unions concerned' (Webb, *History of trade unionism,* p 399).

31 *EJ,* XIX (1909), 517-37.

32 See below, p 41; also Geoffrey R. Elton, *The Tudor revolution in government: administrative changes in the reign of Henry VIII* (Cambridge UP, 1953) and Fisher, 'Commercial trends and policy'.

33 See F.J. Fisher, 'Tawney's century' in Fisher, ed *Tudor and Stuart England,* pp 1-14. In writing this paragraph I have benefitted from the

advice of my colleague, Michael Havinden.

34 See below, pp 65-8.

35 See, for example, Stanley T. Bindoff, *Tudor England* (Harmondsworth: Penguin, 1950), pp 15-16 and Sir John H. Clapham, *A concise economic history of Britain from the earliest times to AD 1750* (Cambridge UP, 1949), pp 213-14, for evidence of population pressure on the land.

36 See below, pp 65-6.

37 See below, pp 67-8.

38 For evidence of sixteenth-century land hunger, see Fisher, 'Tawney's century', p 5 and Joan Thirsk, ed *The agrarian history of England and Wales, IV. 1500-1640* (Cambridge UP, 1967), pp 12, 24.

39 *EcHR*, I (1927-28), 124-34.

40 *EHR*, XLIII (1928), 398-408.

41 *The economic history of England, III. The age of mercantilism* (1st ed Black, 1931), p 248.

42 See above, p 13.

43 PhD thesis, University of London, 1932.

44 'The making of the Statute of Artificers' in Stanley T. Bindoff, Joel Hurstfield and C.H. Williams, ed *Elizabethan government and society: essays presented to Sir John Neale* (Athlone P, 1961), p 56-94.

45 *The enforcement of English apprenticeship.*

46 Notably 23 Henry VI c 12 (1444-5), 11 Henry VII c 22 (1495) and 6 Henry VIII c 3 (1514-15).

47 See below, pp 44-65 also B.L. Hutchins, 'The regulation of wages by gilds and town authorities', *EJ,* X (1900), 404-11.

48 Miss Putnam contends that Tawney was in error when he held (see p 46 below) that the justices were limited by the maximum rates of the statute of 1388 and cites a clause from a statute of the following year: 'But forasmuch as a man cannot put the price of corn and other victuals in certain ... the justices of peace ... shall make proclamation by their discretion according to the dearth of victuals ...' of rates of wages, 'notwithstanding the statutes thereof heretofore made'. See her article, 'Northamptonshire wage assessments of 1560 and 1667', *EcHR,* I (1927-28), 128. Later she suggests (p 130 and note 1) that the assessments of 1560 and 1561 which sanctioned rates above the statutory level represented the earliest example since 1444-5, as far as is known, of a reversion to the policy of 1389-90 and adds that Tawney's interpretation of the act of 1389-90 inevitably leads him to very different conclusions on the policy of Cecil (see below, pp 49-53).

49 By 5 & 6 Edward VI c 8 (1552) a seven-year apprenticeship for clothmaking and putters-out was required but this was modified by 1 Mary, sess 3 c 7 (1553) to exempt cities and towns. This exemption was removed for broadcloth weavers by 2 & 3 Philip & Mary c 11, section 7 (1556) and the act was extended to cover all weaving and clothmaking in broadcloth and narrow cloth (including kerseys) by 4 & 5 Philip & Mary c 5, section 22 (1558).

50 See Bindoff, 'The making of the Statute', p 80.

51 See Cunningham, *The growth of English industry,* 'The policy of Burleigh', pp 53-84.

52 See below, pp 49-50, 177. This document is printed in full in Tawney and Power, *Tudor economic documents,* I, 325-30.

53 Bindoff, 'The making of the Statute', p 88.

54 Bindoff, 'The making of the Statute', pp 80-1. This view significantly modifies Tawney's discussion of the 'Considerations' (see below, pp 49-53.

55 Bindoff, 'The making of the Statute', p 83. The interpretation in these two paragraphs relies heavily on Professor Bindoff's article.

56 *EcHR,* I, 127-8.

57 Bindoff, 'The making of the Statute', p 88.

58 SPD Elizabeth, vol XIX, no 43 in Tawney and Power, *Tudor economic documents,* I, 332.

59 See Putnam, 'Northamptonshire wage assessments of 1560 and 1667', pp 127-9.

60 See Bindoff, 'The making of the Statute', pp 86-7. These proposals must have reached Cecil and if there are grounds for believing that there are some points of similarity with the Statute of Artificers, could it not be asserted, Mr Woodward has suggested, that this provides some basis for arguing that Cecil played a more crucial role in the evolution of the Statute than Professor Bindoff's discussion would allow?

61 *Mr Secretary Cecil and Queen Elizabeth* (Cape, 1955), p 275.

62 See his review of Bindoff, Hurstfield and Williams, ed *Elizabethan government and society* in *EcHR,* 2nd series, XIV (1961), 143-4 in which he hoped that Professor Bindoff's thesis will not be erected into a new orthodoxy until some of the difficulties about it have been explained.

63 *EJ,* VIII (1898), 344. See also William A.S. Hewins, *English trade and finance chiefly in the seventeenth century* (Methuen, 1892), pp vii, 82.

64 'The regulation of wages in the sixteenth century', *EHR,* XV

(1900), 445-55.

65 See below, p 39.

66 See Ellen A. MacArthur, 'The regulation of wages in the sixteenth century', *EHR*, XV (1900), 445-55 and Tawney and Power, *Tudor economic documents,* I, 563-70.

67 This new Appendix is based not only on a search of printed material but also on a circular to archivists and librarians in the autumn of 1969.

68 But it should be noted that 'it was not customary to make a note of every occasion on which assessments were issued, and hence one may presume that many assessments were issued and renewed without such action being placed on record. This supposition is borne out by the evidence contained in the North Riding documents' (*EJ,* XXIV (1914), 220).

69 T.C. Mendenhall, 'A Merioneth wage assessment for 1601', *Journal of the Merioneth Historical Record Society,* II (1955), 204-8.

70 T.S. Willan, 'A Bedfordshire wage assessment of 1684', *Bedfordshire Historical Record Society Publications,* XXV (1947), 130.

71 See below, 201, Professor Heaton notes that in the West Riding each reissue was attended by an ever growing appendix and series of instructions (*EJ,* XXIV (1914), 229). Miss Waterman also mentions that the Kent assessment for 1724 is more detailed than earlier assessments (*EHR,* XLIII (1928), 400).

72 Michael Reed, 'Early seventeenth century wage assessments for the borough of Shrewsbury', *Journal of the Salop Archaeological Society,* LVII (1956), 137.

73 Willan, 'Bedfordshire wage assessment', p 130.

74 *EJ,* VIII (1898), 345.

75 See below, pp 105, 107.

76 See below, p 107.

77 Lipson, *Economic history,* III, 260-1.

78 Lipson, *Economic history,* III, 262.

79 See below, pp 59-61, 102-3, 201-2.

80 See below, p 60. Hutchins notes that 'In London there was evidently some recognised system in the matter, though it was apt to get out of gear. At a meeting of the Court of Common Council, in 1619, a committee was appointed to prepare a statement as to servants' and workmens' wages, "which by the lawe must be ratid at the Sessions after Easter and is nowe much out of order" (*SP Dom Jac* I vol 110,

no 23). In 1655 the Carpenters Company was requested to advise the lord mayor concerning wages'. (*EJ,* X (1900), 406).

81 See below, p 103.

82 *Acts of the Privy Council, 1613-14,* 458, 653, cited in Lipson, *Economic history,* III, 258.

83 Reed, 'Wage assessments', p 138.

84 See below, p 200.

85 Lipson, *Economic history,* III, 264.

86 *EJ,* XXIV (1914), 232.

87 Lipson, *Economic history,* III, 264.

88 See below, pp 81, 159-76.

89 See below, pp 63, 159.

90 D.M. Woodward, 'The assessment of wages by justices of the peace, 1563-1814: some observations', *The Local Historian,* VIII (1969), 293-9, from which article the following examples are drawn.

91 The tail-piece to the 1563 Kent assessment is in similar terms (*Archaeologia Cantiana,* XXII (1897), 319).

92 And changes in the general level of prices ought to be distinguished from short-run fluctuations in the price of grain, foodstuffs and other commodities. Through their control of markets and their ability to regulate prices, the justices could tackle difficulties caused by short-run changes. In addition, local authorities could help in times of need by buying, for example, grain in bulk for resale to the poor. The wage regulation provisions of 5 Elizabeth c 4 were not appropriate for such purposes. See below, pp 61, 167 and Woodward, 'The assessment of wages', p 296.

93 Woodward, 'The assessment of wages', p 295.

94 See below, pp 162-3.

95 Hertfordshire QS records (Hertford CRO). Rates for spinsters, weavers and weavers' servants were added from 1607 onwards, a local response to 1 James I c 6.

96 Reed, 'Wage assessments', p 138.

97 See below, pp 200-1.

98 Review by R.J. Hammond in *EcHR,* X (1940), 181.

99 This paragraph is based on the discussion in Woodward, 'The assessment of wages', pp 297-8;

100 Cited in Woodward, 'The assessment of wages', p 296.

101 Woodward, 'The assessment of wages', p 297.

102 Hewins' opinion in 1892 was that 'It is difficult to say in what manner the Justices used the power which the Government placed in their hands, or whether they really tried to enforce their awards' (*English trade and finance,* p 85).

103 See below, pp 82-5, 111-58.

104 M.W. Beresford, 'The common informer, the penal statutes and economic regulation', *EcHR,* 2nd series, X (1957), 221-39 and especially 227-8.

105 *The enforcement of English apprenticeship,* p 190.

106 MS sessions books, II, Mich 43 Elizabeth (Devon RO, Exeter). This was, Mrs Davies notes, in connection with a wage assessment of the previous spring (*The enforcement of English apprenticeship,* p 215 and note 28). See also Hewins, *English trade and finance,* p 85. Five sub-committees were appointed especially to attend to this matter in the different districts.

107 Probably at Westbury. Wiltshire MS sessions rolls, no 3, Trinity 3 James I (*The enforcement of English apprenticeship,* p 202). See also Heaton, *EJ,* XXIV (1914), 219-20.

108 See below, pp 111-12, 130, 148-9.

109 See below, p 114.

110 *English trade and finance,* pp 83-5.

111 See below, p 85.

112 See below, pp 118-19.

113 Woodward, 'The assessment of wages', p 294.

114 Willan, 'Bedfordshire wage assessment', p 135.

115 See below, pp 192-5, 202.

116 Clapham, *Concise economic history,* p 215.

117 For some suggestions about further work, particularly for local historians, see Woodward, 'The assessment of wages', p 298.

THE ASSESSMENT OF WAGES IN ENGLAND BY THE JUSTICES OF THE PEACE

R. H. TAWNEY
(1913)

I Introductory

The authoritative assessment of wages in England is a subject which extends from the first Statute of Labourers passed in 1349 to the repeal of the wage clauses of the Statute of Artificers in 1813. In the present essay I shall deal with a strictly limited portion of this wide field.[1] I shall consider only the assessment of wages as it was carried out under the Statute of Artificers of 1563, which superseded the earlier legislation and reorganised on a wider basis and in a more elastic shape the system which it had introduced, and I shall confine myself mainly to the operation of that statute in the century and a half after it was passed. I shall therefore leave on one side both the regulation of wages by the state in the fourteenth, fifteenth and early sixteenth centuries and the rules with regard to the remuneration of labour made independently of statute law by gilds and municipal authorities, except in so far as it may be necessary to consider these in order to interpret the Elizabethan legislation. Nor shall I deal with the attempts to revive that legislation as a means of protecting the wage-earner against exploitation which were made both by philanthropists and by bodies of organised workers at the end of the eighteenth and at the beginning of the nineteenth centuries. The latter topic is an extremely interesting one, but it involves considerations peculiar to the rise of modern industrial conditions and quite foreign to the circumstances in which the assessment of wages was administered as a working system. A discussion of the earlier Statutes of Labourers prior to 1563 would take us into fields which, except for Miss Putnam's admirable work,[2] have been scarcely explored, and the political conditions of which are so remote from those of the Tudor age as to require a separate dissertation.

The industrial code of Elizabeth is a topic which has received considerable attention from English economic historians, and with regard to which there has been in the last few years both an increase of material and a change of standpoint. On the one hand a good deal of new evidence has come to light. When Thorold Rogers called attention to the subject in his *History of agriculture and prices in England,* he could print only 12 assessments of wages made by the justices. This number of assessments has been increased by subsequent historians, notably Dr Cunningham,[3] Miss McArthur[4] and Professor Hewins.[5] But even the latter, whose list of assessments was more complete than that of any other writer, tells us that he knows only of 47. Since these authors made their contributions the anticipation that other assessments were only waiting to be discovered has been substantiated both by the explorations of private investigators among Quarter Sessions records and by the work of the Historical Manuscripts Commission and of the Victoria County History. As will be seen from the tables given below, I calculate that the number of distinct and complete assessments at present (1914) available for analysis is 73, and that when their reissues and references to other assessments are included the total number known with certainty to have been made is not less than 112. Moreover the assessments are only part of the new material which calls for treatment. Mere tables of wages by themselves tell us little except that the justices were administering the law. They require to be related to the general social conditions of the age, and to be viewed as a piece of regulation as characteristic of the economic environment of the sixteenth and seventeenth centuries as, in a widely different sphere, factory legislation is of modern industry. The view which we take of them must clearly depend upon our view of the part which the wage-worker played in the economy of the period when the Statute of Artificers was passed; and the work of recent investigators of industrial and agrarian conditions has done something to supply us with the background which is essential to the interpretation of economic legislation, and which, in the days of Thorold Rogers, was almost entirely lacking.

On the other hand not only have materials been increased, but standpoints and canons of criticism have been considerably modified since attention first began to be paid to the subject. The change of opinion among historians as to the objects and merits of the economic legislation of the old regime is a curious illustration of the influence of contemporary problems upon historical judgements. The naive and self-confident philistinism of the committees of the House of Commons which pronounced judgement in the early nineteenth century both upon the authoritative regulation of wages and the statutory system of apprenticeship ('The age of Elizabeth' reported one of them, 'was indeed glorious, but it was one in which the true principles of commerce were not rightly understood') may perhaps be regarded as so obviously the outcome of immediate and pressing material considerations as to fall below the horizon of serious history. It is, however, instructive to compare the views of Thorold Rogers with those of subsequent writers. The greater part of Rogers' work was done during a period when, though the combination laws had long been repealed, the legal status of trade unions was still precarious, and when the distrust of the interference of the state with questions of work and wages which (in spite of occasional agitations for factory legislation) characterised their leaders down to about 1889, was still extremely strong. That distrust Rogers, himself a mid-nineteenth-century radical, shared to the full, and it is no injustice to his services as a pioneer among English economic historians to say that it coloured his estimate of Elizabethan legislation. He condemned the apprenticeship clauses in the Statute of Artificers for the reasons long ago advanced by Adam Smith, that they were a bar to the mobility of labour from one occupation to another, and created a monopoly of skilled workers at the expense of an unprivileged residuum. He condemned with far greater vehemence the wage clauses in the same act, dismissed the allusion in its opening words to the need of making wages keep pace with advancing prices as 'the hypocrisy which the Preamble of an Act of Parliament habitually contains' and described the whole system as 'a conspiracy concocted by the law and carried out by parties interested in its success ... to cheat the English workman of his wages'.[6] Clearly there lies behind these full-blooded denunciations the assumption that the intervention of the state in matters of wages was an object of detestation to the workers concerned, that it invariably operated to prevent wages from being as high as they would have been under a regime of free competition, and that, in short, the prescribing of rates of payment in the sixteenth century was open to the same objections as would fairly be adduced against a similar policy in the nineteenth century.

Rogers' criticism of the Statute of Artificers, though it has passed into the text books and has been repeated in some works of a more serious order,[7] has been considerably modified both by subsequent research, and by the different point of view from which more recent writers have approached the subject. The latest study[8] of apprenticeship in England by no means endorses the verdict of the early nineteenth century as to the inutility or harmfulness of a compulsory system. The exploration of town records shows the assessment of wages to have been a policy to which the word 'conspiracy' is peculiarly inappropriate, since it was carried out independently of any national enactment by a large number of town authorities. A comparison of the act of 1563 with the legislation of earlier periods, which Rogers did not bring into relation with it, shows that his view that it was the grand beginning of the English workman's troubles, is quite unjustified, and that there is some evidence to suggest that on occasion it was used not to lower but to raise wages. Moreover a fuller appreciation of the objects and conceptions of the statesman of the sixteenth and early seventeenth centuries has modified the standpoint from which their economic policy is regarded. The age of 'Tudor despotism' is no longer contrasted with that of constitutional government as darkness with light. Its tendencies are seen to have been in some respects popular, and its attention to the administrative supervision of economic conditions is congenial to modern historians, who are constantly confronted in their own age with the task of securing what Tudor statesmen called 'good order' in industrial matters. In particular it is realised that the assessment of wages cannot be treated, in the manner of Rogers, as though it were something unique, instead of being, what it really was, one part of the absolute monarchy's general system of economic regulation. It requires to be related to the poor laws, to the attempts made to check enclosures and to prevent evictions, to the fixing of prices and the limitation of the rate of interest, the three last of which measures might, if Rogers' canons of criticism were adopted, be described as a conspiracy to cheat the English landlord, employer, and money-lender of their profits. Miss Leonard's[9] description of the personal government of Charles I from 1629-1640 (a period in which several attempts were made by the central government to enforce the assessment of wages), as 'remarkable for more continuous efforts to enforce socialistic measures than have been made by the central government of any other great European country', is an exaggeration which errs almost as much in one direction as Thorold Rogers did in another. The policy of 'thorough' was at best, as its two advocates are constantly reminding us, a sadly slipshod affair. But she does well to emphasise the fact that the assessment of wages was part of a general system of government intervention in economic matters, which was on the whole endorsed by the public opinion of the age, and that it must be judged in relation to that system, not as an isolated freak of arbitrary despotism.

II The act of 1563 and its antecedents

The Statute of Artificers (5 Eliz c 4) was passed in January 1563.

After reciting in the preamble that the existing statutes affecting apprentices, servants, and labourers are both mutually contradictory and unsatisfactory on the ground that the rise in money prices has made the rates of wages paid to them out of date, so that 'the said laws cannot conveniently, without the greatest grief and burden of the poor labourer and hired man, be put in due execution', it proceeds to repeal such legislation as concerns 'the hiring, keeping, departing, working, wages or order of servants, workmen, artificers, apprentices, and labourers', and to lay down a large number of provisions which may be grouped under five heads. First there are a series of clauses designed to secure stable and regular employment.[10] A list of thirty occupations is set out in which contracts of services are to stand for not less than one year at a time, and in which a quarter's notice is to be given before either party can terminate the contract. All persons who are unmarried or under the age of thirty years, who have been engaged three years in any of the above occupations, and who neither have a certain minimum of real or personal property, nor are employed by any gentleman or nobleman, nor are working on a farm of their own, may be compelled by the justices to work for any employer in any of these industries who desires their services. Second, an attempt is made to secure a sufficient supply of labour for agriculture. All persons between the ages of twelve and sixty who are not otherwise employed, and who have not a certain minimum of real or personal property laid down in the act, may be compelled to serve as labourers in husbandry in times of hay or corn harvest. Justices and constables may require 'all such artificers and persons as be meet to labour' to serve by the day for the mowing or inning of corn, grain and hay; and youths between the age of ten and eighteen may be bound as apprentices to husbandry. Thirdly, there are certain provisions as to apprenticeship, the object of which is partly to secure that youths are adequately trained, partly to prevent the overstocking of industries with juvenile workers, partly to secure an adequate supply of labour for employers, partly to preserve social distinctions by preventing free movement from one grade into another. After the first of May following the passage of the act, no one may practice 'any art, mistery or manual occupation' without first serving a seven years apprenticeship. In certain industries there must be at least one journeyman to the first three apprentices employed and an extra journeyman for every apprentice beyond that number. In cities, towns corporate, and market towns, merchants engaged in the export trade, mercers, drapers, goldsmiths, ironmongers, embroiderers or clothiers may take as apprentices only either their own children or else the children of parents with a certain minimum property qualification. Fourth, provision is made for the assessment of wages. Justices of the peace in counties, and mayors, bailiffs, or other head officers in cities, are, at their first general sessions after Easter in every year, after taking the advice of 'discrete and grave persons', and 'conferring together respecting the plenty or scarcity of the time or other circumstances necessary to be considered' to 'rate and appoint the wages as well of such of the said artificers ... or any other labourers, servants or workmen whose wages in time past hath been by any law rated and appointed, as also the wages of all other labourers, artificers ... which have not been rated'. They are to make a return of their assessments into Chancery; whereupon the Lord Chancellor or Lord Keeper, after submitting them to the Privy Council, may cause them to be printed and despatched to the respective counties concerned before the following 1 September, in the form of a proclamation. Masters giving more than the rates fixed are liable to a fine of £5 and 10 days imprisonment, servants taking more to twenty-one days imprisonment, The hours of labour are to be as follows: In summer not less than from 5 am to between 7 and 8 pm with 2½ hours interval for meals; in winter from dawn to night with the same break. Finally an attempt is made to facilitate the working of the whole system of regulation by restricting the mobility of labour. No one who is employed in agriculture or in any other of the occupations mentioned in the statute may leave the city, town, parish, hundred or county where he was last employed, unless he obtains a 'testimonial with the seal of the said City or of the Constable or other head Officer and of two other honest householders of the City, Town, or parish where he last served, declaring his lawful departure ..., which testimonial shall be delivered unto the said servant and also registered by the parson of the parish'. Anyone having a servant who has not got such a testimonial is to be fined £5, and the servant who migrates without one is to be imprisoned and whipped.

In the following pages we shall be concerned only with the wage clauses of this famous act. But they cannot be treated in isolation from the general system of which they were a part. To understand their significance it is necessary to give a short account of the type of intervention which preceded the Statute of Artificers, and which to some extent it replaced. It was closely related on the one hand to the economic activity of town authorities, and on the other hand to the attempts which had been made to regulate wages by statute. A characteristic common to all Tudor legislation upon economic matters, and accounting for the readiness with which its very drastic provisions were accepted by the classes concerned, was that so far from being an original departure, it almost invariably proceeded by erecting into a national system regulations which had long been the common property of minor authorities. Thus the statutes against depopulation, which forbade the conversion of arable land to pasture and limited the number of sheep which a man might keep, did little more than aim at constructing a universal customary out of the local customs of thousands of manors all over England. The famous Elizabethan poor law was based on the experiments made for nearly a century by the most enterprising, or the most unfortunate, localities. The statute of 1563 was no exception of the rule. In drawing up its great industrial code, the state only applied on a national scale what had long been the practice of a large number of towns.

That this was so in the matter of apprenticeship, of the restrictions imposed on the mobility of labour, of the compulsion to work which was to be brought to bear upon the unemployed requires no proof. The municipal records of the fifteenth and sixteenth centuries are full of regulations limiting the entry into occupations, providing for the expulsion of 'foreign' immigrants, requiring the workless man to stand every morning with his tools in the market-place and hire himself to the first person demanding his services. And the clauses in the act relating to the assessment of wages were to almost an equal extent grounded in the industrial practice of the towns. True, rules on the latter subject are not so common in municipal records as are rules on the former. Outside the larger towns the number of permanent wage workers was small; the typical 'workman' even in the sixteenth century was still a master craftsman; and the public was sufficiently protected against exploitation by the regulations fixing the price of goods. Nevertheless, as far as the more important boroughs are concerned, there is ample evidence to show that from very early times it was the practice for corporations to fix, quite independently of any national legislation on the subject, the wages of journeymen, and to punish those by whom their ruling was broken. The records of London, Leicester, Norwich, Beverley, Coventry, Gloucester, Chester, Bury St Edmunds, Southampton, Reading, and Nottingham all offer examples of the practice. The crafts which are most commonly the object of regulation are those connected with building (carpenters, tilers, sawyers, masons, etc) but the wages of porters, bowyers, bakers, and several different classes of workers in the woollen industry are often fixed as well. The mention of the latter industry raises the interesting point that the wages of the persons engaged in it are frequently treated in a quite special manner, the town authorities, when they deal with spinners, walkers, and weavers being frequently concerned with establishing not a maximum but a minimum wage.[11] I shall return to this matter later in speaking of the assessment of the wages of woollen workers under the act of 1563. I mention it now in order to enter a *caveat* against the conclusion that gilds and town authorities, as a rule, fixed a minimum, while the state fixed a maximum, wage, which one writer,[12] has drawn from the instances of minimum wage regulations which undoubtedly are to be found in municipal records. The distinction which should be based upon them is not a distinction between the action of the state and the action of local bodies, but between the policy of both types of authority towards workers in the woollen industry and their policy to all other classes of wage earners; for the state itself treated wages in the woollen industry in a special way. Apart from this particular industry there is no doubt that towns, like the national government, were concerned with establishing maximum rates of payment and minimum hours of labour. In a few – a very few – cases, gilds direct that workers are not to accept less than a certain price. But in almost every instance which I have examined gilds and town authorities act together to fix the terms of the contract between employer and employed, and it is hardly to be doubted that the masters who governed the gilds were frequently the rulers of the town. When journeymen's associations are mentioned they are either denounced, and threatened with proceedings under 3 & 4 Edward VI c 3, or are bound over not to inconvenience masters by raising wages. Two documents will illustrate with sufficient clearness the type of municipal regulations of which I am speaking. The first comes from Coventry[13] in 1553:

'(Enacted) That no master carpenter or sawyer shall take for his wages from Candelmas to Allhallentyd above viiid a day, and for a journeyman or a sufficient servant above 6d a day, and also that no master Tyler or rough mason during the said time shall take above 7d a day, and for their sufficient servant not above 5d a day, and no dauber during the said time shall take above vid a day, nor his servant above vd; nor no common labourer during the said term above vd a day'.

The second comes from Chester[14] in 1576. It will be noticed in the first place, that though at this time the Statute of Artificers has been passed for 13 years a town goes on regulating wages quite independently of it; and in the second place, that though the woollen industry is the object of regulation, the wage fixed is a maximum, not a minimum.

'It was then and there ordered by the said Mayor, Alderman Sheriffs and Common Council that the rate, price, and weight, of spinning, carding and weaving, walking, fulling and dyeing of wool hereafter following shall be from henceforth observed and kept, and that no manner of persons or person within the city shall take or receive for spinning and handcarding of one weight of wool above 6d, nor for stock carding of every stone of wool above 6d, nor for weaving any piece of woollen cloth containing xxii yards in length above 12d, nor for walking any such piece of cloth above 8d, nor the shearman for dressing any such piece of cloth above 10d, nor for the dyeing of any stone of wool above 16d.[15]

Rules of this kind, entering sometimes into greater, sometimes into less, detail, are typical. The establishment of a maximum wage was in fact a settled part of municipal policy from the thirteenth to at least the seventeenth century. Since the earliest example comes from the year 1264,[16] nearly a century before the first Statute of Labourers, and the latest which I have noticed from 1634, a period when the personal government of Charles I was making exceptional efforts to get the Statute of Artificers successfully administered, municipal action must be regarded as having anticipated that of the state, and having run parallel to, and continued independently of, the intervention of the justices. To the small oligarchies of master craftsmen and traders who governed most sixteenth century towns the wage clauses of the Statute of Artificers must have come as an extremely welcome enforcement of their traditional policy.

If the assessment of wages was in accordance with the ideas of the town bourgeoisie it was equally in line with those of all the rural classes, great and small, who were interested in the employment of labour. Of the labour problem in the rural districts I shall have something to say later, when I come to speak of the economic aspects of the assessment of wages. The establishment of a maximum wage by the state had been in origin an attempt to help those classes out of the difficulty created by the great plague of 1348-49. The act which set the precedent, however, for subsequent legislation was not the first Statute of Labourers, but an act of 1389 (13 Richard II c 8), which placed the assessment of wages in the hands of the justices of the peace subject to a statutory maximum imposed by Parliament. It was this act, re-enacted in 1445 (23 Henry VI c 13), 1496 (11 Henry VII c 22), and 1514 (6 Henry

VIII c 3), which Elizabethan statesmen found ready to hand as the embodiment of traditional wisdom on the subject of state interference with wages; which they examined, partially preserved, and partially improved upon.

They improved upon both it and the experiments of the towns in two ways. In the first place, though the main ideas of the Statute of Artificers had been applied for centuries to particular trades, particular localities, or particular problems, the statute of 1563 made a new departure by dealing in one comprehensive measure with all the principal relationships surrounding the contract between employer and employed. In the second place, it abolished the statutory maximum which had hitherto limited the justices' discretion in the assessment of wages, and thus made it possible for them, in the not very probable contingency of their thinking wages too low, to make the scales which they drew up slide freely in both directions. The former innovation was one which was peculiarly congenial to the ideas of the age. Both political reasons – a worship of the state amounting to idolatry – and economic reasons – the destruction of customary relationships by the swift changes of the preceding half century – caused the establishment of a great industrial code to be an expedient foreshadowed by several writers in the first half of the sixteenth century. To many of the better minds of the generation which grew up between 1530 and 1540 the world seemed to have experienced within their memory a complete collapse of the forces making for stability in economic life. Whether politicians who noted the absence of 'good order' in industry, or moralists denouncing the exploitation of the weak by the powerful, or municipal authorities lamenting that 'the wretched life of ociosite or idleness is the rote of all vice and engendreth slothe, poverty, miserie and other inconveniences as voluptuositie and all other vayne things', what struck them most was the fact that the dislocation of traditional standards seemed to be general, all-pervading and increasing. It was this universal disorganisation which explains why it is that scientific economic thought really begins in England about the middle of the sixteenth century. What supplied the stimulus to it then was what gave it its impetus both in the eighteenth century and in our own day, namely the existence of grave practical evils. People had been accustomed from time immemorial to ascribe a rise in prices to the covetousness of brewers and bakers and the uncharitableness of artificers and merchants. Now they saw all prices rising together, and to attribute price movements to the exorbitant demands of some particular monopolist was no longer a satisfactory explanation. They had seen groups of peasants evicted by a tyrannous landlord. Now there was a complete alteration in the balance between the life of the country and the life of the towns. They had grumbled often enough that the justices did not do their duty in fixing wages. Now the disturbance of customary levels of remuneration had brought with it an upward movement in wages, which, though it did not correspond with the upward movement in prices, carried them well beyond the statutory maximum by which the justices' discretion had been limited. The bewilderment which the collapse of traditional standards produced is expressed very clearly by one of the few contemporary writers who understood it, in the dialogue composed probably about 1549, and called *Discourse of the Commonweal of this Realm of England,* where husbandman blames landlord, and landlord artificer, and artificer merchant, and merchant foreign exporter, for a movement for which none of them is primarily responsible, but which occurs, in the words of the writer, 'as in a press where the foremost is driven by him that is next him, and the next by him that follows him, and the third by some violent and strong thing which drives him forward'[17] The demand for a measure of economic reorganisation as comprehensive as these changes themselves was expressed in several works, of which the *Dialogue between Reginald Pole and Thomas Lupset,* composed by Starkey, Henry VIII's chaplain, about 1536, may be taken as typical.[18] Starkey's programme, though in some respects more drastic than the Statute of Artificers, is in others a most remarkable anticipation of its main provisions, and shows that the sort of regulation which it contained was such as political thought found congenial. He proposed to compel parents either to apprentice their children, when they reached the age of seven, to a craft, or to send them to school; to empower the authorities of cities and the curate in every village, together with 'the gentleman chefe lord of the same' to inquire into the characters of all persons who have no settled occupation, and to appoint officers 'to see that there be no idle persons without craft or means to get a living', suggestions which anticipate both the compulsory apprenticeship of the act of 1563, and the clauses which authorised the justices of the peace to compel persons who had practised certain occupations for three years to work in them for any master requiring their services. Equally illuminating as a comment upon the Statute of Artificers is his lamentation over the growth in the number of beggars, over the tendency of one craft to encroach upon the province of another, and over the emigration from the country districts. These were precisely the evils which the act tried to meet by giving justices power to compel unemployed persons to labour in husbandry, and by stratifying social classes by means of the clauses providing that no parent who had not a certain property qualification should apprentice his child to certain occupations. The belief in the necessity of an all-comprehensive system of regulation was, in fact, a commonplace. When the act of 1563 was passed, it was welcomed as meeting an urgent need. 'In times passed' ran a memorial stating 'The causes whie bothe lawfull artificers and unlawefull artificers do desyer to have the statute towchinge them to be put in execution and obs'vid' addressed to the government in 1573, and urging the better administration of the act, 'while order was observed among artificers, they found their trades and occupations such a stay of living that by means thereof they might maintain themselves in all things necessary for their calling ... But since disorder hath entered among them and increase of offences grown, they have found their trades and occupations so uncertain and their earnings and gettings so abated that they want to maintain themselves with things necessary ... Wherefore to stay the further increase of such offences, they do become suitors and earnestly desire to have the said Statute executed and observed'.[19]

But what of the other new departure in the act of 1563, the removal of the statutory maximum to wages? This was a policy which was not so readily accepted. It is a curious illustration of the tyranny of an established idea that the proposals first made by the government should have apparently aimed simply at re-enacting a maximum wage by act of parliament, and that the decision to leave the assessment of actual rates to the justices for their yearly revision, which was the only original[20] feature in the Elizabethan wage policy, should have been adopted as an afterthought, probably as the result of debate in parliament. That this was so is suggested by a document which a fortunate chance has preserved, and which appears to be an outline of the bill[21] before its introduction, and of certain other measures as well, drafted by Cecil, in accordance with his usual practice, for preliminary consideration. It throws such an extremely interesting light upon the ideas of the statesman who was principally responsible both for the act of 1563 and for the other economic legislation of Elizabeth's reign, that I may be pardoned for quoting it at some length.[22]

Considerations delivered to the Parliament 1559

1. Vagabonds – That the Statute 1 Ed. VI cap 3, concerning idle

persons and vagabonds being made slaves, now repealed, be revived with additions.

2. Labourers and servants – That the statutes Richard II cap 3 that no servant or labourer at the end of his term depart out of the hundred where he dwells, etc and 13 Richard II cap 8, ordering the Justices to appoint by proclamation the wages of artificers, be confirmed, with the addition that no man hereafter receive into service any servant without a testimonial from the master he last dwelt with, sealed with a Parish seal kept by the Constable or Churchwarden witnessing he left with the free license of his master, penalty £10. So, by the need of the masters servants may be reduced to obedience, which shall reduce obedience to the prince and to God also; by the looseness of the time, no other remedy is left but by awe of the law to acquaint men with virtue again; whereby the Reformation of religion may be brought in credit, with the amendment of manners, the want whereof has been as a thing grown by the liberty of the Gospel.
3. Husbandry – That the statutes of 4 Henry VII cap 9 for re-edifying houses of husbandry to avoid the decay of towns and villages, and 5 Ed. V cap 5 for maintenance of husbandry and tillage be put in execution.
4. Purchase of lands – No husbandman, yeoman, or artificer to purchase above £5 by the year of inheritance, save in cities, towns and boroughs, for their better repair; one mansion house only to be purchased over and above the said yearly value. The common purchasing thereof is the ground of dearth of victuals, raising of rents etc.
5. Merchants – No Merchant to purchase above £50 a year of inheritance, except aldermen and Sheriffs of London, who, because they approach to the degree of knighthood, may purchase to the value of £200.
6. Apprentices – None to be received apprentice except his father may spend 40/- a year of freehold, none to be apprenticed to a Merchant except his father spend £10 a year of freehold, or be descended from a gentleman or merchant. Through the idleness of these professions so many embrace them that they are only a cloak for vagabonds and thieves, and there is such a decay of husbandry that masters cannot get skilful servants to till the ground without unreasonable wages.

The document then goes on to matters into which we need not follow it, such as the education of the nobility, the necessity of securing a supply of bullion and the erection of tariffs against imported articles. The important point for us is to compare Cecil's draft with the shape which legislation finally took in the hands of parliament. It will be seen that while a considerable part of it was actually embodied either in the Statute of Artificers or in other acts, its general tendency is at once more conservative and more repressive then the statutes which actually became law. It proposes for example to re-enact an extremely brutal act of 1547 providing that a vagrant should after the third conviction become the slave of anyone arresting him, which had been repealed only two years after it was passed. The suggestion was quite in accordance with the legislation of the first half of the sixteenth century, when the economic causes of unemployment were not understood. But, as a matter of fact, the Elizabethan poor law legislation proceeded upon the quite different principle of distinguishing between the man unemployed for personal reasons, who was to be punished, and the man unemployed for economic reasons, who was to be 'set on work'; and forty years later Cecil's own son, then secretary of state in his father's place, penned a memorandum[23] preliminary to the introduction of the poor relief measure of 1597, which altogether threw overboard his father's earlier ideas. The impracticable rigour of Cecil's views with regard to the suppression of vagrancy should be remembered in considering his proposals for the regulation of wages. It will be noticed that while he makes the object of the enforcement of maximum wages perfectly clear by his allusion to the 'unreasonable wages' demanded by servants in husbandry,[24] what he actually recommends is simply the re-enactment of the second Statute of Labourers passed 170 years before. What can only be called the unreasoning conservatism of this suggestion is doubly noteworthy in view of the extreme improbability that the act which Cecil wished to see re-enacted was ever successfully enforced. Our information about the assessment of wages in the fifteenth century is, it is true, very meagre. The justices were not required, as under the act of 1563, to make returns to Chancery of the rates fixed, and it is not until the organisation of the Tudor bureaucracy that a close supervision of local authorities by the Council begins to supply us with masses of material in the shape of letters to justices, orders, and proclamations. We have only two assessments made under the act of 1389, one from Coventry[25] in 1420, and one from Norfolk[26] in 1431, a proclamation[27] issued in 1452 directing that labourers and artificers should take such wages as were fixed by the statutes, one or two cases of men being brought before the courts for taking excessive wages[28] and a few records of attempts on the part of town authorities to insist that labourers should 'offer themselves to be hired to labour for their living according to the King's laws and Statutes provided for labourers'.[29] Rules were made in the city of London in 1514, 1521 and 1538 in pursuance of the act of 1514 assessing wages[30] and in Coventry rough masons and daubers were directed 'to take such wages as is limited them by the statutes hereupon made'.[31] While, however, researches into the administration of the act in the fifteenth century similar to those which Miss Putnam has made for the years 1349-1359, may possibly show the justices to have been more active than our scanty evidence suggests, they are not likely substantially to modify the picture of the general inefficiency of the acts in the fifteenth century, and still more in the sixteenth century, which we got from other sources. The rolls of parliament[32] are full of complaints that the justices are not doing their duty, that masters who refuse to pay more than the legal maximum find themselves without workmen, that men escape service by pretending to be living upon their own holdings. The passage of subsequent acts raising the maximum suggests that economic forces were too strong for the law. And of course the depreciation of money which took place with increasing rapidity from the accession of Henry VIII intensified all difficulties. In the very year after the last act of the old model was passed, in 1515, it was found necessary to allow workers connected with the building trades in London to take the higher rates[33] which had been customary before it. The fearful hardships which spasmodic attempts to enforce the legal maximum involved were described in burning words by More. 'They invent and devise all meanes and crafts ... how to hire and abuse the worke and labour of the poor for as little money as may be'. The context shows that the reference is to legislation.[34] Ten years before Cecil drafted his bill, Hales pointed out that in a time of rising prices servingmen could not possibly live on 'their old stinted wages'. That sad precocious child, Edward VI, in a catalogue of the signs of the evil days in which his lot was cast, had set down that 'labourers have enhanced their wages and artificers the price of their workmanship'.[35] It is not surprising, therefore, that Cecil's proposal to re-establish a fixed statutory maximum, a maximum which, if his proposals are to be taken literally, was to stand at the figures settled when the purchasing power of money had been at least from three to four times what it was in the middle of the sixteenth century, should have roused bitter resentment. 'The business', writes one of Cecil's agents to him, 'touching what wages workmen should take, was much cried out upon'.[36] The remarkable thing is that the re-enactment of the old maximum rates should ever have been thought possible for a moment. The episode is a comment upon the views of those writers who speak as though the Tudor regime were that of an enlightened bureaucracy using the resources of scientific administration to pursue a farsighted and clearly conceived economic policy. The whole economic environment had been revolutionised by the fall in the value of money, and here is the ablest statesman of the Elizabethan age on his knees before mediaeval precedents, till (apparently) the country gentlemen in the House of Commons bring him up to date! Clearly in the early years of Elizabeth economic rationalism was not a mighty force.

III Was the act carried out?

The first question to be considered in relation to the wage clauses of the Statute of Artificers concerns their administration. To what extent did the justices of the peace fulfil the obligations to 'rate and appoint wages' once a year, which was imposed upon them by the act of 1563? An answer to this question must be based, in the first instance, on a statistical survey of the evidence at our disposal, and such a survey I attempt to give in the two tables set out below. Table II groups assessments according to their dates, table I to the districts – counties or boroughs – for which they were made. It will be seen from the first two columns of table I that the total number of complete and different assessments which are at present known to exist is seventy-three, and that, in addition to these, we have twenty-four assessments which appear to be mere reissues or repetitions of assessments already made. The total number of wage lists, therefore, which are at present known to be extant is ninety-seven.

Seventy-three original and independent assessments, twenty-four reissues of assessments already made, though representing a considerable increase over the documents known to exist when Professor Hewins and Dr Cunningham treated the subject, is not a large number to be produced by an act which applied to the whole of England and Wales, and which was nominally in force for a period of exactly two hundred and fifty years. It is not surprising, therefore, that most economic historians, with the exception of Thorold Rogers (who expressed the opinion that the actual course of wages did follow the justices' assessments down to 1813, but who did not produce any satisfactory evidence for his statement, and, indeed, could not do so, owing to the extremely small number of assessments which he had before him) should have held that the wage clauses of the act of 1563 were largely inoperative; inoperative not merely in the sense that assessments, when made, were not enforced, but in the sense that it was only on quite exceptional occasions that they were made at all, except, perhaps, during a limited period after the passage of Cecil's bill into law. Professor Hewins[37] and Dr Cunningham[38] agree in thinking that, though the act may possibly have been administered fairly frequently during the first eighty years or so after its enactment, the fall of the Stuart monarchy, which involved the weakening, and later almost the complete cessation, of interference by the central government in local economic conditions, brought anything like the regular assessment of wages to an end. Such opinions seem to me, however, to be considerably overstated. The view that the constitutional changes brought about by the destruction of the old regime were such as to make it improbable that the act was ever carried out subsequently with the same regularity as during the reign of Elizabeth and of the first two Stuarts appears to be based on reasoning of an *a priori* character which requires several qualifications. It is not easily reconciled with the actual records of assessments which we possess. A glance at table II will show that, as a matter of fact, the reigns of James I and Charles I are not a period for which we possess many assessments, and that assessments do not by any means cease with the years 1640 or 1642. On the contrary there are twenty-five assessments for the 40 years from 1650 to 1689, as against thirteen for the years 1600 to 1639. After 1660 the century-long rise in prices came to an end. Prices began to fall, and the downward movement in prices was naturally an opportunity for trying to force a similar movement in wages. This was avowedly the reason for the assessment of wages by the authorities of the city of London in 1655: 'Wee, the Mr. and Wardens of the Company of Carpenters, in pursuance of your lordships desire for the reducing of the excessive wages of Labourers and Workmen in these times of great plenty, we humbly conceive to be sufficient that Labourers take for wages but 16d a day only etc'[39] and it is probable that the operation of the same motive elsewhere is the explanation of the comparatively numerous assessments of the Restoration period.[40] Moreover the analogies which may be adduced – and the argument is admittedly one from analogy – to

TABLE I ASSESSMENTS BY COUNTIES AND BOROUGHS

County or Borough	Number of complete assessments exclusive of reissues	Number of reissues	Orders continuing assessments already made	Assessments referred to, but not included above	Action ordered by Privy Council
Buckinghamshire	4				
Cambridgeshire	-				1
Cardigan	1				
Cheshire	-			1	
Derbyshire	2			1	
Devon	3				
Essex	2			1	1
Gloucestershire	3			1	
Hertfordshire	1				
Kent	1				
Lancashire	1				
Lincolnshire	5			1	
Middlesex	1			1	
Norfolk	1				1
Northamptonshire	2				
Nottinghamshire	1			1	
Rutland	2				
Shropshire	1	5		1	
Somerset	9			1	
Suffolk	2				1
Warwickshire	5	4	1		
Wiltshire	6		82		
Worcestershire	1				
Yorkshire, ER	1				
Yorkshire, NR	2			1	
Yorkshire, WR	1	6			
Chester	5	1			
Colchester				1	
Kingston upon Hull	1				
Lancaster	1				
Leicester				1	
Lincoln	1				
London	3	8	4		
New Sarum (Salisbury)	1			1	1
Reading				1	
St Albans	1				
Sandwich	1				
Southampton				1	
Warwick	1				
TOTAL	73	24	87	15	5

TABLE II ASSESSMENTS BY DATE (DECADES)
Number of assessments, including reissues which can be dated

1560-69	5	1670-79	3
1570-79	2	1680-89	7
1580-89	1	1690-99	1
1590-99	11	1700-09	6
1600-09	3	1710-19	5
1610-19	3	1720-29	3
1620-29	1	1730-39	10
1630-39	6	1740-49	-
1640-49	4	1750-59	1
1650-59	12	1760-69	3
1660-69	3	1770-79	-

Total: 90

suggest that with the decline in the administrative activity of the Privy Council the assessment of wages declined also will not bear examination. It is, of course, perfectly true that the victory of parliamentary government, which carried with it as a corollary the abolition of 'administrative law', did involve a laxity in the control of local affairs which, in the course of time, and in certain departments of administration, produced something like complete anarchy. The attempts for example, which had been fitfully made under James and Charles, to protect the peasantry by checking enclosures involving depopulation, came to an end with the restoration of parliamentary government in 1640, and Laud lived to be reminded in the day of his ruin of the sharp words with which he had barbed the fine imposed by the commission for depopulation upon an enclosing landlord.[41] The effective enforcement upon parochial authorities of their statutory obligations to relieve the aged and infirm and to set unemployed persons to work, was replaced, when the pressure of the Council upon the justices was removed, by a neglect which resulted in each board becoming a law to itself, so that, by the middle of the eighteenth century, there were in England almost as many poor law systems as there were counties. But the analogy between these types of intervention and the assessment of wages is an extremely superficial one. Interference in disputes between landlord and tenants over commons and copyholds, insistence on the efficient administration of the Elizabethan poor law, these things came to an end in 1640, not because there was any general prejudice in favour of laisser-faire – of any general economic policy parliament was quite innocent – but because these were just the matters to which the of Dr Cunningham's volume appeared in 1903, evidence showing the existence of at least thirty-two assessments not mentioned by him has come to light. Nor can much weight be allowed to the utterances of contemporary writers, which imply that assessments were habitually made. Smith[45] and Lambard[46] in the sixteenth century, Shepperd[47] in the seventeenth, certainly speak of the assessment of wages as being one of the ordinary duties of a justice of the peace. But then so does Fitzherbert[48] at an earlier date, when there is little doubt that the acts fixing wages were not administered; and, in any case, little reliance can be placed on the general statements of authors of legal textbooks.[49] What suggests that the assessments in our possession must not be taken as representing anything like the full activity of the justices is, first, the existence of references in official documents which show that numerous assessments were made that have not come down to us, and secondly the fact, which is apparent from the Quarter Session records, that in some counties and cities it was the custom to continue existing assessments by order from year to year, so that the administration of the law was receiving attention from the justices, even when no new assessments were made.

The first point may be illustrated by the examples of Derbyshire, Essex, the North Riding of Yorkshire, Reading and Leicester. The earliest assessment which we possess from the first county is one of 1634, and, in default of further information, the absence of others might be taken as evidence that the administration of the act of 1563 was neglected in Derbyshire till that date. That this would be an error is proved by the fact that a document[50] of the year 1618 mentions the delivery to the clerk of the peace (probably by a servant of one of the justices) of 'three several rolls of parchments containing the rates of servants wages'. The only full assessment known to exist for Essex was made in 1651. But there remains the preamble of an assessment drawn up in 1612: '23. April 1612. Roll and schedule of the Particulars of Wages for all manner of artificers and servants; set forth by the Justices of the Peace for the Co. Essex; under the seals and signatures of the same Justices'.[51] There is no complete assessment for the North Riding of Yorkshire before the year 1658. But presentments[52] of offenders for breaches of the wage clauses of the Statute of Artificers, made at intervals between the years 1608 and 1647, showed that at least one assessment, and probably more than one, had been issued by the justices before that date. The Quarter Sessions records of the same county show no assessment under the year 1691. But since an order interests of the triumphant landed gentry, who wanted to be free to increase their rent rolls and to escape the poor rates, were opposed. The fixing of maximum wages by the action of the justices stood upon a quite different footing. The system had been originally introduced, and had been re-enacted in 1563, in order to protect not the wage-earners but the wage-payers, and though this object was not incompatible with occasional attempts by the Privy Council to use the act to fix in certain industries a minimum, there is no reason whatever to suppose that the policy of fixing a maximum wage was other than highly popular with the employers of agricultural labour, whose complaints of the 'unreasonableness' of the workers demands are quite common in the latter part of the seventeenth century. The Commonwealth[42] government in April 1649 directed justices to assess wages, and Petty, one of the few writers who suggests that assessments were regarded as a grievance by the poor, writes in 1662 as though they were a not uncommon practice: 'Besides it is unjust to let any starve, when we think it just to limit the wages of the poor, so as they can lay up nothing against the time of their impotency and want of work'.[43] Hence, while the use of the wage clauses of the Statute of Artificers to fix a *minimum* certainly was bound up with the administrative intervention of the Privy Council, and thus terminated in 1640,[44] the use of them to enforce a maximum – the normal object of assessing wages – certainly was not; and to suggest that the latter policy must have disappeared with the former when the period of absolutism came to an end, is to confuse the general purpose of the act with an occasional deviation from it. The probabilities of the case are at one, in fact, with the direct evidence of documents, in suggesting that the assessment of wages was carried out as regularly in the forty years after the outbreak of the Civil War as in the forty years before it.

To say this, it may be answered, is not to say much. The question remains whether the ninety-seven assessments, which are all that have as yet been unearthed, can be taken as in any way representing the full activity of the justices, or whether there is reason to suppose that the act was more regularly administered than this small number of detailed tables would indicate. To this question the answer must be given that the scantiness of the specimens available for analysis must certainly not be taken as implying that for the years and places for which no assessments exist, no action was taken by the justices in pursuance of the law. It is not merely that new assessments are constantly being discovered, though this, indeed, is striking enough; I estimate that since the third edition made in 1692[53] directs 'the same rates of wages ... to stand this year as they were appointed and settled by order of this court last year', an assessment must have been made in the preceding year.[54] For Reading and Leicester no assessments at all have survived. But in 1598 offenders against the act were being tried in the court of the mayor of Reading[55] while from Leicester there is conclusive evidence that the act received attention regularly from 1564 down to at least 1603 and possibly longer. The records[56] of that borough show that in every year of that period a certificate was forwarded by the borough authorities to Chancery, setting out the wages of servants, labourers, and artificers. Similar evidence of the enforcement of the act at a time for which few assessments are known to exist is supplied by the registers[57] of the Privy Council, which prove that assessments were issued by the authorities in London on at least eleven occasions between 1563 and 1596. This source of information is, it is true, disappointing. It comes to an end with the passage of the act of 1598 (39 Eliz c 12) relieving justices of the duty of making returns of their assessments to Chancery. Further, there is no reason to suppose that a formal letter was always or usually written by the Council to the Lord Keeper directing him to print the assessments which had been made, and it would, therefore, be quite erroneous to regard the small number of entries in the Privy Council registers as implying that no assessments were made upon other occasions. What these entries, and other references of the kind mentioned above, do prove, is that wages were assessed in many years and places for which no assessments have yet been discovered, and that it would, therefore, be quite erroneous to use the absence of assessments as proof that the act was administered with laxity. They show that the assessments in our possession are a mere residuum of a much larger number which have perished. In each of the instances mentioned above the absence of assessments might have led us to argue that the act was a dead letter, and in each instance the inference would be wrong. From these and similar miscellaneous references I estimate that we know that at least fifteen assessments were made of which we have no particulars. That is a minimum figure; but it brings up the number of assessments of whose existence we have proof from 97 to 112. More important, it suggests that a very large number of assessments must have perished, without leaving any trace whatever behind them.

In the second place, when the regularity of the administration of the act is being considered, due weight must be given to the practice of continuing existing assessments by order of Quarter Sessions in years in which no full assessment was made. Such orders are of course, evidence for the practice of assessment as complete as the issue of actual rates,[58] and prove conclusively that an omission on the part of the justices to publish fresh rates did not necessarily imply a failure upon their part to comply with the law. Miss McArthur[59] has shown, for example, that during twenty-one out of the twenty-eight years immediately following the passage of the act of 1563 the authorities of the city of London either issued assessments or issued orders continuing existing assessments. My own investigations have led me to believe that this continuous activity was by no means exceptional. The practice of the Wiltshire[60] justices supplies a case in point. In that county new assessments were made at various dates in the seventeenth century, 1602, 1603, 1605, 1635, 1655, 1685. But the fact that assessments were made in this county only at long intervals does not prove that the administration of the act was at a standstill in the intervening years. As far as the letter of the law went the justices were discharging their statutory duties if they renewed the old rates without a change. This they did in Wiltshire every year from 1603 to 1696, with the exception of an interval of eleven out of the whole ninety-three years, four out of the eleven being those from 1642-3 to 1645-6, when country gentlemen had sterner work in hand than the routine business of Quarter Sessions. The question whether regular confirmation of rates fixed many years before was due to mere carelessness, or was justified by the fact that conditions had not altered, is of course, quite another matter. When the clerk of the peace read out a schedule containing, like that drawn up for Wiltshire in 1603, some 200 separate items, and asked whether it was to be continued or revised, somnolent justices meeting in a bar parlour were probably disposed to have a high opinion of the wisdom of their predecessors. On the other hand it would certainly be wrong to assume that the frequent reissue of old assessments necessarily implied negligence. On the economic objects and effects of the policy something will be said later. But one may point out here that the assessment of wages in the sixteenth and seventeenth centuries did not involve the problem of readjusting them in accordance with constantly fluctuating economic conditions, which confronts any authority interfering with wages at the present day. The practice with regard not only to wages but to prices and the rate of interest was based on the idea that values were objective realities, which could, as it were, be held in position, irrespective of the higgling of the market. In the slowly moving life of the time, with its almost stationary population, and its absence of rapidly growing industries, there was, in general, not the same reason for changes in the rates of remuneration as exist to-day. One such reason there was. Food prices fluctuated violently, far more violently than they do in modern industrial communities. If movements in wages had been adjusted with any accuracy to movements in prices, it would have been necessary for them to take place not only from year to year, but from month to month, and, indeed, almost from day to day.[61] The machinery for dealing with such temporary oscillations was not so much, however, the Statute of Artificers, as the regulation of markets and the fixing of the prices of food supplies. It cannot therefore be assumed that the admitted omission of the justices to make wages correspond with the short-period fluctuations necessarily implies that they failed to carry out the intentions of the act.

To sum up this part of my discussion: the view taken by most economic historians that the wage assessment clauses of the act of 1563 were, except on special occasions, a dead letter, and that whatever vitality they had under Elizabeth and the first two Stuarts disappeared after the Civil War, must be regarded as, to say the least, not proven.[62] In the first place, there was no reason why the rise of parliamentary government should have had the effect of making justices of the peace less disposed to fix maximum wages, nor does the actual distribution of assessments over different periods bear out the conclusion that it had. In the second place, the discoveries recently made of new assessments and the considerable number of references proving that assessments were made which have not come down to us, show that those which we possess are a remnant of a much larger number. In the third place, the fact that in years when no new assessments were made, the justices nevertheless attended to the duties imposed upon them by law, suggests that the mere absence of assessments cannot in itself be taken as an indication of laxity of administration.

IV The motives for the assessment of wages in non-textile trades

In what light are we to regard the system of regulating wages which was set up by the Statute of Artificers? Are its opening words, with their declaration that 'wages are in divers places too small ... respecting the advancement of prices' to be taken as indicating a paternal solicitude on the part of the government for the well-being of the wage earning classes? Or should we follow Thorold Rogers in discounting this pious preamble as mere hypocrisy, and see in the assessment of wages simply one outcome of the enduring instinct of the governing classes in favour of using the law to buttress their economic privileges?

Between the hypotheses of philanthropy and class tyranny it is not, perhaps, necessary to make a definite choice. The mediaeval ideal of equity in bargaining, of which the fixing of wages was one expression, was based on the assumption that it was possible to do substantial justice to the interests of all parties to a contract; and though there are some indications that in the seventeenth century puritanism, with its insistence on the duty of labour, and its severe condemnation of luxury, led to a harsh view being taken on the moral evils supposed to result from high wages, the establishment of a maximum wage did not in itself necessarily involve any more injustice to the wage-worker than the establishment of a maximum price did to the dealer. That, as far at least as all trades except the textile industries were concerned, the principal object of the assessment of wages was to prevent them rising above the level thought 'reasonable' by the justices, there is no doubt whatever. Quite apart from the connection between the act of 1563 and the earlier Statutes of Labourers, both the wording and the administration of the law leave no room for uncertainty as to its purpose. It imposes penalties on those who pay or accept more, not on those who pay or accept less, than the legal rates. A form commonly employed in the assessments is that 'wages shall be such and no more than are hereafter set down'. When punishment is incurred by masters and workmen, it is invariably for exceeding the figure fixed by the justices. The writers of legal text-books all state that the wage was a maximum. The cases to be considered later, in which a minimum was established, are of a special and peculiar character, and in no way invalidate the conclusion that, as a general rule, the object and effect of assessments were to prevent the worker demanding more than a certain sum for his labour.

To say this, however, is neither to substantiate Rogers' charge of hypocrisy, nor to imply that, in the circumstances of the age, the establishment of maximum rates was a piece of intolerable tyranny. In the first place, there is the minor point that the view sometimes expressed as to the discrepancy between the preamble of the act and its substance appears to have been formed in forgetfulness of the fact that it was one, and the least harsh, of a series. As a matter of fact the wage clauses did exactly what the preamble indicated that they should do. They substituted a sliding scale for the fixed maximum imposed by previous statutes. The effect of this is seen in the words with which assessments frequently begin, stating that they are made 'in respect and consideration had of the great dearth and scarcity of things at this present', or 'having a special regard ... to the prices at this time of all kinds of victual and apparel, and all other necessary charges, wherewith artificers, labourers and servants are more grieviously charged than in time past'. Whether the movement of wages did in fact correspond to the movement of prices is, of course, another question. As will be shown later, there is good reason for believing that in most districts it did not. But that should not be allowed to obscure the fact that the statute of 1563 made possible a movement of legal rates, which, under the earlier acts, had been out of the question. By directing yearly assessments it certainly fulfilled the declaration of its preamble, that it was enacted in order to 'yield unto the hired person both in the time of scarcity and in the time of plenty a convenient proportion of wages'.

In the second place, the policy of fixing a maximum wage must be interpreted with reference to the general economic circumstances of the Tudor age. The two fundamental facts in the social structure of the sixteenth century were the wide distribution of property and the scarcity of wage labour. It is, of course, quite true that the process of commutation which, in spite of the existence of backwaters where the remnants of labour services still lingered on, was virtually complete by the reign of Elizabeth, can only be explained by the existence of a considerable number of persons who were available for employment as hired labourers. It is true also that the agrarian revolution which was taking place with growing rapidity from 1450 onwards resulted in the increase of a landless proletariat dependent upon wages for its livelihood. But though forces were at work to replace the mediaeval wage problem, which consisted in the scarcity of labour, by the modern wage problem, which consists in its abundance, they certainly had not by the middle of the sixteenth century proceeded so far as to effect any substantial alteration in the balance between the relatively large number of property holders and the relatively small number of wage workers. Statistical evidence on this subject is naturally not very easy to obtain, but such as it is, it confirms the view that except in those parts of the country, like East Anglia, where a large population was employed in the textile industries, the family entirely dependent for its livelihood upon wage-labour was in rural districts the exception. That this was the case is suggested in the first place, by such incidental evidences of economic status as are supplied by the descriptions of offenders presented for justice. In the Quarter Sessions records[63] of the North Riding, for example, at the beginning of the seventeenth century, the large number of yeomen and husbandmen presented is very striking. Out of 3780 persons mentioned in recognisancies in the records[64] of the Worcestershire Quarter Sessions between 1591 and 1643, 667 are described as labourers, 1303 as husbandmen, 1810 as yeomen, the latter always, and the second usually, implying a holder of land. The more detailed evidence of manorial surveys points in the same direction. Taking 52[65] manors in the sixteenth century, I find that of the 1664 customary tenants upon them rather more than one-third, 562, had less than 5 acres of land, while of these 255 had more than 2½ acres, and only 167 are entered as holding no land other than gardens. In Norfolk or Suffolk, the proportion of landless cottagers, is as one would expect, considerably larger, and, of course, though the head of a family held land, he had usually a family of sons who would be employed for a time, at any rate, by the large farmers of the district. But such figures suggest that the proportion of persons holding land in sixteenth-century England was still large; while if we approach the matter from the other end, and examine the staffs employed both on demesne farms and by small landholders, we shall be inclined, I think, to say, that the number of employees, even when there is no reason to suspect any sweeping change in the direction of pasture farming, was singularly small. On the demesne farms of 22 religious[66] houses in Leicester, Warwick and Sussex there were on the eve of the Dissolution 255 hinds, and 76 women servants, an average of about 11 hinds and about 3 women to each farm. Best[67] narrates how he worked a considerable farm of Yorkshire with 4 men, 2 boys, and 2 maidservants; and we read of a village[68] where in the latter part of the seventeenth century, 13 freeholders farmed 580 acres with the aid of only 10 menservants before enclosure, and of 7 afterwards. The smallness of the permanent staff of wage-workers suggests that at times of unusual pressure, labour must generally have been drawn from men who normally were occupied on their own holdings, and quite explains why the Statute of Artificers empowered the justices to press artisans for work on the land during the corn and hay harvest.

A recollection of the large part which was played in sixteenth-century England by the small property holders should warn us that to estimate the wage policy of Tudor and Stuart governments by presuppositions drawn from the experience of modern industrial communities is an error in the very foundations of the subject. In countries where the 'Great Industry' has developed, the vast majority of the population are workers for wages; the principal social problem is the problem of wages; to fix a maximum wage by law would be to depress the price of something, which is already, often, a drug in the market. In the England of the Tudors and Stuarts, though the proportion of the people employed as wage-labourers was growing, the typical 'workman' was not a wage-labourer, but a small master craftsman or a landholding peasant. The economic problem which received most attention both from writers and statesmen was not the problem of wages, but that of usury and prices, matters which were felt acutely by the man who had to stock his farm or his shop with borrowed capital, and who was easily exploited by a large dealer who cornered the supplies of raw materials or food stuffs. The wage labourers scattered between the interstices of a society based on property were often in a strong position relatively to their employers. To check by law the demands which they might make was often no doubt a grievance analagous to that of the speculator in grain, who found his profits swept away when prices were lowered by a proclamation from the Privy Council, or when an energetic justice inspected his barns and exposed to compulsory sale below the market rates the corn which he had hoarded against a time of scarcity. The object, however, of assessing wages was not to benefit a privileged oligarchy of employers at the expense of the vast majority of workers, but to protect one class of workers against another.[69] The system is evidence not so much of the defencelessness of the wage-worker against oppression as of the fact that he was often able to drive a hard bargain with a master who was not much better off than himself.

Such an account of the economic environment which produced the system of assessing wages will not seem fanciful to anyone who studies contemporary complaints of the difficulties caused by the scarcity of labour. One must of course enter a caveat against taking the arguments of employers or of those who write from the employers' standpoint *au pied de la lettre.* But their statements, even when discounted, harmonise too well with what we know from other sources, to be other than reliable. To give an extreme example of the situation which sometimes arose one may cite in the first place the difficulties of the English colony of Massachussetts. The experience of the colonists is worth attention, because the scarcity of labour which is to be expected in a new country naturally causes the problem to be seen there in its simplest form. The journal of Winthrop,[70] the governor of the colony, gives us an insight into the situation produced by the high prices of labour. 'The scarcity of workmen had caused them to raise their wages to an excessive height, so as a carpenter would have three shillings a day, a labourer two shillings and sixpence etc and accordingly those who had commodities to sell advanced their prices sometimes double that they cost in England ... which the Court taking knowledge of, made an order that carpenters, masons, etc should take but two shillings a day, and labourers eighteen pence, and that no commodities should be sold at above fourpence in the shilling more than it cost for ready money in England'. 'I may upon this occasion report a passage between one Rowley and his servant. The master being forced to sell a pair of his oxen to pay his servant his wages, told his servant he could keep him no longer, not knowing how to pay him next year. The servant answered he would serve him for more of his cattle. "But how shall I do" saith the master, "When all my cattle are gone?" The servant replied, "You shall serve me, and so you may have your cattle again"'. The answer scandalised the decorous Winthrop, and if the servant had made it in England, the neighbouring justices would probably have made him rue his impudence. But though the economic conditions of a colony were peculiar, there were times, even in England, when the wage earner could make his own terms. Side by side with the remarks of a statesman like Cecil as to difficulties caused by the high price of agricultural labour, one may set a complaint from a rural community which is all the more remarkable, in that it comes from the latter part of the seventeenth century. 'We desire' say the grand jury of Worcestershire in 1661 'that servants' wages may be rated according to the Statute, for we find the unreasonableness of servants' wages a great grievance, so that servants are grown so proud and idle that the master cannot be known from the servant, except it be because the servant wears better clothes than the master'.[71] It would, at any rate, be a grave error to think of agricultural labourers in the sixteenth and seventeenth centuries as the helpless victims of economic oppression. Combination to raise wages was, of course, forbidden by statute, nor need we place much reliance on the statements of writers like Roger Coke[72] and the author of *Britannia Languens* (1680), who find a stick with which to beat the Elizabethan poor laws in the alleged fact, that by making the worker independent of his master, they are 'the principal, if not the only, reason of the excessive wages of servants as well as of labourers, who will neither serve nor labour'. Quite apart, however, both from trade unionism and parochial relief, there were two methods of raising wages to which the workers could have recourse. In the first place they could practice passive resistance by refusing to enter the labour market, and, instead of working for an employer, employing themselves at home.[73] This alternative, which in modern England, at any rate, is beyond the reach of the worker whose wages are reduced, was made possible by the predominance of small scale production both in agriculture and in many, though not all, branches of manufacturing industry. The peasant could work on his own holding, the village weaver for customers who dealt with him direct, the village joiner in doing odd jobs for his neighbours. That it was used as a lever for raising wages is proved by the orders which justices found themselves obliged from time to time to issue, directing that since 'young people both men and maids ... will not go abroad to service, without they may have excessive wages, but will rather work at home at their own hands, whereby the rating of wages will take little effect, therefore no young men or maids fitting to go abroad to service ... shall remain at home ... but shall with all convenient speed betake themselves to service for the wages aforesaid'.[74]

In the second place, there was nearly always the possibility of turning from employment with a master to some sort of rough subsistence farming. In the sparsely populated England of the Tudors the land under cultivation was everywhere an island set in an ocean of unreclaimed barrenness, and well into the eighteenth century the wastes available for occupation by settlers were enormous. As a consequence, the worker who was discontented with the terms offered for his labour could often make an independent, though precarious, living, by squatting upon unoccupied land, and working for himself. It was, indeed, in this process of spontaneous colonisation that many of the peasants displaced by the spread of pasture-farming found an alternative to wage-labour, and in the seventeenth century the issuing of licenses for the erection of cottages on waste lands by able-bodied men who had come with their families from a distance became a regular part of the business of Quarter Sessions. The economic effect of the existence of these reservoirs of unoccupied territory is indicated by the lamentations of contemporary economists over the high wages which they enabled workers to demand.[75] 'In all or most towns, where the fields lie open' writes a pamphleteer, 'there is a new brood of upstart intruders or inmates ... loiterers who will not work unless they may have such excessive wages as they themselves desire'.[76] 'There is with us now' states another, whose words offer a striking parallel both to the story told by Winthrop and to the complaint of the Worcestershire grand jury, 'rather a scarcity than a superfluity of servants, their wages being advanced to such an extraordinary height, that they are likely ere long to be masters and their masters servants, many poor husbandmen being forced to pay near as much to their servants for wages as to their landlords for rent'.[77]

That such complaints were exaggerated, that the workers would have given a very different account of their conditions, is highly probable. But the fact that it should have been possible to make these statements with any show of verisimilitude shows how radically different was the situation of the wage worker at the time when the fixing of maximum rates was enforced from that with which the modern world is acquainted. Remembering the multitude of small property holders and the comparative fewness of the families who had no holdings of land at all, we shall be in a position to understand the extreme suspicion with which petty farmers and craftsmen regarded any attempt at independence on the part of their employees, and to realise that the assessment of wages may have been a policy popular not only with the governing classes who sat on the county bench, but with large bodies of humble people; for humble people were property holders and employers themselves. Readers of [George Bernard Shaw's] *John Bull's other island* [1904], will remember the horror with which the Irish peasant, who had just acquired land under the land purchase acts, greeted the proposal to pay the labourer, Patsy Farrell, 20s a week. The attitude of the yeomen and small masters in the England of the sixteenth and seventeenth centuries towards the Patsy Farrells of their day was much the same. In the 'Distributive State' to which some modern admirers of small-scale agriculture and small-scale industry look as an ideal, the laws regard with an eye that is anything but favourable the claim of the wage-earner to make the best bargian for himself that he can. Happily for him, the economic conditions which produced a demand for the assessment of his wages were such as to facilitate his escape from a life of continuous wage-labour. If the establishment of maximum rates had been widely regarded as oppressive we should almost certainly have heard of some petitions, some riots, against it, such as were made so frequently by peasants who resisted enclosures. That nothing of the kind has come down to us from any bodies of agricultural labourers is evidence of some weight for the belief that the interference of the state with wages was not regarded as an intolerable grievance.

V The economic motive for the assessment of wages in the textile trades

There was, however, another side to the wage-policy of the Tudors and Stuarts than that which we have hitherto considered. If the labour problem in agriculture arose in the sixteenth and seventeenth centuries, as in the middle ages, from the scarcity of wage-workers, the labour problem in the textile industries was nevertheless of a quite modern character, and consisted in the inability of large bodies of artisans to resist the reductions forced upon them by their employers. It was the attempts spasmodically made by the government and some boards of justices to use the Statute of Artificers to maintain a standard wage in the textile trades, which has led to the suggestion that its general effect was to protect the worker against exploitation. In reality the policy pursued towards workers in the woollen industry was a special departure arising from the peculiar circumstances of that trade. The production of woollen cloth was the branch of manufacture in which, in the sixteenth century, capitalism had proceeded furthest. There were, of course, a certain number of independent weavers who worked to the order of purchasers in their own immediate neighbourhood. There were also, especially in the northern counties, a large number of small masters, of a type that survived in the West Riding of Yorkshire well into the nineteenth century, who bought their own raw materials, marketed the finished product themselves, and were not far removed in economic status from the two or three journeymen whom they employed. But these were the irregular forces of the industry, not the main army. In the principal 'clothing counties', Norfolk and Suffolk, Wiltshire, Gloucestershire, Somerset and Devon, several causes had combined to supersede the simple organisation under which the same individual was at once merchant, master, and artisan, to specialise in separate hands the commercial and industrial sides of the industry, and thus to run the greater part of it into a capitalistic mould. For one thing, a large part of the cloth manufactured in the south and east of England was exported to continental markets. For another thing, the collecting, sorting, and distributing of raw materials was a business in itself. Different kinds of wool were produced in different parts of the country. Different kinds of cloth required different kinds of wool, and it was therefore common for wool produced in one county to be distributed for manufacture over half a dozen different counties far removed from each other and from its place of origin. 'The places of growing and the places of converting are as far distant as the scope of this kingdom will give leave. The wools growing in the counties of Worcester, Salop, and Stafford, are spent partly in Worcester, and a great part of them in the counties of Gloucester, Devon, and Kent, and much of them in Southampton. The wool of the counties of Lincoln, Northampton, Rutland, Leicester, Warwick, Oxford and Bucks are thus dispersed: one sort of it is carried into the North parts, to Leeds, Wakefield, Rochdale, etc, and another sort is carried part of it into the East parts, to Norwich ... and part of it into the West parts into Exeter ... some wools growing in Norfolk are brought three score miles or more to London and from thence carried eight score miles or more into North Wales, then draped into cloth and so sent back again and sold in London'.[78] The result was that the commercial side of the industry passed into the hands of a special body of capitalist entrepreneurs, who bought and sold on a large scale and could afford to take risks and wait for their returns. The actual operatives were no longer independent craftsmen, but entirely dependent on these great 'clothiers' for their employment. One outcome of the over-shadowing of the artisan by the entrepeneur was the tentative growth of a rudimentary factory system. A large number of towns in the sixteenth and seventeenth centuries, when confronted with the difficulty of finding work for the unemployed, used to lend money to capitalist clothiers to establish what were factories[79] in all but name. The most general consequence, however, of the spread of capitalism in the textile industries was not the appearance of a factory system, which was hampered both by the laws forbidding the engrossing of looms, and by the fact that most of the families engaged in the production of cloth could not easily be massed together, since they practised agriculture as a bye-employment. It was the so-called 'commission-system', under which a single great clothier provided the raw materials worked up in hundreds of cottages, paid the artisans their wages, and collected the finished product for the home or foreign market when the process of manufacture was over. It was calculated that in Suffolk in the reign of James I one large merchant would keep 500 workers employed.

The natural outcome of the organisation of the industry on a capitalistic basis was the appearance of complaints as to low wages and payment in kind. In 1539 the weavers of Suffolk were complaining exactly in the manner of the handloom weavers in the early nineteenth century. 'The rich men the clothiers be concluded and agreed among themselves to hold and pay one price for weaving, which price is too little to sustain householders upon, working night and day, holiday and week day, and many weavers are thereby reduced to the position of servants'.[80] 'The rich clothier' said an observer 'that buyeth his wool of the grower in the wool counties in the winter time hath it spun by his own spinsters, and woven by his own weavers and fulled by his own tuckers, and all at the lowest rate of wages'.[81] A draft bill[82] of 1593 states that spinners are driven to embezzle yarn, and weavers to weave faulty cloth, because 'necessity doth many times enforce them thereunto for lack of sufficient wages and allowances for the workmanship at the hands of the clothiers'. The fixing of maximum wages directed by the Statute of Artificers was obviously not a remedy for such conditions. On the other hand, in view of the interference with wages being a traditional part of the policy both of town authorities and of the government, the step involved in fixing a minimum wage was not a long one.[83] It was taken first by the former. At intervals from the middle of the fifteenth century onwards the court leet of Coventry, where the journeymen weavers and the masters had already (in 1429) made a collective bargain[84] binding the latter to pay the journeyman a third of the value of every cloth woven, was busy with the issue of ordinances regulating wages in the woollen industry. In 1452 any spinner who was given more than two and a half pounds of wool to spin was directed to bring his or her complaint before the sherriffs, who were to pay the spinner for his labour, and to confiscate the spindles provided by the employer.[85] In 1460 it was enacted that all weavers, fullers, spinners, and carders should be paid in ready money. In 1514 clothiers who gave out wool to spinners were ordered not to put more to each weight than two and a half pounds, and to pay in ready money 5d per pound for the best quality, and 4d for inferior qualities.[86] In 1524 a price list was drawn up for weaving. The usual rule was made as to payment in ready money, and payments were fixed for standard patterns of cloth, ranging from 5s for the heaviest, to 4s 6d for medium weights, and 3s 4d for the lightest. This was followed by a similar list for walkers, 'for a low-priced cloth 3/6, and for a middle cloth 4/- and for a fine cloth 5/-, and for a very fine cloth as the owners and he can agree'.[87] What was done at Coventry in the way of protecting the journeymen against exploitation seems to have been a fairly common practice on the part of town authorities, though not so general as the attempts to protect the consumer by fixing maximum wages in the building industries. At Norwich in 1502 a body of woollen weavers requested the authorities to enact a rule fixing 20d as the minimum price for cloth of a certain quality.[88] At Reading in the early seventeenth century the Court of the Borough fixed the rates of spinners at '13d a padd for spinning ordinary work, and so ratably for better work', and when the workmen in a local woollen factory partly financed by the town complained that their wages were too low, appointed three arbitrators to report upon the dispute.[89] In 1648 the common council of Nottingham, who had followed the common practice of lending capital to a clothier provided he would start work in the town, fixed a fairly elaborate scale of prices for spinning and carding different kinds of wool.[90]

These examples, though not sufficient to prove that the fixing of minimum rates was a common practice, do at any rate point to the conclusion that there was a disposition to treat workers in the textile industry in a different way from the great mass of labour, and that in fixing minimum rates for workers in that industry, the state would have some experience which it could follow. It was not, however, till the latter part of the reign of Elizabeth that this aspect of the wage problem began to receive attention from the government. In 1593, a year in which, owing to the failure of the harvest, distress was unusually severe, four bills[91] were drafted which can still be examined in the Public Record Office. One of them need not detain us long. It is headed 'The rate of the wages for clothiers to give unto their spinsters and weavers'; it is simply a list of piece-prices for spinning and weaving, with certain provisions as to the pattern of tools to be used, containing six rates for the former and eleven rates for the latter; there is no preamble and no enacting words, and it was intended perhaps to appear as a schedule to any acts which might be passed upon the subject. The other three drafts are more elaborate. They deal not only with wages, but with frauds practised on clothiers by spinners and weavers – of which they complain in terms almost identical with those used by the commission on handloom weavers in 1835 – with the length of cloth to be woven, and with that bugbear of sixteenth century statesmen, the speculator, 'yarn choppers or jobbers' who 'for their own private gains, without having any regard to the maintenance of the Commonwealth, using no trade either of making woollen cloth or any other thing made of woollen yarn ... do ... buy up and get into their hands so great quantities of woollen yarn'. There is some difference between the bills in the matter of wages. One of them does not set out any 'list' in detail, but enacts that the wages of spinners of warps shall be advanced 30 per cent, that those of spinners of wefts and those of weavers shall be advanced 25 per cent, and that the clauses in certain acts allowing clothiers to make cloth of a length greater than that fixed by law shall be repealed, on the ground that the effect of them has been that 'divers poor artificers, as spinners, weavers, tuckers, carders, clothworkers, and divers others have been secretly and most unconscionably deceived, oppressed and wronged in their labours, for that the masters and owners of the said long clothes neither have given nor do give wages answerable to the great length of the said clothes'. The other two bills set out a list of piece-prices for spinning and weaving, fix a fine of 12d for every penny that a 'clothier shall withold or detaine ... contrary to the charitable intent of this Statute', but provide that where higher rates have hitherto been paid than those contained in the bills, they shall continue to be paid in the future. Neither of these measures became law. But their existence proves that the idea of fixing a minimum wage for workers in the woollen industry was one to which the government was prepared to give consideration. Ten years later Parliament returned to the subject, this time with some result. By an act of 1603 (1 James I c 6) the Statute of Artificers was re-enacted with the addition of three significant clauses. The first stated that there had been some ambiguity in the act of 1563, which had resulted in its being uncertain whether the justices had power to rate the wages of workers other than those engaged in husbandry and other than those whose wages had been assessed under previous acts. It accordingly enacted that it was to be interpreted as giving authority to assess the wages of any 'Labourers, Weavers, Spinners, and Workmen whatsoever'. The second clause definitely laid down that as far as workers in the woollen industry were concerned the rates fixed were to be a *minimum*, and that clothiers were to be fined for paying less, not for paying more, than that rate. It is so important that I quote it in full: 'And furthermore, be it enacted by the authority aforesaid, that if any clothier or other shall refuse to obey the said order, rate, and assessments of wages, as aforesaid, *and shall not pay so much or so great wages to their weavers, spinsters, workmen or workwomen, as shall be set down, rated, and appointed,* according to the true meaning of this Act, that then every clothier and other person or persons so offending shall forfeit and lose ... for every such offence to the party grieved ten shillings'. The third clause took the important step, without which that just quoted would have been of little value, of forbidding clothiers who were also justices of the peace to take part in assessing wages 'for any weaver, tucker, spinster, or any other artisan that dependeth on the making of cloth'.

If the statute of 1603 is strictly construed it would appear to have directed the justices to fix a minimum, not a maximum, rate for workers in *all* occupations, not only for those engaged in the manufacture of cloth. If this was its intention it does not appear to have been carried out. Subsequent assessments allude to 5 Elizabeth c 4, but scarcely ever contain any reference to 1 James I c 6 and, as has been explained, above, they usually say that wages are not to be *more* than a certain amount. It is plain, however, from the references in the statute to clothiers, that its main object was to empower the justices to fix a minimum for the woollen industry, and though evidence as to the effect of this part of it is not so abundant as could be desired, there is no doubt that both local authorities and the central government did from time to time administer it in this sense. To see the line taken by the former we may examine the dealings of the justices of Wiltshire, one of the most important of the cloth manufacturing counties, with the wages of spinners and weavers. My first example[92] comes from the year 1602. The drafting of piece rates for the woollen industry was an extremely technical matter, involving expert knowledge as to qualities of wool and yarns, breadth of looms etc. What the justices did, therefore, was to ask the clothiers who gave out the materials and the weavers who worked them up in their cottages to submit a statement of the prices which they thought reasonable. In 1602 a piece list, – 'the just proportions of the severall works usually put forth by the clothiers of the county of Wiltshire both to the weavers and spinners with the valuation of the wages according as every sorts of work do deserve by reason of the fineness of the wool and spinning of every sort of work' – was signed by seven clothiers and six weavers, and was submitted to the justices. The justices confirmed it as it stood, and reissued it in 1605[93] with certain trifling variations. It would be too much to say that the justices ratified a collective bargain which had already been made by the representatives of the employers and the workmen, for one does not in these documents find traces of a permanent organisation among either party, nor would it have been lawful for them to combine to alter working conditions prescribed by the state. It is evident, however, that the justices did not simply settle matters over their heads, and that some attempt was made to ascertain the opinion of the industry before thrusting the rough hands of Quarter Sessions into its delicate mechanism. Moreover the fixing of rates was certainly regarded as an advantage by the workmen concerned. This is proved not only by the part which the journeymen weavers took in preparing the price list, but by the fact that they later petitioned the justices to enforce the assessment of wages as a means of protecting them against their employers. In 1623 the artisans engaged in the Wiltshire cloth-making industry were in deep distress. 'May it please you' they write to the justices 'to be informed of the distressed state of most of the weavers, spinners, and others that work on the making of woollen cloths, that are not able by their diligent labours to get their livings, by reason that the clothiers at their wish have made their work extremely hard, and abated wages what they please. And some of them make such their workfolk to do their household businesses, to trudge in their errands, spool their chains, twist their list, do every command, without giving them bread, drink, or money for many days labours. May it please you, therefore, for the redressing of these enormities done by Clothiers, to appoint certain grave and discreet persons to view the straitness of works, to assess rates for wages according to the desert of their works, now especially in this great dearth of corn, that the poor artificers of these works of woollen cloths may not perish for want of food, while they are painfull in their callings'.[94] The justices responded to this appeal. They issued an order summoning the clothiers and workmen to meet them at Devizes; directed the observance of the piece-list, which was already nominally in force, though broken by the clothiers; and ordered its publication on market-day at Devizes 'in order that workmasters and workmen alike may take notice thereof, and that the workmen who desire that the same rates may stand, may be the better satisfied'.

The fixing of minimum rates for artisans in the woollen industry had not the same reasons for commending itself to the justices as had the fixing of maximum rates for other classes of workers. It is, therefore, not surprising that the interference of the Privy Council should often have been required in order to induce them to do their duty. To see its economic activities at their height one must, of course, turn to the period between March 1629 and April 1640, when 'that noise', as Laud called parliamentary debate, was silent. The government's intervention to control economic conditions was one side of the attitude which found its more famous expressions in arbitrary taxation and the enforcement of conformity in religion, a natural outcome of the authoritarian conception of the state held by Charles and his advisers. It did not imply any popular sympathies, but simply a desire to prevent agitation by removing the material causes of discontent, and incidentally to put pressure on the middle and upper classes, who were the stronghold of religious and constitutional opposition.[95] To levy fines upon an enclosing landlord was a convenient financial expedient. The bishops who punished the usurer, or the dealer who charged extortionate prices, before the Courts[96] of Star Chamber and High Commission had an excellent opportunity of expounding the duty of obedience to the established authorities, and scolded the offender with all the more gusto when he was suspected of being a puritan as well. In the matter of wages there was no general change of policy. From a letter[97] which the Derbyshire justices wrote to the government in 1631 stating, in reply to a circular from the Council, that 'we find none presented to us that ... refuse to work for reasonable wages', it is plain that in the case of agricultural labourers the fixing of maximum wages still went on. But attempts to get the justices to carry out their obligation of fixing minimum rates for workers in the cloth-manufacturing industry were made more regularly than either before or since. In 1629[98] the Council wrote to the earl of Warwick and the justices of Essex directing them to take steps to raise the wages of the weavers of baize who worked in the neighbourhood of Braintree and Bocking. In September[99] 1630 they circularised the justices of Norfolk, Suffolk, Essex, Cambridge, all cloth manufacturing counties, and the mayor of Norwich, stating that 'the Statutes of 5 Eliz & 1 Jac have so carefully provided against these inconveniences it were a great shame if, for want of due care in such as are specially entrusted with the execution of these lawes, the poore should be punished in these times of scarcity and dearth', and requiring them to see to the assessment of wages.[100] To these instances, which I take from Miss Leonard's *The early history of English poor relief,* one may add the example offered by the proceedings of the government in the matter of the cloth trade of Sudbury and the neighbouring parts of Suffolk and Essex. They illustrate excellently the grievances of the workers, the attitude of the Privy Council, and the difficulties of the justices.

The question was first raised by a petition addressed to the Council in February 1630 on behalf of the workers in the trade by one Sylva Harbert.[101] It stated that the clothiers of Sudbury had reduced the wages of combers, spinners and weavers to such an extent that 'they (who in times past maintained their families in good sort)... are constrained to sell their beds, wheels, and working tools', and asked the government to interfere. The Council directed that the petition should be forwarded to a committee composed of the justices of Suffolk and Essex together with two aldermen of Sudbury, who were instructed to call before them representatives of both parties, to insist on wages being raised to the level hitherto customary, and to bind over any refractory person to appear before the Council. The clothiers began[102] by attempting to show that Sylva Harbert had no real grievance, but had acted at the malicious instigation of a third party who had a grudge against one of them. The committee, after examining the complaints of the workpeople, decided that they were justified, and drew up a price list for spinners and weavers which forbad deductions ('fines'), and stated the length of reels to be used for the yarns. They informed the Council, however, that the reason alleged by the manufacturers for reducing wages was the competition of the trade in other parts of the country, and that 'if the like order be not more general than to Sudbury, and to towns adjacent, it must necessarily be their ruin and utter undoing'. The justices assessment runs as follows: 'Essex. An order made at our Meeting at Halsted in the said countie the eight day of Aprill anno dmi 1631 by vertue of an order from the Lords of the Cownsell.

It is ordered and agreed uppon by us whose names are here-Suff. shall paye unto the spynsters for spynnings of every seaven knotts, one penny, and to have noe deduccon of their wadges, and that the keele wheron the yard is reeled to be a yard in length and not longer. And we doe further order, that for all the white sayes under five pounds weight the Saymaker shall give unto the weaver 12d the pound for the weavinge thereof, and for the Sayes that shall be above five pounds and under Tenne pounds to give 12d the pound abatinge 6d in the peece for the weaving thereof, and for the mingled Sayes conteyninge eight or nyne pounds nyne shillings, and soe proporcionally, as it shall conteyne more or less in weight. This our order to contynewe untill the fiftenth daye of Maye next ensuinge, Excepte from the Cownsell there shall be other order taken.

Tho. Wyseman	R. Wareyn
Willi Maxey	Ri. Skynner
Dra. Deane	Benjamine Fisher'[103]

This eminently reasonable request does not appear to have received any attention from the government. But it continued to lend an ear to the complaints of the Sudbury wage-earners. In 1637 three weavers again approached the Star Chamber with the complaint that, not content with reducing their wages, a manufacturer named Thomas Reynolds insisted on their accepting payment in truck 'dead commodities, such as they cannot put off, and at a far undervalue, he himself refusing to take them again without great abatement, making merchandize of the petitioner's labours'.[104] The Star Chamber found on enquiry that Reynolds was a bad character who had already been punished for a similar offence – 'this way of oppressing and abusing poor weavers hath been ordinary with him' – and committed him to the Fleet till he should have repaid the wages due, together with the plaintiff's costs. Having complied with the order of the Court, he was released a week later.[105]

What has been said above of the objects of the assessment of wages may now be summarised. The principal aim of the wage clauses of the Statute of Artificers was to prevent the scarcity of agricultural labour driving wages above the point thought 'reasonable', and at the same time to allow that point to be shifted upwards by the justices as prices rose. In the textile industries, however, where owing to the development of a capitalistic organisation, the wage problem was of a different character, the policy of fixing a minimum wage had been pursued by town authorities from an early date. It was given statutory sanction by the act of 1603 and was enforced at intervals both by the justices of the peace and by the Privy Council. After the constitutional revolution of the seventeenth century the assessment of maximum wages continued; but the fixing of a minimum for artisans in the cloth manufacturing industry, which was opposed to the interests of the wealthier classes, fell into desuetude. The clause in the act of 1604 stating that doubt had been expressed as to whether the wage clauses of the act of 1563 applied to other than labourers in husbandry shows that even in the generation immediately following the passage of Statute of Artificers there was a tendency to limit its application; and in the reign of Anne (if not before) it was definitely decided by the judges that only the wages of agricultural workers fell within the jurisdiction of the justices; – 'the statute extends only to service in husbandry, not to gentlemens' servants, nor to journeymen with their masters'.[106] Memories of the earlier practice survived, however, into the latter part of the eighteenth century, and prompted the demands for the establishment of a minimum wage advanced both by the Gloucestershire weavers in 1756, and by many other bodies of textile operatives at the time of the rise of the factory system.

VI The effects of the assessment of wages

It remains to ask what was the economic effect of the system of assessing wages. On this question I can throw little light. I will begin by describing the procedure in making assessments, and examining the movements in wages as set out in some of them, and then go on to say what I can of the actual administration of the law.

By the act of 1563 the justices were directed to consult 'grave and discrete persons', and to confer together 'concerning the plenty and scarcity of the time, and other circumstances necessary to be considered'. The view taken of the administration of the act must depend to some extent upon the degree to which the justices are thought to have complied with these instructions. Did they take the trouble to obtain the necessary economic information before issuing their rules? or did they act entirely upon their own discretion? That some attention was paid by the justices to the movements of prices is suggested by the allusions to them which are frequent in the preambles of assessments. That they went further, and made any regular attempt to secure advice from persons qualified to judge as to the economic conditions of the wage-earners is, as far at any rate as agricultural labour is concerned, extremely improbable. In one case, indeed, we do get a hint of inquiries preceding the issue of rates. In 1648 the inhabitants of the eastern division of the hundred of Portbury in Somerset[107] called the attention of the justices to the fact that twenty-three years before the wages in their district had been fixed by the 'two next Justices', and stated that the assessment was now disobeyed. Accordingly Quarter Sessions referred the matter to a committee of three 'to examine the said proportion or rate, and to certify the true state thereof at the next General Sessions'. But in no instance is there any evidence that the views of the wage workers themselves were in any way consulted. The agricultural labourers were then, as in 1914, entirely unorganised. The justices, who were mainly country gentlemen, were naturally biassed in favour of keeping down their wages. The course which they seem to have followed when it was thought desirable to take the opinion of persons other than those of the county bench was to refer the matter to the grand jury. As judicial charges show, the presentment of 'labourers or servants' who 'take any more wages than the rate of wages allowed by the Justices'[108] was part of its ordinary duties. What more natural than that it should be consulted when rates were being fixed? The records of Wiltshire, Worcestershire, and Somerset supply examples of what was probably a common practice. In the former county[109] an assessment of 1625 which considerably raised the wages of workers in husbandry was embodied in the grand jury's presentment. In Worcestershire[110] the grand jury addressed the justices with some vigour in 1661, remonstrated with them for failing to administer the Statute of

Artificers, and, among other demands, requested that servants' wages might be assessed according to law. In Somerset[111] eight assessments were issued between 1647 to 1655. The formula most commonly used is, first, 'This Court desired the Grand Jury to present their opinions what wages they thought fit to be set and assessed'; second, 'the presentment of the grand inquest' containing the rates proposed; third, 'This Court doth approve thereof'. It is scarcely necessary to point out that the intervention of the grand jury, consisting as it generally did of gentry and yeomen, was anything but a protection to the wage-earner. If the exhortation addressed by George Fox to the Nottingham justices, 'not to oppress the servants in their wages, but to do that which was right and just to them' was not always necessary, the cause was not the good will of the 'grave and discrete' persons, but the comparatively strong position of the agricultural labourer.

In the case of workers other than those employed in agriculture it was easier for the justices to take expert advice. We have already seen that in fixing the wages of spinners and weavers in Wiltshire they consulted both the employers and the journeymen. In the towns gilds and companies supplied an obvious source of information. In Chester in 1588 wages were fixed by the mayor with 'the advise and consultation of divers others of the city'[112] and in 1607 the London justices specially directed the wardens of the London companies to attend the meeting at which wages were to be assessed.[113] Whether the intervention of a gild was a safe-guard to the wage-earners or to their employers depended entirely upon its constitution. In the smaller towns, where capitalist industry was little developed, and where therefore, the gap between master and man was still only a narrow one, gilds seem occasionally, as at Bristol, Norwich, Coventry and Carlisle, to have prevented the reduction of wages below a certain minimum.[114] In most cases, however, the gild was only too ready to be used by the justices as a means of preventing a rise in wages inconvenient to the masters by whom it was governed, and to assist them in seeing, in the words of the authorities of Bury St Edmunds, that 'every journeyman do serve according to the Queen's Majesty's Statutes'.[115] In Chester, where there was much complaint of the great exactions of 'the artizans and servants belonging to the corporation of Wrights and Slaters', the mayor fixed their wages, and compelled the governors of the Society to enter into bonds to see that the rates settled by him were observed.[116] In London many of the companies had, by the middle of the seventeenth century, developed into extremely aristocratic and exclusive bodies. It is not surprising, therefore, to find the wardens of the Company of Carpenters making recommendations to the Lord Mayor 'in pursuance of your lordship's desire of our opinion for the reducing of the excessive wages of labourers and workmen'.[117]

According to the preamble of the act of 1563 the justices should have made wages move in correspondence with prices. The question how far they did this is not easily answered, partly because there was no common form in which assessments were issued, so that it is often impossible to compare different assessments made for the same county, even when there is only a few years between them; partly because, though we know the general course of prices, we do not know their local variations. By way of testing whether there was any close correspondence between wages and prices, I set out below an index number of wheat prices,[118] and of the rates assessed at different dates in one borough and four counties. They are as follows:

Chester		*1570*		*1597*
Wages		100		141.7
		1571–81		*1593–1602*
Wheat prices		100		209
Rutland		*1563*		*1610*
Day wages		100		104.16
Yearly wages		100		101.2
Wheat prices		100		274.6
Devon		*1594*		*1654*
Day wages		100		107.04
Yearly wages		100		132.4
Wheat prices		100		135.4
Wiltshire	*1603*	*1635*	*1655*	*1685*
Wages	100	125	137	150
	1603–12	*1633–42*	*1653–62*	*1680–92*
Wheat prices	100	117	134	97
Gloucestershire		*1632*		*1655*
Day wages		100		131.3
Yearly wages		100		108.1
		1623–32		*1653–62*
Wheat prices		100		108.1

It will be seen that there is a rough parellelism between the rise of wheat prices and the rise of wages in Wiltshire up to 1655, and of yearly wages in Devon up to 1654. For the rest, there seems to be no correspondence at all. At Chester wages rise by over 40 per cent when prices rise by 109 per cent; in Rutland wages rise by under 5 per cent, when prices rise by 174 per cent. In Wiltshire, where prices and wages move with the same correspondence up to 1655, wages rise after that date and prices fall, Even if the means for making a comparison were more satisfactory than they are I doubt very much whether any close correspondence would be established. It was hardly to be expected that the justices who saw prices doubled would meet the situation by doubling wages. They themselves belonged to a class which felt the rise severely, for the rents of their copyhold and freehold tenants were fixed, while they were buying everything dearer. An advance in wages as great as the advance in prices would have benefited the worker while aggravating their own difficulties. Moreover all sorts of factors influenced wages besides the movement in prices. Custom was very powerful, and on 22 May 1735 the Lancashire board appealed to the fact that wages have always been lower in the northern part of the country than elsewhere as a justification for refusing to raise them: 'The said county being eighty miles in length, we think the more northern parts thereof ought not to demand so much, but be content with what the custom of the county hath usually been'.[119] After the Civil War the scarcity of labour forced wages up, and the assessments, as the Gloucestershire justices pointed out, had to follow the market rate.[120] A motive which tended to raise the price of agricultural labour while lowering that of artisans was the interest of the country gentlemen in preventing a shortage of the former. This is probably the reason why the wages of workers in husbandry were advanced in Wiltshire on the recommendation of the grand jury, in 1635, while those of other classes of wage earners were unaltered; and why in Warwickshire the wages of certain classes of agricultural workers were fixed at a much higher rate in 1672 than in 1657, while those of masons, tilers, plasterers and bricklayers were reduced by from 75 to 100 per cent.[121] Such a double movement was a simple method of ensuring that the supply of agricultural labour would be sufficient. It is not surprising, therefore, that wages and prices should not have risen and fallen together.[122]

When assessments were made, were they operative in practice, or did the market rate of wages move quite independently of them? The methods employed to secure the observation by employer and workman of the legal rates were very various. Under the Act of 1563 the justices were bound to forward their assessments to the Court of Chancery. The Privy Council was to examine them, to have them printed if they were approved, and to send them, in the form of a proclamation, to their respective counties before 1 September, where sheriffs and justices were to cause them to be proclaimed on market days and to be posted up in some conspicuous place. When the act of 1598 relieved the justices of the necessity of forwarding their assessments to London for confirmation, the ordinary practice was to send them to the sheriff of the county with the request that they should be published in every city and market town. Sometimes however, the justices sent them to the constables direct, and on one occasion, in 1680, they ordered that, with a view to giving them publicity, the rate should 'be read every Quarter in their Parish Church or some other convenient place upon Sunday or festival day after morning prayers'.[123] Occasionally special expedients were adopted for discovering breaches of the assessments. In Buckinghamshire,[124] for example, a special 'governor of labourers' was appointed in every township in the Chiltern Hundreds in 1562 to supervise the movements and hiring of labourers, and to present masters who gave too high a rate of wages. In Devon[125] in 1601 the justices divided themselves into sub-committees to deal specially with offenders in different parts of the county. In the North Riding of Yorkshire[126] in 1610 on account of 'much complaint, as well by masters as servants, of sundry abuses commited against the Statute of Labourers and Apprentices' the justices decided that in the future they would hold an additional summer sessions every year for the purpose of hearing cases under the act. It was, however, the parish constables who supplied the hinge upon which the whole system turned. For the justices to supervise the actual hiring and discharge of labour, was of course, out of the question. But when the machinery of the law was working properly no man could get a master, and no master could get a man, without the constables knowing the terms of the bargain. It was the duty of the workman to show the constables (or the curate or churchwarden) a testimonial from his last master. It was the duty of the employer to register with the constables the names of his labourers and the wages at which they were engaged, and to notify to him anyone who left his service without giving the statutory notice of one quarter. The whole system depended in fact, on the presence of a third party at every contract made between master and man; it was only workable in so far as publicity was given to the engagement of labour, and it was for this reason that rules are so frequently made requiring young people to go into service, unemployed workmen to stand in some conspicuous place until they find an employer, employers to hire publicly and not in secret, masterless men to take masters. The man who had labour to sell was in fact treated exactly like the corndealer. Neither was to be allowed to forestall the market or to take advantage of an exceptionally good offer to force up the price. Neither could pick his purchaser or refuse to sell except upon his own terms. Hence, when the machinery was working properly, the constables had in their possession a register of persons hired and of the wages offered to them, which they could compare with the assessments issued by the justices, and by means of which they could check any alteration in wages which might subsequently be made or demanded.

That in some districts and at some periods the constables succeeded in keeping in close touch with their duties is proved by the appeals which the justices made to them for information, and by the presentment of offenders who break the law. The punishment of offenders at Reading has already been mentioned. In the court of the manor of Ingoldmells[127] in Lincolnshire, fourteen persons were summoned in 1567 'before the steward appointed to execute the Statute of Labourers'. In the North Riding of Yorkshire, there were numerous presentments of both masters and journeymen for paying and taking more than the statutory rate of wages, or otherwise evading the act: 'John Bulmer of West Cottam, husbandman, for hiring servants without recording their names and salaries before the chief constable'; 'the inhabitants of Thirkleby ... for refusing to give the names of their servants and their wages to the constables of the said Town and to the head constables', 'the inhabitants of Kilbourne for giving their servants more wages than the Statute doth allow'; 'Thomas Gibson of Easingwold for retaining and accepting into his service one Will Thompson without showing to the Head Officer Curate, or Churchwarden, any lawful testimonial'; 'Thomas Wawne yeoman for giving wages ... Rymer his servant to exceeding the rate set down by the Justices';[128] such examples show that in parts of the country the administration of the statute was a reality. Occasionally we find particulars of wages which show that the market rate and the legal rate coincided. In Rutland,[129] for example, where an assessment was made in 1610, the High Constable's list of persons hired between 1626 and 1642 proves that the rates then fixed were closely followed. In Derbyshire[130] the masons and labourers who worked at Chatsworth in 1693 obtained the rates per day, 1s 4d and 10d, which had been fixed by the assessment of 1648. Usually, however, the evidence which could enable us to determine whether assessments when made were effectively carried out is lacking. There are no presentments of offenders for exceeding the legal rates in the manuscript proceedings of the Warwickshire Quarter Sessions which I have examined from 1610 to 1680.[131] Nor have I found any in the records of other counties which have been printed, with the exception of those contained in the proceedings of the North Riding Quarter Sessions. As far as my evidence goes at present, which is not very far, the legal rate often differed considerably from the market rate, and usually fell short of it. In Buckinghamshire[132] for example, some workmen in the building trades were being paid in the latter part of the sixteenth century a wage more than double that fixed by the assessment of 1562, and though the legal scale was considerably raised in the latter part of the following century it was still exceeded by the actual rates paid by masters. In the eighteenth century at any rate, the courts seem to have countenanced the evasion of the act by ruling that a master might 'reward a deserving servant, over and above his wages, according as he shall decide; so it be not by way of promise or agreement upon his retainer'.[133] While, therefore, it is probable that the practice of assessing wages tended to keep them down by setting up a standard to which the master could appeal, it is also probable that it was evaded without much difficulty by the exceptionally competent journeyman, or by the master who was in difficulties through a shortage of labour.

Notes

1 I desire to acknowledge the assistance of Mr J.G. Newlove of Ruskin College and of Miss Drucker who have kindly helped me to collect materials for this article.

2 Bertha H. Putnam, *The enforcement of the statutes of labourers during the first decade after the Black Death, 1349-1359* (New York: Columbia UP, 1891).

3 William Cunningham, *The growth of English industry and commerce* (2nd ed Cambridge UP, 1907), pp 37-44, Appendix A, pp 887-97.

4 *EHR,* XIII (1898), XV (1900).

5 *EJ,* VIII (1898).

6 James E. Thorold Rogers, *Six centuries of work and wages: the history of English labour* (10th ed T. Fisher Unwin, 1909), pp 398-9.

7 Gustaf F. Steffen, *Studien zur Geschichte der englischen Lohnarbeiter* (Stuttgart, 1901-5), I, 339.

8 Olive J. Dunlop and Richard D. Denman, *English apprenticeship and child labour: a history* (T. Fisher Unwin, 1912).

9 Ellen M. Leonard, *The early history of English poor relief* (Cambridge UP, 1900), p 164.

10 See below, p 153.

11 See below, p 169.

12 *EJ,* X (1900).

13 Mary D. Harris, *The Coventry leet book or mayor's register* (Early English Text Society, 1907-13), under the year 1553.

14 Rupert H. Morris, *Chester in the Plantagenet and Tudor reigns* (Chester, 1893), p 409.

15 See below, p 105.

16 Mary Bateson, *Records of the borough of Leicester* (London, 1899-1923), III, 105, 186.

17 *Discourse of the common weal of this realm of England,* ed Elizabeth Lamond (Cambridge UP, 1893), p 100.

18 Edited by Kathleen M. Burton (Chatto & Windus, 1948).

19 *SPD Elizabeth,* 93, no 27.

20 I am aware that Miss MacArthur (*EHR,* IX (1894) infers (a) from Sir Anthony Fitzherbert, *The boke for a justyce of the peace* (London, 1538) and (b) from the *Rotuli Parliamentorum* (London, 1767-77), III, 268b and 269, that the sliding scale was not first introduced in 1563. This is correct. But before 1563 its movement was limited by a statutory maximum.

21 *HMC Salisbury,* I, 162-5. I have to thank Professor G. Unwin for referring me to this document.

22 For a summary of recent discussion of this view, see above, pp 16-18.

23 *HMC Salisbury,* VII under November 1597: 'Notes for the present Parliament'.

24 See below, p 177.

25 Harris, *Coventry leet book,* p 21.

26 *EHR,* XIII (1898).

27 *HMC Various,* IV, 201.

28 Morris, *Chester,* p 366.

29 Morris, *Chester,* p 356.

30 *EHR,* XV (1900), 449-50.

31 Harris, *Coventry leet book,* III, 653.

32 *Rot Parl* III,269,330,352;IV,330-1,253;V,110.

33 *EHR,* XV (1905), 450.

34 Sir Thomas More, *Utopia* (Pitt Press Series, Cambridge UP, 1879), p 162.

35 King Edward's remains: 'a discourse about the Reformation of many abuses'.

36 *EJ,* VIII (1898), 342.

37 *EJ,* VIII (1898).

38 Cunningham, *Growth of English industry,* pp 43-4.

39 *EJ,* X (1900).

40 See below, p 162.

41 *SPD Charles I,* I, 499, no 10.

42 Samuel R. Gardiner, *History of the commonwealth and protectorate, 1649-1660* (Longmans, 1894-1903), I, 39-40.

43 Sir William Petty, *A treatise of taxes and contributions* (London, 1662), chapter I.

44 See below, p 173.

45 Sir Thomas Smith, *De republica anglorum: the maner of gouernment or policie of the realm of England* (London, 1583), lib. III, chapter 19. 'The Justices of the Peace doe meete also ... sometimes to take order for the excessive wages of servants and labourers'.

46 William Lambard, *Eirenarcha or of the offices of the justices of peace* (London, 1582).

47 William Sheppard, *Whole office of the county justice of peace* (London, 1652).

48 Sir Anthony Fitzherbert, *The boke longyng to a justice of the peace* (London, 1538); see also *EHR*, IX (1894).

49 See below, p 107.

50 *VCH Derbyshire*, II, 182-3.

51 *HMC Tenth Report, part IV* (1885), p 491.

52 *NRQSR*, I, 148; II, 114, 141, 202, 220; IV, 270.

53 *NRQSR*, II, 218.

54 See below, p 102.

55 John M. Guilding, ed *Reading records* (London, 1892-), I, 445.

56 Bateson, ed *Records of Leicester*, III, 114.

57 *EHR*, XV (1900), 451-4.

58 See below, p 103.

59 *EHR*, XV (1900), 451-4.

60 *HMC Various*, I, 161-75.

61 See below, p 167.

62 See below, p 191.

63 *NRQSR*, lists of recusants, passim.

64 John W.W. Bund, ed *Worcestershire county records: calendar of the Quarter Sessions papers* (Worcester Historical Society, 1899-1900), II.

65 For details see Richard H. Tawney, *The agrarian problem in the sixteenth century* (Longmans, 1912), pp 63-6.

66 Alexander Savine, 'English monasteries on the eve of the dissolution' in Paul Vinogradoff, ed *Oxford studies in social and legal history* (Oxford: Clarendon P, 1909-27), I, 223-6.

67 *Rural economy in York, being the forming books of H. Best, 1641* (Surtees Society, XXXIII, 1857).

68 Joseph Lee, *A vindication of a regulated inclosure* (London, 1656).

69 See below, p 187.

70 John Winthrop, *A journal of the transactions and occurrences in the settlement of Massachusetts* (Hertford, Conn: 1790), I, 112 (1633); II, 228 (1645).

71 *HMC Various*, I, 322-3.

72 Roger Coke, *A discourse of trade* (London, 1670).

73 See below, p 179.

74 *HMC Various*, I, 132; see also Arthur H.A. Hamilton, *Quarter Sessions from Queen Elizabeth to Queen Anne* (Sampson Low, 1878), pp 163-4, for an order made in 1657 that 'Masterless persons should have Masters within a month'.

75 See below, p 179.

76 Pseudonismus, *Considerations concerning common field and enclosures* (London, 1654).

77 Pseudonismus, *A vindication of the considerations concerning common field and enclosures* (London, 1656).

78 *SPD James I*, LXXX, no 13 (quoted in George Unwin, *Industrial organisation in the sixteenth and seventeenth centuries* (Oxford: Clarendon P, 1904), pp 188-9.

79 *HMC Fifteenth Report, part VIII* (1895), pp 17, 44 (Lincoln); Guilding, ed *Reading records*, II, 273, 357; III, 7, 25.

80 *VCH Suffolk*, II, 259.

81 *SPD James I*, 80, no 13 (1615) quoted in Unwin, *Industrial organisation*, Appendix A, II.

82 *SPD Elizabeth*, 244, no 126.

83 See below, p 169.

84 Harris, *Coventry leet book*, I, 94: 'Oct. 24, 1424. Indenture between master weavers and journeymen ... and the journeymen may have the third part of the payment for weaving cloth, as well less as larger, which they weave with their masters, as they used to have'.

85 Harris, *Coventry leet book*, II, 271.

86 Harris, *Coventry leet book*, III, 640.

87 Harris, *Coventry leet book*, III, 689.

88 William Hudson and J.C. Tingey, ed *Records of the city of Norwich* (Jarrolds, 1910), II, 106.

89 Guilding, ed *Reading records*, III, 46-7, 252.

90 W.T. Baker, ed *Records of the borough of Nottingham, being a series of extracts from the archives of the corporation of Nottingham,* V (London and Nottingham, 188?), pp 259-60.

91 *SPD Elizabeth,* 244, nos 126, 128, 129, 130.

92 *HMC Various,* I, 162.

93 *HMC Various,* I, 168.

94 *HMC Various,* I, 94.

95 See below, p 172.

96 Samuel R. Gardiner, ed *Reports of cases in the Courts of Star Chamber and High Commission* (Camden Society, new series, XXXIX, 1886), Attorney General v Archer (see especially Laud's remarks); Attorney General v Taylor and others (both these in the Star Chamber); also before the Court of High Commission, the case of Mr Viccars of Stamford, a Puritan minister who adds overstrict opinions about usury to his other heterodoxies.

97 *SPD Charles I,* 202, no 54: 'We doe not find upon our enquiry that the Statute for laborers and ordering of wages is deluded...'.

98 Privy Council Register, Charles I, V, 399, quoted in Leonard, *Poor relief,* p 160.

99 Quoted in Leonard, *Poor relief,* p 162.

100 See below, p 171.

102 *SPD Charles I,* 197, no 72.

103 *SPD Charles I,* 189, no 40.

104 Privy Council Register, Charles I, XIII, 389-90.

105 Privy Council Register, Charles I, XIII, 442.

106 William Salkeld, *Modern reports or select cases adjudged in the Courts of King's Bench, Chancery, Common Pleas and Exchequer* (London, 1700), II, 442: Trin 3. Anne. Cf William Blackstone, *Commentaries on the laws of England* (Oxford: Clarendon Press, 1765-9), 426-8.

107 Somerset Quarter Sessions Records, XXV, 66, no 13.

108 *The Harleian Miscellany* (London: Dutton, 1808-11), II: Sargeant Thorpe's charge to the Grand Jury at York assizes, 20 March 1648.

109 *HMC Various,* I, 169.

110 *HMC Various,* I, 322-3.

111 Edward H. Harbin and M.C. Dawes, ed *Somerset Quarter Sessions records* (Somerset Record Society, XXIII, XXIV, XXVIII, XXXIV,

1907-19), III.

112 Morris, *Chester,* p 367.

113 *EHR,* XV (1900).

114 *EJ,* X (1900).

115 *HMC Fifteenth report,* Appendix, part VIII, p 139.

116 Morris, *Chester,* p 436.

117 *EHR,* XV (1900).

118 I take the prices on which my index number is based from Steffen, *Studien zur Geschichte der englischen Lohnarbeiter.*

119 Frederick M. Eden, *The state of the poor or an history of the labouring classes in England from the conquest to the present period,* 3 vols. (London, 1797), III, appendix, p cvi.

120 Rogers, *History,* VI, 694: '... Which afterwards, since these troubles, have been increased, and in the year 1655 were thus assessed...'.

121 Warwickshire QS records. See below, p 180.

122 See below, p 166.

123 *VCH Lincs,* II, 336.

124 *VCH Bucks,* II, 69.

125 Hamilton, *QS.*

126 *NRQSR,* I, 204.

127 William O. Massingberd, ed *Court rolls of the manor of Ingoldmells* (Spottiswoode, 1902), p 285.

128 *NRQSR,* I, 27, 60, 105.

129 *Archaeologia,* XI (1794), 200.

130 *VCH Derbyshire,* II, 182-3.

131 See below, p 113.

132 *VCH Bucks,* II, 67-8.

133 Richard Burn, *The justice of the peace and the parish officer* (London, 1766), IV, 130-2.

WAGE REGULATIONS UNDER THE STATUTE OF ARTIFICERS

R. KEITH KELSALL
(1938)

Preface

So many economic historians have, in the past, been attracted by the Elizabethan labour code as a subject of study, that it may be as well to explain what gap this book is intended to fill. Briefly, it is hoped to provide a rather fuller treatment of wage assessment under the Statute of Artificers than has hitherto been published. In doing this my indebtedness to Professor Tawney's work will be constantly apparent – indeed, so far as suggestive ideas are concerned, it would be hard to improve upon his masterly analysis, published in *Vierteljahrschrift für Sozialund Wirtschaftsgeschichte* in 1914 [and reprinted above, pp 38-91]. What one can perhaps do, however, is to bring forward additional evidence on many different points, which may lead to changes in emphasis. This additional evidence comes, in the main, from sessions records. A large number of these has been published since 1918, several since the appearance of volume three of Lipson's *Economic history of England* in 1931. (Lipson, incidentally, apparently overlooked one or two that were published long before that date, notably the *Somerset Quarter Sessions records*). Full use has been made of this new printed material, but an attempt has also been made to utilize some of the unpublished records, most of which will not be printed for many years if, indeed, they are ever published.

The scope of the present study is at once narrower and wider than the title would suggest. Thus on the one hand, it has already been satisfactorily established that there was little novelty about Elizabethan labour legislation, that precedents both national and local lay to hand. Again, the full significance of the Gloucestershire clothiers' eighteenth century struggle against wage assessment, leading to the exemption of the woollen industry, and of the early nineteenth century efforts to revive assessment, has been brought out elsewhere. To neither of these questions is anything more than incidental reference made in the following pages, not because their importance is not appreciated, but simply because the records examined throw no additional light upon them, and mere repetition of what has already been so well said seems pointless. For the same reason, it has not been thought necessary to recapitulate what is known regarding poor law practices, or the functions of justices, high constables and petty constables, or the development of industrial organisation and similar questions. The relevance of this knowledge to the subject under consideration is not, of course, denied; but those who read this book can be relied upon to fit it into the appropriate setting for themselves, without the reminders which would be necessary in a general text. On the other hand, the present study embraces not merely the assessment of wages itself, but other closely allied parts of the Elizabethan labour code. Naturally, some selection had to be made, and the group of subjects centring on apprenticeship was excluded.

Finally, there are three points in particular on which I anticipate criticism, where I should like to say a few words in defence of the procedure here adopted. The first is that more use has not been made of early treatises on the practice of justices, which Dr Putnam has done so much to make more readily available. In this book we are, in the main, concerned with the administration of an Elizabethan statute, and the offences, penalties and procedure to be followed are, on the whole, clear enough. True, there are doubts – as to the exact functioning of the high constable's 'petty sessions', for instance – but these and similar difficulties are of a type which can only, in my opinion, be resolved by a close examination of sessions records in different parts of the country, and on which general treatises shed, at best, an uncertain light. Nor, according to Professor Tawney, should too much reliance be placed on the evidence of Lambard and the others as to the regularity, in different periods, of the practice of assessment.

Secondly, some will no doubt feel that too much space is devoted, in what follows, to irrelevant detail as, for instance, in the discussion of the exact wording of entries in sessions minutes. It seems to me, however, that the subject under review has now reached a stage at which, before fresh advances can be made, rather careful examination of the nature of the evidence on which many of our conclusions are based is necessary. It is perhaps not generally realised, for instance, how much individual judgment sometimes enters into the apparently simple task of distinguishing an entry in sessions minutes involving reissue of the existing scale from one involving the promulgation of a new scale. In these circumstances the more collective experience (for guidance in making such judgments, and for estimating the probable error in conclusions) is made available, the better. [A list of all known assessments, brought up-to-date to 1970, is printed as Appendix A.W.E.M.]

Thirdly, it may be felt that more use should have been made of the material available, that there should have been comparison of assessed rates in the same area at different dates, and in different areas at the same date. I do not myself feel, however, that the conclusions which usually emerge from comparisons of this type – to the effect, say, that wages in the north were higher than those in the south, and that the general movement of wages was in an upward direction – quite justify the labour involved in arriving at them. Moreover, so far as general comparisons are concerned, it is unlikely that more information can be gleaned from the existing material than has been done by Miss Hindmarsh, to whose unpublished London University thesis my attention was only drawn when the present study was virtually completed.

Acknowledgements

I should like to record my indebtedness to the following persons who have helped me by granting permission to examine records, by allowing me to print material, or in other ways.

Sir William Beveridge, Miss E.M. Brown, Mr Leonard Chubb, Mr B.C. Duddles, Mr J.W.F. Hill, Sir Godfrey MacDonald of the Isles, the Dowager Duchess of Norfolk, Rev Prebendary T.F. Palmer (Somerset Record Society), Dr S.A. Peyton, Miss M.E. Rayner, and Professor R.H. Tawney (who very kindly read the book in manuscript and made a number of helpful suggestions).

The clerks of the peace of the parts of Holland and Lindsey in Lincolnshire, of Norfolk, Staffordshire, Suffolk, and the East and West Ridings of Yorkshire, and their staffs.

The incumbents of numerous parishes in Lincolnshire and Yorkshire.

The Librarians of Canterbury, Chester, Hull, Hull University College, Ipswich, Manchester University, Norwich, Queen's College Oxford, and St Albans, and their staffs.

The mayor of Hedon.

The town clerks of Aldebrugh, Beverley, Great Grimsby, Great Yarmouth, Hertford, Hull, Ipswich, Scarborough, and Thetford, and their staffs.

I Assessments and reissues

Workers in the field of wage assessment labour under one serious initial handicap, in that there is no certainty as to where, for any particular county or borough, the assessments themselves may be found. For the first years of the statute's operation, it is true, the procedure was reasonably clear. Justices were, at Easter Sessions, to rate wages and certify them into Chancery: if approved, they would then be issued as proclamations, and copies sent to the counties of origin for distribution, in compliance with the statute (5 Eliz c 4, sec 11).[1] Although the entries in the Privy Council register suggest that the central government performed its functions in this matter,[2] we are dependent on the survival of proclamations for most of our knowledge regarding the rates laid down by the justices at this period. Those proclamations incorporating assessments which have survived are clearly only a fraction of the original number, and there does not seem to be much likelihood of discovering more at the present time. After 1597, however, certification into Chancery ceased to be necessary (39 Eliz c 12). The position in the East Riding at the middle of the seventeenth century seems, incidentally, to have been that certification into Chancery was still believed to be necessary – the justices in 1647 ordered the clerk of the peace to 'certifie upp above the rates of servants wages and procure proclamations thereupon according to the forme of the statute'.[3] I know of no other case, however, in which this mistake was made. The problem of locating assessments was not rendered any easier by the change in procedure. The clerk of the peace was, it is true, responsible for keeping the parchment rolls on which the rates decided on were engrossed. In some cases he may have kept them separately from other sessions papers, as appears to have happened at Hull; in other cases they were filed in the general sessions bundles;[4] more commonly they were treated as of purely ephemeral interest, and were lost or destroyed. The absence of the parchment rolls themselves is not always, however, a sign that the rates assessed cannot be found, for several other possible sources exist. In the first place, where minutes of proceedings at Quarter Sessions were kept, an entry relating to this matter was sometimes made, usually among administrative entries but occasionally[5] as presentments; it was not usual, unfortunately, actually to copy the rates into the minutes, though occasionally this was done.[6] A second possible place of record was the book of sessions orders. Early researchers relied largely on this source, and were led into the error of supposing that, if no mention of assessment was included amongst the orders, no action in the matter of assessment was being taken by the justices.[7] It would be equally wrong, however, to assume that order books could safely be ignored in this connection, for in some districts the assessed rates were issued as orders,[8] whether this was a misconstruction of the terms of the statute or not. It is worth mentioning, incidentally, that although it was originally (5 Eliz c 4 sec 11) laid down that the wages should be assessed at Easter Sessions, entries are sometimes found in minute or order books under later sessions, either because action had been accidentally or intentionally postponed (a 1604 statute, 1 Jac I c6, sec 5, authorised rating of wages at *any* general sessions), or because the clerk had forgotten to make the entry at the time. Numerous instances of this are to be found, for example, in the Ipswich and Norwich sessions records.[9]

Lack of mention of assessment in minute and order books is not, however, conclusive evidence either that an assessment was never made, or that one no longer survives. Thus in some cases minute books ignore the administrative, as distinct from the judicial, side of the justices' activities altogether, for example, the sessions books at Great Yarmouth; while in other cases, despite the silence of the minutes, cases where rates of wages higher than those assessed were given or received show that the normal machinery must have been functioning as in Nottinghamshire in 1603-61.[10] A final possibility is that the copies transmitted to the high constables or petty constables may have survived, perhaps having been entered in petty constables' books of memoranda along with other instructions periodically received.[11] Oddly enough the distribution of large numbers of printed copies, which became quite a usual means of publication of the assessed rates in the last quarter of the seventeenth, and in the eighteenth century,[12] has not apparently meant the survival of several copies of each of the known assessments for that period. Nevertheless, a careful search of parish chests in those parts of the country where no lists of their contents have been published would probably yield a certain number of additional copies, some of which had not hitherto been recorded.

Assessments, when made, did not always apply to the entire county.

Thus in those counties where each of the four sessions was duplicated (whether by adjournment or otherwise) as for instance in Suffolk, Lindsey, Holland and Kesteven, it naturally followed (and was recognised by the Statute, 39 Eliz c 12, sec 2) that wages were rated separately at the duplicated Easter Sessions. Thus separate Suffolk assessments might be drawn up the same Easter, in the seventeenth century, for the four divisions of the county in sessions held at Beccles, Woodbridge, Ipswich and Bury. (The arrangement for duplication of sessions by adjournement in Suffolk is explained in some detail in Devreux Edgar's diary).[13] In counties where duplication was not indulged in, it was sometimes necessary to try and achieve the same result by so wording the general assessment as to distinguish between different areas within the county. Examples of this practice are found in Buckinghamshire, where a distinction was drawn between the Vale and the Chilterns,[14] in Lancashire, where rates in the 1725 assessment were qualified by the statement 'but the said county being near eighty miles in length, we think the more northern part thereof ought not to demand so much, but be content with what the custom of the country hath usually been';[15] that this represented a change of practice in Lancashire is suggested by an order of 1620 that the justices at their several sessions should rate wages within their several divisions;[16] and in Oxfordshire, where provision seems to have been made in the form of the assessment for a distinction between the North and South Divisions.[17] Assessment by divisions, though it obviously had much to commend it, has made things more difficult for research workers – when two assessments, or copies, for the same county and the same or adjacent years have survived, there is often no indication as to whether the differences between them are to be explained by careless copying, or by their being for separate divisions. Several instances of this difficulty will be found in the list in Appendix A. Another complicating factor was the existence of privileged jurisdictions within the county. An extreme case is to be found in Hertfordshire, where about one-third of the county area, the liberty of St Albans, had its own Quarter Sessions; in this instance the practice appears to have been to use the same *form* in drawing up a scale of wages, and at least on the one occasion for which we have information – two 1631 assessments – very similar rates.[18] Almost every county had, of course, within its area some borough with its own Quarter Sessions. Normally, this must have meant that the usual tendency for town wages in the crafts to exceed those in the surrounding country was reflected by a separate borough assessment, with appropriately higher maxima. However, if I am right in thinking that the 1631 assessment in the Town Clerk's custody is for a division of the *county,* the complete absence of anything directly related to the assessment of wages – including mention of receiving or giving higher rates, or refusing to work for the assessed rates – amongst the reasonably full records of the borough of Hertford, suggests that in some cases the justices of these privileged areas may (by choice or by necessity) have allowed the matter of wage assessment to be dealt with at Quarter Sessions for the county as a whole. It was stated that 'the mayor and steward and one burgess were to be justices of the peace for the borough, but their jurisdiction seems not to have excluded that of the county magistrates'.[19] The magistrates of the borough of St Albans seem to have combined with the liberty magistrates for wage assessment purposes *inter alia;* this, at least, seems to be a reasonable interpretation of the wording of an entry in the Corporation records, dated March 1587 – 'it was reported that it was agreed at the Sessions holden immediately after Easter for the liberty and borough that the rate of wages ... should remain the same as before, and this was confirmed'.[20] That the grant of separate Quarter Sessions did not always and necessarily carry with it the right to assess wages separately is at least hinted at, moreover, in the wording of an assessment for the county of Lancaster in 1725 – 'which rates ... we ... have hereby ordered not be exceeded in any part of the county ... and we do think fit that in every town-corporate, within this county, this our order be by the mayor or chief officer or officers there caused to be proclaimed'.[21] And even in the two cases where one would have thought the right of the town to draw up its own wage-scale unlikely to be surrendered or allowed to lapse – Exeter and Oxford (an assessment for Exeter has been printed)[22] – two scholars have, without actually raising the issue, spoken as if the county rature was valid there also.[23] One would, however, be safe in suggesting that, whatever is thought about these particular cases, the normal town with its own Quarter Sessions rated wages separately. Such assessments are, unfortunately, not always easy to distinguish from assessments for a division of the county, particularly where only a truncated copy survives. The 1682 Suffolk assessment printed by Thorold Rogers,[24] for instance, may, on the evidence he gives, equally well be for Bury St Edmunds as a borough, or for the Bury division of Suffolk.

It is, of course, of vital importance in the study of the rating of wages by the justices to be able to distinguish between a new assessment and a reissue, without alteration, of a previous scale. (For the purpose of the list in the appendix, any alteration in the existing rates constitutes a new assessment). Such a distinction is not difficult to draw where the wording used in order or minute books admits of only one interpretation. 'Wages to be as last year', or 'rates of wages continued' are clear enough; even 'rates of wages confirmed' can safely be regarded as evidence of reissue if, in a particular series of records, the wording used in case of setting new rates is known to differ from it. Ambiguity can, however, easily arise. For one thing, how much reliance is to be placed on a date referred to in the phrasing of a subsequent reissue? In Tawney's opinion,[25] the inclusion in the 1692 sessions minutes of the phrase 'the same rates of wages ... to stand for this year as they were appointed and settled by order of this Court last year',[26] justified the assumption that a new North Riding assessment had been drawn-up in 1691. Yet even wording of a still more definite character has, on occasion, proved misleading. We know, for example, that although in the early years of the eighteenth century reissues for Hertfordshire were in the form 'as at Easter Sessions 1700', the Easter 1700 assessment was itself merely a reissue of that of 1695.[27] Another rather odd use of words is to be found in the records of the same county. There is an order at Easter Sessions 1687 that rates be continued, though a new assessment was drawn up at that very sessions.[28] Presumably 'continued as now assessed' is to be understood, on the analogy of a similar case at Ipswich, 'rates ... to be continued as they are now newly assessed and appointed by the Court'.[29] It should be added, incidentally, that reissues were, when the need arose, proclaimed or printed and distributed as if they were new assessments,[30] a circumstance which naturally makes it even harder to distinguish the two. From a legal point of view there was, of course, no distinction; but this is small compensation to the student of economic history, to whom the reissue of the existing rates without alteration is a very different matter from a revision of the scale.

The number of known reissues is, of course, very much larger than the number of known new assessments. The Kent assessment of 1563 was reissued without alteration until at least 1589.[31] In Wiltshire, the 1605 assessment was apparently reissued for nearly thirty years, that of 1635 for nearly twenty, and that of 1655 for another thirty.[32] In Ipswich, reissues are found for every year in the period 1618-46, and most of the years 1608-49.[33] In the West Riding, the 1647 assessment probably remained in force up to 1671.[34] In Shropshire, reissues are to be found for many of the years between 1653 and 1669;[35] reissues exist for all but two of the years between 1692 and 1712;[36] while the

1732 assessment was apparently issued without alteration up to 1739.[37] Reissues, with gaps, are to be found in the first half of the eighteenth century for Devonshire,[38] while the 1679 spinners' rates for that county were renewed without change up to 1790.[39] The Middlesex records show reissues for practically every year between 1610 and 1725,[40] while the Warwickshire assessment of 1738 held good, we are told, until 1773.[41]

What interpretation are we to place on all this reissuing of existing scales? One point at least is clear – that unless an unbroken series exists, care should be taken not to assume too much. Thus, despite the run of reissues for Middlesex just mentioned, a scholar who has worked through these records thinks (on evidence of a court order requiring punishment for overpayment) that a new assessment was probably made about 1682;[42] even so, the absence of presentments for infringing the assessment between 1660 and 1760, in view of the court's own statement in 1694 that there was widespread disregard of the assessed rates, suggests that reissue was, in that county and period, largely a matter of form.[43] Reissues have been held to be significant as showing at least a certain amount of administrative activity on the part of the justices.[44] Tawney would, however, go further than this – 'such orders are ... evidence for the practice of assessment as complete as the issue of actual rates'.[45] My own feeling is that the significance of a run of reissues cannot be judged in isolation, that it must be considered in conjunction with several other factors, of which lack of change in the cost of living or in the demand for labour, a certain relation between assessed and economic rates, and the known activity of justices and those acting on their instructions in publishing rates and presenting those infringing these rates are the most important. The presence of any one of these factors may be sufficient to convince me that reissue was more than a matter of form, as for instance, when the Suffolk justices go to the expense of having the rates reprinted and distributed.[46] On the other hand, the absence of any corroborative evidence of one of these types strongly predisposes me to believe that the monotonous reissue of a thirty-year-old order does not mean the practice of assessment in any sense that matters.

Turning to the assessments themselves, the most noticeable feature about them is their astonishing variety in form and in types of work covered. Some are very lengthy, include piece-rates as well as time-rates, and go into detail on such matters as allowance for livery and for board and lodging. The Hull form used in the late seventeenth and early eighteenth centuries also details the charges of porters for carrying goods of varying types to different parts of the town and it would be of interest to know whether this was done in other ports. Others are extremely short as, for instance, the Norwich assessment of 1657 – 'wages for men servants by the year £3, women servants 40s and meat and drink, master workmen of carpenters, tilers, masons, reeders and the like to have 18d a day and their labourer 12d a day'.[47] A tendency for assessments to become less detailed, which might be inferred from a comparison of Northamptonshire assessments for 1560 and 1667,[48] is not borne out by comparison of Kent assessments of 1563 and 1724,[49] of Hull ratures of 1570 and 1721, or of Holland schedules of 1563 and 1680. Such an apparent tendency is sometimes to be explained by the practice of merely mentioning those rates which were to be altered, or by that of assessment by divisions.[50] Indeed, the Act of 1603, (1 Jac I c 6) by removing any ambiguity as to whether those outside husbandry and the 'enumerated occupations' were covered must, one would think, have tended to make assessments more, rather than less, detailed. Conversely the repeal in 1757 of the Act of 1756 had a contrary tendency; but few assessments survive after that date. Miss Hindmarsh found seventeenth-century ratures more detailed than those of an earlier date. Assessments were, of course, modified to meet changing needs and conditions, but the exact significance of these alterations cannot normally be grasped by those without detailed local knowledge. Such changes of form took place in Hertfordshire, for example, between 1631 and 1678 or 1687,[51] the 1631 form dating back to at least 1592.[52] Differences between one town and another, or one county and another, in the range of occupations covered are presumably to be explained, *inter alia,* by the relative strength of their trade associations. There is more than a hint of this in the sentence appearing in the 1621 Faversham assessment – 'Smithes, shoomakers, and other trades worke by Rate wee knowe not'[53] – and in the New Sarum declaration that it was best not to meddle with rates for certain classes of work.[54] Outside the towns the position was different, hence the statement in a Holland rature for 1563 – 'the saide servaunties, and apprentyces of Husbandry, Labourers, and Artificers hereafter named, and al other Artyfycers not named, shall have and take the several wages hereafter appoynted and not above'.[55] There were, of course, ample precedents for interference by the mayor and other town officers in the fixing of wages within the different crafts, so that we sometimes find such interference still taking place, after 1563, quite independently of the wage assessment provisions of 5 Elizabeth c 4. In Chester, for instance, it was in 1576 ordered by the 'Maior, Aldermen, Sheriffs, and Comen Counsaile, that the rate price and weighte of spyninge, cardinge, wevinge, walkinge, fullinge and dyinge of woll hereafter followinge shalbe from hensfurthe observed and kept, viz., that no manner of person or persons within this citie shall take or receyve for spyninge and hande cardinge of one waight of woll above sixe pens, ... nor for weveinge any peece of wollen cloth ... contayninge xxii yards in length, above twelve pens ...'.[56] Time-rates for work of some of the types mentioned in the order had already been laid down in assessments under the statute,[57] but not piece-rates.

The extent to which adjacent counties acted in concert in their wage assessment policy is a matter of some interest. A glance at the list of assessments in Appendix A suggests that, on a number of occasions, the same factors must have led to the rating of wages roughly simultaneously by different groups of justices. This is probably why there are several assessments in 1647 and the following year; the justices of Lindsey, Kingston-upon-Hull and the East Riding were presumably influenced by the same considerations in 1669; there is evidence that this was so in East and North Yorkshire in 1679-80; and concerted action between the justices of three adjacent counties is suggested by the ratures of 1687 for Buckinghamshire, Hertfordshire and Oxfordshire. We know that the East Riding justices sought the advice of their fellow magistrates in the other two Ridings on wage assessment on at least one occasion. An East Riding order of 1721 was to the effect 'that such of his Majesties Justices of the Peace for this Riding as shall appear at the next Assizes held for the County of York be desired to meet any or such of his Majesties Justices of the Peace as shall also appear for the other two Ridings in order to settle servants and labourers wages that they make a report thereof against the next Easter Sessions'.[58] On the other hand, the known dates of reassessment in East Anglia suggest that the different groups of justices involved acted independently of each other in this matter, as will be seen from the accompanying table. Information regarding assessed rates at the same date in adjacent areas tends to be inconclusive, as there are so many doubts about the comparability of different categories of work.

Earlier writers have been led, by an examination of the dates of known assessments and reissues, to certain conclusions regarding periods of general activity in the rating of wages. Hewins, for example, suggested that activity was greatest in seven short periods (1563-7, 1591-6,

EAST ANGLIAN ASSESSMENTS AND REISSUES
1631-1663

(Blanks normally indicate absence of records)

	Ipswich	*Suffolk*	*Norwich*	*Norfolk*
1631	Reissue		Reissue	
1632	Reissue		Reissue	
1633	Reissue		Reissue	
1634	Reissue		Assessment	
1635	Reissue		Reissue	
1636	Reissue		No mention	
1637	Reissue		Reissue	
1638	Reissue		Reissue	
1639	Reissue		Reissue	
1640	Reissue		Assessment	
1641	Reissue		Reissue	
1642	Reissue		Reissue	
1643	Reissue		Reissue	Reissue
1644	Reissue		Reissue	
1645	Reissue		Reissue	
1646	Reissue		Reissue	
1647	No mention		Reissue	
1648	Reissue		No mention	
1649	Reissue		Apparent Reissue	
1650	No mention	Reissue	Assessment	Reissue
1651		Reissue	No mention	Reissue
1652	Reissue	No mention	Reissue	Reissue
1653	Reissue	Reissue	Reissue	Reissue
1654	No further	Reissue	Reissue	Reissue
1655	mention	Reissue	Reissue	
1656		Assessment	Reissue	
1657		Reissue	Assessment	
1658		Reissue	Reissue	
1659		Reissue	No mention	
1660		Reissue	Reissue	
1661		Reissue	Reissue	Assessment
1662		Reissue	Reissue	Assessment
1663		Reissue	No further mention	Reissue

1608-12, 1619-21, 1632-4, 1651-5 and 1682-8), and that special reasons could be assigned for this.[59] Although this is clearly true up to a point (as will be shown in subsequent chapters), it is hardly a statement that would be made today. There are few periods of more than a year or two, until we reach the second half of the eighteenth century, for which evidence of activity in some part of the country is lacking. Even at the height of the Civil War the administrative work of Quarter Sessions was not everywhere suspended, while during the Commonwealth the Statute of Artificers was still regarded as a valuable piece of social legislation.[60] To attempt to go further than this, and calculate an annual or decennial 'density' on the basis of known assessments and reissues would be, except for one or two groups of abnormal years, statistically valueless, however; for one thing, the years after 1670 or so would be unduly weighted by the volume of sessions records which has survived and been printed for that period. Tawney, it is worth noticing, does not regard the evidence of the authors of legal textbooks as to the regularity of the practice of assessment as carrying much weight.[61] Only for particular localities – and then only with certain important reservations – are we justified, in my opinion, in making any general statements regarding periods of activity.

Finally, it may be said that a position has now been reached at which, so far as the practice of assessment in any particular area is concerned, the onus of proof rests on those who think the rating of wages was not practised. Cases in which there is no evidence of assessment at *any* date within a given Quarter Sessions area are becoming more and more rare. There is the case of Hertford, mentioned earlier in this chapter, but there lack of authority may have been the obstacle. Cases in which there is positive evidence that wages were never assessed are not, so far as I know, on record. Court's suggestion that wage assessment was not practised in Worcestershire, Warwickshire and Staffordshire in the sixteenth and seventeenth centuries is disproved by the data given in Appendix A.[62]

Notes

Chapter I

1 The statute is printed in A.E. Bland, P.A. Brown and R.H. Tawney, *English economic history: select documents* (Bell, 1914), pp325-33 and Richard H. Tawney and E.E. Power, *Tudor economic documents* (Longmans Green, 1924), I, 338-50. I have followed their numbering of the sections.

2 *EHR*, XV (1900), 448.

3 East Riding QS books, October 1647.

4 Elizabeth W. Gilboy, *Wages in eighteenth-century England* (Cambridge, Mass, Harvard UP, 1934), p 247.

5 Eg Edward H.B. Harbin and M.C. Dawes, ed *Somerset Quarter Sessions records* (Somerset Record Society, XXIII, XXIV, XXVIII, XXXIV, 1907-19), III, 40, 66-7.

6 Eg Norwich Court books, August 1657; Holland QS minutes, Easter 1714.

7 Sidney A. Peyton, ed *Minutes of proceedings in Quarter Sessions held for the parts of Kesteven in the county of Lincoln, 1674-1695* (Lincoln Record Society, XXV, XXVI, 1931), p cxi.

8 *EJ*, XXIV (1914), 221.

9 Eg Ipswich QS minutes, 20 September 1619; Norwich Court books, 26 September 1656.

10 Henry H. Copnall, ed *Nottinghamshire county records: notes and extracts from the Nottingham county records of the seventeenth century* (Nottingham, 1911), pp 65-6.

11 *EHR*, LII (1937), 283.

12 Eg Suffolk QS Order books, April 1729; *NRQSR*, VII, 50 and William J. Hardy, ed *Hertford county records* (Hertford, 1905), I, 338.

13 For the duplication of sessions in Lincolnshire, see *VCH Lincs*, II, 337.

14 Eg William Le Hardy, ed *Buckinghamshire Sessions records*, I. 1678-1694 (Aylesbury, 1933), pp 227-9.

15 *Annals of Agriculture*, XXV (1796), 312.

16 Ernest Axon, ed *Manchester Sessions, I. 1616-1623* Lancashire and Cheshire Record Society, XLII, 1901), p 113.

17 May S. Gretton, *Oxfordshire justices of the peace in the seventeenth century* (Oxfordshire Record Society, XVI, 1934), p lxiv.

18 For similarity of *form*, compare Hardy, ed *Hertford CR,* I, 8-12 with Robert Cluttbuck, *The history and antiquities of the county of Hertford* (London, 1815-27), I, xxii-xxiv.

19 *VCH Herts*, III, 496.

20 Arthur E. Gibbs, ed *The corporation records of St Albans* (St Albans, 1890), p17.

21 *Annals of Agriculture*, XXV (1796), 312.

22 *HMC Exeter*, pp 50-1.

23 Gilboy, *Wages*, pp 110-11 and William G. Hoskins, *Industry and trade in Exeter 1688-1800* (Manchester UP, 1935; University of Exeter, 1968), p 130.

24 James E. Thorold Rogers, *A history of agriculture and prices in England* (Oxford: Clarendon p, 1882-1902), VI, 698-9.

25 See above, p 59.

26 *NRQSR*, VII, 128.

27 William Le Hardy, ed *Hertford county records* (Hertford, 1928-35), VII, 3, 14, 26, 36, 48, 58, 68.

28 Le Hardy, ed *Hertford CR*, VI, 400.

29 Ipswich QS records, Easter 1656.

30 Eg Suffolk QS order books, April 1748; R.L. Kenyon, ed *Shropshire county records: orders of Shropshire Quarter Sessions,* I, 109.

31 *EHR*, XLI (1926), 273.

32 *HMC Various*, I, 161-75.

33 Ipswich QS records.

34 *EJ*, XXIV (1914), 228.

35 Kenyon, ed *Salop CR*, I, 5, 14, 26, 56, 64, 88, 95, 98, 102, 106.

36 Kenyon, ed *Salop CR*, I, 140, 146, 151, 162, 167, 180, 187, 193, 198, 205, 212, 219, 224, 229, 233, 236; II, 4, 8, 11.

37 *EJ*, IV (1894), 516.

38 Gilboy, *Wages*, p 88.

39 Hoskins, *Industry and trade,* P 130.

40 Eric G. Dowdell, *A hundred years of Quarter Sessions: the government of Middlesex from 1660-1760* (Cambridge UP, 1932), p 149.

41 Arthur W. Ashby, *One hundred years of poor law administration in a Warwickshire village* (Oxford: Clarendon P, 1912), p 176.

42 Dowdell, *QS*, p 149-50.

43 Dowdell, *QS*, p 150.

44 *EHR*, XLIII (1928), 402.

45 See above, p 60.

46 Suffolk QS order books, April 1748.

47 Norwich QS minutes, August 1657.

48 *EcHR*, I (1927-28), 130.

49 *EHR*, XLIII (1928), 400.

50 *EHR*, LII (1937), 287.

51 Hardy, ed *Hertford CR*, I, 292; VI, 400.

52 Hardy, ed *Hertford CR*, I, 8-12.

53 *Archaeologia Cantiana,* XVI (1886), 270.

54 Nora Hindmarsh, 'The assessment of wages by the justices of the peace, 1563-1700' (University of London PhD thesis, 1932), p 160.

55 A copy of this proclamation is in the library at Queen's College, Oxford.

56 Rupert H. Morris, *Chester in the Plantagenet and Tudor reigns* (Chester, 1893), p 409; see also above, pp 45-6.

57 Morris, *Chester,* pp 367-8.

58 East Riding order book, July 1721.

59 *EJ*, VIII (1898), 345.

60 Ephraim Lipson, *Economic history of England, III: the age of mercantilism* (Black, 1931), 260-1.

61 See above, p 58.

62 William H.B. Court, *The rise of the Midland industries, 1660-1838* (Oxford UP, 1938), p 59.

II The extent of infringement

It was one thing to draw up and publish a scale of maximum rates of wages (for, except in the cases to be discussed in chapter five, it was a question of maxima and not minima) but quite another to ensure that these rates would not be exceeded. The statute, it is true, prescribed ten days' imprisonment and a fine of five pounds for giving higher wages, and twenty-one days' imprisonment for receiving higher wages (5 Eliz c 4, sec 13), while by fixing a copy of the scale on church doors, proclaiming it on certain market days, and instructing petty constables to acquaint every family with it[1] and high constables to make it known at their petty sessions, the authorities made sure that no one could justifiably plead ignorance. In other ways too, as will be shown later, entering into contracts of service which infringed the assessed rates was both difficult and attended disadvantages. Nevertheless, if it was in the immediate interests of both parties to break the law, and when the agents of the law were overworked, practically unpaid, and perhaps even, on occasion, sympathetic, risks were likely to be taken. What evidence, then, do we possess regarding the effectiveness of the justices' scales? Direct evidence – which is all we shall be concerned with in the present chapter – is of two main types. On the one hand, there are the cases of infringement which were brought to the notice of the justices; while on the other hand, comparison can be made between wages known to have been paid and the corresponding assessed rates. As a matter of convenience, these two types of evidence may be considered separately.

Of what might be called specifically wage-assessment offences there were three (excluding the offence of not being present at the sessions for the rating of wages, which was an afterthought (5 Eliz c 4, sec 12)[2] and not often treated as an offence[3]). They were giving and accepting more than the assessed rates, and refusing to work for the assessed rates. To take the first of these, the bulk of our examples come from the North Riding of Yorkshire. Thus in January 1606-7 the inhabitants of a parish were collectively presented for giving excessive wages;[4] and four other cases were brought up at the same sessions.[5] There were three

cases[6] between then and Easter Sessions 1608, when seven people were presented for this offence.[7] There were two further instances that year,[8] while at the sessions held in January 1608-9 four more presentments are recorded.[9] Except for three cases in 1610-11[10] (one of which is the only instance in the series we know to have concerned daily, as distinct from yearly, wages[11]), one in 1614[12] and one in 1647;[13] there is then complete silence on the subject until, in the early sixteen-eighties, there is an outburst of overpayment associated, in my view, with a temporarily acute shortage of labour. This will be discussed at a later stage in the present study.[14] In Kesteven three cases (one concerned with daily wages[15]) are recorded in 1684,[16] and one instance two years earlier.[17] In Middlesex an instance occurred in 1564,[18] and in Hertfordshire there was one in 1655.[19] In Nottinghamshire we are told there were many presentments for giving and receiving more than the assessed rates in the seventeenth century – one of these was in 1606-7, and another in 1627.[20] In the latter part of the seventeenth century, though in fact wages had been assessed ten years previously, the Buckinghamshire justices observed that, as a result of failure to adapt assessed rates to the needs of the times, 'both masters and servants had been and were subjected to indictments for their disobedience and contempts of the orders of the Court.'[21] To this printed evidence there can be added a few cases which I have come across in the manuscript material examined – two Lindsey instances in 1655[22] and 1658,[23] and two for Suffolk, in 1564[24] and in the seventeen-twenties.[25] Miss Hindmarsh's survey of manuscript sessions records yielded thirty-six Essex cases of giving and receiving excessive wages in twenty-four years of the sixteenth century, masters usually being the offenders.[26] In addition, she mentions a Sussex instance of giving and taking more than the assessed rates in 1683, and four Hertfordshire examples of the same type for the period 1655-66.[27]
sixteen-eighties, already mentioned) only yield four cases (of which two appear to involve daily wages[28]) one in 1607-8, one in 1609, one in 1610, and one in 1612.[29] There is one Kesteven case, in 1684,[30] and one Hertfordshire instance, in 1655,[31] while in 1632 in Wiltshire the tythingmen of Tinhead presented two sawyers, two carpenters and a thatcher 'that doth exceed in taking of wages contrary to the Statute', but reported that they knew of no covenant servants committing the same offence.[32] A few instances can be added from manuscript records consulted, but not many. There is an interesting group of cases in the Thetford (Norfolk) court books, where, under the date 22 April 1571,

it is recorded that four men took wages contrary to the rate. Three of these appear to have been masons' labourers, and their offence was that of taking fourpence a day. The fourth (who, it may be guessed, had taken too great yearly wages) was punished in the stocks, instead of the statutory twenty-one days' imprisonment (5 Eliz c 4, sec 13). After a careful examination of loose sheets relating to Scarborough courts of various kinds, four instances were found, two in 1627[33] and two others representing the presentment twice over of a certain Miles Cooper 'for taking wages above the Statute about August last ... and about 16 July last' – clearly not a yearly wage.[34] Finally, an instance of a brick-layer 'taking and demanding' excessive wages is recorded for Holland in 1675;[35] and two Lindsey examples occured in 1625 and 1655 respectively.[36] Miss Hindmarsh found cases, additional to the 'mixed' types already mentioned, in Northamptonshire in the sixteen-sixties and eighties, (nine instances), in Hertfordshire in 1646 and 1650, and in Surrey in 1669.[37]

The relative scarcity of instances of these two offences is, therefore, plain. It is true that a recent writer, speaking of these offences, observes 'to this aspect the orders of sessions and presentments constanlty refer',[38] but this view would seem to give undue weight to North Yorkshire experience. Other workers in this field have commented rather on their scarcity. Tawney, for instance, found no instances in the manuscript proceedings of Warwickshire Quarter Sessions for the period 1610-80,[39] Heaton comments on the paucity of cases in the West Riding,[40] Cunningham's general impression was that steps were not taken.[41] Turning to the explanation of this scarcity the commonest view is, as one would expect, that it constitutes proof that these sections of the statute were not enforced.[42] In the case of Buckinghamshire, one writer observes 'the laws against masters who gave more than the legal wage were ... not enforced; there are no presentments of such offences, and the bench of magistrates even ordered a master to apy his servant wages that ... exceeded the maximum'.[43] Chambers suggests that the more powerful masters (eg the Duke of Rutland) could safely ignore the Statute 'as their social prestige would reduce, if not eliminate, the risk of prosecution at Quarter Sessions'.[44] Heaton, on the other hand, does not agree that an absence of cases indicates failure to apply the act. 'By its very nature and by its threats of penalties, the act was an easy one to obey'.[45] Hewins, on the strength of Buckinghamshire evidence of 'unjustified' indictments mentioned earlier, reaches the same conclusion from the other side – the laxity of the justices is not necessarily disproved even if numerous cases of overpayment occur in the records.[46] My own view is that we are not justified in inferring from the lack of such cases that the justices' scales had no effect unless *for the same area and date* it can be shown that actual wages in excess of these scales were being paid. Before proceeding to examine this aspect of the matter, however, the third type of wage assessment offence may be dealt with.

It could no doubt be objected that 'refusal to serve for the assessed rates' was not, under the Statute of Artificers, distinguishable as an offence from mere 'refusal to serve'. It is, of course, true that there were a number of circumstances in which a person could be compelled to serve, and that no particular stipulation regarding the rate of wages at which this service should be undertaken was made. Thus those who had been brought up in one of the 'enumerated occupations' (5 Eliz c 4, sec 2), or had been attached to it for three years, and were unmarried, (or, if married, under thirty), who failed to fulfil a minimum property condition, and were not legally retained elsewhere, could be compelled to serve in that occupation at the request of any master (5 Eliz c 4, sec 3). Again, every person between twelve and threescore years, not being already lawfully retained or apprenticed and not having a minimum property qualification, could be compelled to serve in husbandry by the year (5 Eliz c 4, sec 5). Unmarried women between the ages of twelve and forty could, at the discretion of two justices, be compelled to serve by the year or week or day for such wages as were thought fit (5 Eliz c 4, sec 17). At harvest time artificers and persons fit to labour could be compelled to serve *by the day* (5 Eliz c 4, sec 15). Only in one of these cases, it will be noticed, is anything said about wages, and on that occasion what is said is vague enough. The offence 'refusing to work for the assessed rates' was, however, made perfectly clear in two later statutes. Thus in 1572 (14 Eliz c 5) and 1597 (39 Eliz c 4) 'all common Labourers being persons able in Bodye using loytering, and refusinge to worke for suche reasonable Wages as ys taxed and comonly gyven in suche partes' (14 Eliz c 5, sec 5) were declared to be vagabonds and were to be treated as such. This being so the phrase 'refusing to work', where met with in presentments and indictments, is very often accompanied by mention of the justices' rates. For many purposes it would, of course, be sufficient to class several varieties of refusal to work together – living idly, living at one's own hands, refusing to work for the assessed wages. But for this study cases where it is definitely stated that the refusal was of this latter character are of special interest, however much we may regret our inability to determine what proportion of the residue should really be included in this category. For, where this particular aspect of the offence is stressed the refusal, one may infer, amounted to a demand for higher wages than those in the justices' scale – a demand, at least, of a somewhat more direct character than 'living idly' which, however often it may have been an indication of precisely the same maladjustment between assessed and economic rates of wage, must sometimes have had a simpler explanation. The other offences mentioned in this paragraph will be considered in chapter three.

As before, the North Riding and Kesteven provide the bulk of our examples. In North Yorkshire there were five instances in October 1610. Three men were presented 'for denying to worke emongest their neighbours in Harvest, and for departing forth of the Libertie for greater wages';[47] while at a special sessions held later in the same month a man was presented for refusing to thatch 'for such wages as is allowed', and another for refusing to thresh under fourpence a day, though this last entry is crossed out.[48] In 1614 a rough-waller was presented for, *inter alia,* refusing to work for statute wages, and going forth of the Riding 'into other cuntryes to worke in sommer so as his neighboures cannot have his worke in hay-time and harvest'.[49] Three instances are to be found in the Kesteven minutes for the sixteen-seventies – one in 1675 and two in 1678.[50] There are one or two early Middlesex examples in the fifteen-sixties,[51] while the Oxfordshire justices decided in 1694 that if a certain William Wakelin of Whately did not work 'at such rates as the town shall allow' the next justice should send him to the house of correction.[52] Finally, so far as the printed materials go, the West Riding justices in 1641, acting on 'the generall complainte of the inhabitants of these partes, that servants refuse to worke for reasonable wages, and cannot be hired for competent allowance as formerlye, makeing advantage of the much busines of the times' ordered that the Statute should be observed;[53] while, on the other hand, the justices of a Derbyshire wapentake reported, ten years earlier, that none were presented to them for living out of service and refusing to work for reasonable wages.[54] Two Holland cases were noted in the manuscript materials examined, one in 1673 and one in 1678.[55] Such, meagre as it is, is the evidence available on refusing to work for the assessed rates.

Turning now to the comparison of assessed with *actual* rates it will be remembered that Hewins took Thorold Rogers to task for comparing averages deficient in northern wages with northern assessments and concluding that the market rates were higher than assessed rates.[56] Hewin's own view was that the justices' scales could be accepted as representing current wages in the various counties at the time they were promulgated.[57] Almost inevitably, everyone whose researches have brought him into contact with assessments has associated himself with one or other of these views. No study of the rating of wages would be complete, therefore, without some mention of this controversial topic; so that, unsatisfactory as the evidence is in most respects, some attempt must be made to review it here. In the North Riding, daily rates paid to thatchers in 1681 and masons and carpenters in 1687 and 1691 by the Topcliffe churchwardens were in accordance with the juctices' scale of 1658[58] (a new assessment was, it is true, drawn up in 1680,[59] but it is unlikely – as will appear in the discussion[60] of the circumstances making that assessment necessary – that daily rates were altered). The Miscellaneous Corporation Accounts show Scarborough masons in 1657 and carpenters in 1667 to be receiving slightly higher rates but this was, of course, a normal feature of town economy, and wages there were in any case separately assessed. In the West Riding, where even the rates for clothworkers were maxima, we are told that 'the average daily earnings of the weaver in the seventeenth century were ... well below the maximum fixed by the assessment of 1647';[61] and that up to about 1730 the wage lists were being enforced, but not thereafter.[62] It would appear from wages recorded in Captain Bosseville's account book relating to Penistone, however, that there were divergencies between assessed and economic rates earlier than that. Thus a carpenter was paid 1s 2d a day in 1694, though 12d was the maximum a master carpenter who took charge of a building and had two or three under him was allowed to take; while numbers of men mowing and women haymaking were overpaid in 1693, although the 1691 husbandry wages were correct. A joiner at Masham appears from the churchwardens' accounts to have been overpaid in 1669. In the East Riding, the wages given in the account book of Philip Constable of Everingham are in accordance with the rature of 1669.[63] Those in a Welwick farmer's accounts,[64] given under the heading 'servants and their wages' are not so in all cases, however. Thus, although we have no knowledge of the assessed rates current in the years 1659-67, if the 1669 rature is any guide to them two maidservants must have been overpaid in 1659 and 1660; and the same would be true of some women harvesting in 1666 and a thatcher in the previous year. Moreover four maidservants were definitely overpaid in 1673 and the four following years, by comparison with the highest rates given in the 1669 assessment, as were two men who were paid higher wages in 1674 and 1675 than that applicable to a bailiff of husbandry; though the majority of the wages recorded were below the appropriate maxima.

Turning to Lancashire, a comparison of the 1725 assessment and the wages given by Arthur Young in 1768 shows remarkably little difference between the two.[65] In Derbyshire there are indications that mid-seventeenth century payments to day labourers in husbandry were in accordance with the 1634 rature; and that masons and their labourers in 1693 were receiving the amounts given in the 1648 assessment.[66] Rutland yearly wages recorded at statute sessions between 1626 and 1634 are said to have been in accordance with the rature of 1610,[67] it is, of course, unlikely that failure to comply with the assessed rates would be officially recorded by the master breaking the law. For the same reason, our knowledge that the wage agreements recorded in the Norwich court books did not infringe the official scale is not, perhaps, of very great value. In Warwickshire (where the 1738 rature was reissued until 1773) there is evidence that unemployed labourers were, in 1770, receiving allowances supplementing their wages which brought their earnings above the justices' rates, and in 1778 the justices overpaid a thatcher,[68] in the latter case, however, we do not know that the 1738 scale was even officially recognised. Two bills of repairs for work done on Magdalen Bridge in 1688-9[69] include some wages which appear to be in excess of those allowed by the 1687 assessment[70] for Oxfordshire; Mrs Gilboy, too, found large discrepancies between masons' and carpenters' actual wages and those given in the rature of 1701,[71] but her *agricultural* information is for too late a period to enable any inference to be drawn in that case.[72] The Buckinghamshire position is very similar to that of Oxfordshire. Here, too, wages were reassessed in 1687, and market rates seem to have been out of alignment with this scale. The justices themselves ordered a master to pay his servant a wage at a yearly rate exceeding the maximum allowed, while we are told that 'the regular rate for ordinary labour seems already to have been 1s a day with but little variation, though the legal amount was 8d at most; but in the more skilled work the difference as usual was even greater. Instead of 1s 2d a bricklayer was entered as receiving 2s, a carpenter 1s 6d, and a plumber, whose trade did not appear in the scale of wages, had 2s 6d a day'.[73] Nor did the increases in yearly rates sanctioned in the 1765 rature anything like keep pace with the increases in amounts actually paid to workers on a comparable basis.[74] Turning to Hertfordshire, it appears from various accounts for work done for the county town that the assessed rates were exceeded. Thus in July 1629 a mason was paid 9d for half a day's work, the summer rate for artificers of the best sort in the 1631 rature being only 1s 4d a day; a carpenter was, however, paid at the correct rate on the same occasion. In April 1633, according to the miscellaneous accounts for the town of Hertford, a carpenter was paid at the rate of 1s 6d a day; and artificers (either carpenters or masons) were getting 1s 6d and 1s 8d in 1635 and 1636 (two instances of 1s 6d a day occur in the winter of 1636, the official winter maximum being 1s), a carpenter in July 1637 getting 1s 9d a day. It may, of course, be objected that rates in the town would naturally be somewhat higher than those in the surrounding district. One writer finds still greater discrepancies between assessed and actual rates in Hertfordshire.[75] His case is based, however, on a comparison of a labourer's 1s a day in a 1659 account[76] and 10d and 1s a day for work on the highways in 1672[77] on the one hand, and the winter rate for general labour – 4d or 5d a day – in the St Albans liberty assessment of 1631.[78] Quite apart from the obvious dangers of comparing rates separated by such long periods of time, the assessed rate that should have been chosen for comparison is certainly that *without* meat and drink – 10d in the 1631 assessment. Wages given to carpenters in a 1683 bill[79] fall within the limits laid down in the 1678 rature.[80] Wages mentioned by yearly servants in three petitions alleging non-payment, one in 1635-6, one in the latter half of the century, and one in 1732,[81] accord with the assessed rates then current. An eight-pound-a-year wage mentioned in a 1680 petition,[82] however, exceeds by three pounds the highest wage given in the 1678 assessment.[83] Comparison of bricklayers' and carpenters' bills for county work with the 1724 Kent rature shows the actual rates to be considerably higher than those assessed,[84] and the position with regard to the Gloucestershire assessment of 1732 is similar.[85] This, as Mrs Gilboy points out, is particularly significant since the bills concerned had to be examined by a committee of justices.[86] A comparison between the daily agricultural rates assessed for Gloucestershire in 1732 and Arthur Young's figures for 1768 does not, however, show any marked disparity.[87] Roughly the same position is found in eighteenth-century Devonshire – higher rates than those rated in the building trades,[88] particularly in the towns, but no very noticeable discrepancy in daily rates in husbandry.[89]

What conclusions can we draw from the evidence examined? In the first place, there is clearly a tendency for assessed and actual rates to diverge in the eighteenth century. Secondly, this tendency is, on the whole, most marked in the building trades and least marked in daily rates for work in husbandry. Thirdly, there is some doubt as to whether the assessed rates for the *county* ever had much relevance to *town* conditions; where towns rated their own wages, of course, this particular difficulty did not arise. Fourthly, the case of a divergence between assessed and economic rates before, say, the sixteen-eighties is still not proven; such material as is readily available suggests comformity between the two in that period, but a fuller examination of unpublished early farm account books and churchwardens' accounts might, in some districts, disprove this. Miss Hindmarsh, after working on manuscript materials different from those used in this study, came to the conclusion that, up to the middle of the seventeenth century, market and assessed rates corresponded fairly closely;[90] but that in the second half of the century there was a definite failure to restrain market rates for skilled labour (except in husbandry) from exceeding the assessed rates.[91] This failure she attributes not to magisterial laxity (though she admits the scarcity of recorded proceedings against those infringing the official scales)[92] but to the growth of a tendency to combination amongst journeymen and small masters which marked the break-up of the older types of guild, and other well-known tendencies accompanying these developments.[93] With the general outlines of this picture one could hardly quarrel, though it is perhaps a little more clear-cut than the uncertain and rather contradictory nature of the evidence justifies.

Notes

Chapter II

1 *EJ,* XXIV (1914), 230.

2 Tawney and Power, *Tudor economic documents,* I, 344.

3 Cf *EJ,* IV (1894), 513.

4 *NRQSR,* I, 60.

5 *NRQSR,* I, 60.

6 *NRQSR,* I, 87, 105.

7 *NRQSR,* I, 111.

8 *NRQSR,* I, 122, 127.

9 *NRQSR,* I, 142-4.

10 *NRQSR,* I, 202, 207, 209.

11 *NRQSR,* I, 202.

12 *NRQSR,* II, 37.

13 *NRQSR,* IV, 270.

14 See below, pp 181-6.

15 Peyton, ed *Kesteven QS minutes,* p 216.

16 Peyton, ed *Kesteven QS minutes,* pp 216, 228.

17 Peyton, ed *Kesteven QS minutes,* p 138.

18 John C. Jeaffreson, ed *Middlesex county records* (Middlesex County Records Society, 1886-1892), I, 50.

19 Hardy, ed *Hertford CR,* I, 112.

20 Copnall, *Notts CR,* p 66.

21 William A.S. Hewins, *English trade and finance* (Methuen, 1892), p 86.

22 Lindsey QS rolls, 1655.

23 Lindsey QS rolls, 1658.

24 Ipswich QS records, 1564.

25 Book of Precedents and Indictments, p 89.

26 Hindmarsh, 'Assessment of wages', p 129.

27 Hindmarsh, 'Assessment of wages', p 284.

28 *NRQSR*, I, 171, 202.

29 *NRQSR*, I, 99, 171, 202, 266.

30 Peyton, ed *Kesteven QS minutes*, p 228.

31 Hardy, ed *Hertford CR*, I, 112.

32 Benjamin H. Cunnington, ed *Records of the county of Wiltshire ... of the seventeenth century* (Devizes: G. Simpson, 1932), pp 105-6.

33 Scarborough sessions records, 9 April 1627.

34 Scarborough sessions records, 7 January 1638-9.

35 Holland QS minutes, Xmas 1675.

36 Lindsey QS rolls.

37 Hindmarsh, 'Assessment of wages', pp 284-5.

38 Peyton, ed *Kesteven QS minutes*, p cxi.

39 See above, p 85.

40 *EJ*, XXIV (1914), 231.

41 *EJ*, IV (1894), 513.

42 *EJ*, IV (1894), 513.

43 *VCH Bucks*, II, 71.

44 Jonathan D. Chambers, *Nottinghamshire in the eighteenth century* (P.S. King, 1932), p 279.

45 *EJ*, XXIV (1914), 231.

46 Hewins, *Trade and finance*, p 86.

47 *NRQSR*, I, 202.

48 *NRQSR*, I, 220.

49 *NRQSR*, II, 53.

50 Peyton, ed *Kesteven QS minutes*, pp 35, 86, 93.

51 Jeaffreson, ed *Middlesex CR*, I, 63.

52 Gretton, *Oxfordshire JPs*, p lxxix.

53 John Lister, ed *West Riding Sessions records, 1611-42* (Yorkshire Archaeological Society, Record series, LIV, 1915), p 333.

54 *VCH Derby,* II, 182; Bland, Brown and Tawney, *English economic history,* p 389.

55 Holland QS minutes, Michaelmas 1673, Xmas 1678.

56 Hewins, *Trade and finance,* p 83.

57 Hewins, *Trade and finance,* p 87.

58 *NRQSR,* VI, 3-4.

59 *NRQSR,* VII, 45.

60 See below pp 181-6.

61 Herbert Heaton, *The Yorkshire woollen and worsted industries* (Oxford UP, 1920), p 115; *EJ,* XXIV (1914), 234.

62 *EJ,* XXIV (1914), 232.

63 *EHR,* LII (1937), 284-6.

64 Welwick byelawmen's and miscellaneous accounts book.

65 Gilboy, *Wages,* pp 174-5.

66 *VCH Derby,* II, 182-3.

67 Rogers, *History,* VI, 693.

68 Ashby, *Poor law administration,* p 176.

69 Gretton, *Oxfordshire JPs,* pp 69, 94.

70 Gretton, *Oxfordshire JPs,* pp lxii-lxiv.

71 Gilboy, *Wages,* p 110.

72 Gilboy, *Wages,* p 89.

73 *VCH Bucks,* II, 71.

74 *VCH Bucks,* II, 84.

75 *VCH Herts,* IV, 228.

76 Hardy, ed *Hertford CR,* I, 130.

77 Hardy, ed *Hertford CR,* I, 233.

78 Clutterbuck, *Hertford,* I, xxii-xxiv.

79 Hardy, ed *Hertford CR,* I, 339.

80 Hardy, ed *Hertford CR,* I, 292.

81 Hardy, ed *Hertford CR,* V, 209; I, 207; VII, 238.

82 Le Hardy, ed *Hertford CR,* VI, 332.

83 Hardy, ed *Hertford CR,* I, 292.

84 *EHR,* XLIII (1928), 404.

85 Gilboy, *Wages,* p 110.

86 *EHR*, XLIII (1928), 404.

87 Gilboy, *Wages,* p 87.

88 Gilboy, *Wages,* pp 110-11.

89 Gilboy, *Wages,* pp 88-9.

90 Hindmarsh, 'Assessment of wages', pp 105-6.

91 Hindmarsh, 'Assessment of wages', p 301.

92 Hindmarsh, 'Assessment of wages', p 282.

93 Hindmarsh, 'Assessment of wages', pp 332-51.

III Complementary parts of the policy: I

As we have seen, several sections of the Statute of Artificers made it an offence for people fulfilling certain conditions to refuse to work under given circumstances. There was an additional deterrent to living idly, in that a statute of 1572 laid it down that 'all and everye persone ... able to labour, haveinge nor Land or Maister, nor using any lawfull Marchaundze Crafte or Mysterye whereby hee or shee might get his or her Lyvinge' and with no legal means of support was to be treated as a vagabond (14 Eliz c 5, sec 5). There were, indeed, under these and other statutes, ample means provided for taking proceedings against masterless men and women, boys and girls, in the parishes in which they were settled, and the justices were not slow to avail themselves of them. The apprenticing of poor children and the provision of a parish stock for setting the poor on work – expedients which there is no need to discuss here – represented, in fact, only part of a policy of which the compelling of everyone who could legally be forced to do so to obtain a service, or go to one found for them, was another important element. The printed records of sessions provide numerous examples of the latter (other than those given in the previous chapter) and would, no doubt, yield still more but for the fact that a single justice had authority to order the idle able-bodied to work.[1] In the North Riding, it is true, instances are rare. A mother was presented in 1610 for keeping her son at home idly,[2] and there is a case of refusal to serve in 1619;[3] but, except for two women being presented in 1670,[4] there is no further mention of the matter until the temporary labour shortage of 1680-2, when the justices employed all the means at their command, and naturally found their powers of compelling to go to service of value in this emergency.[5] The Kesteven minutes provide an instance, in 1692, of someone for whom the overseers have found a service being threatened, in case of refusal, with the house of correction, 'there to remayne till she doe goe'.[6] At a Shropshire sessions held three years earlier two women were given three months to provide themselves with services, with the alternative of the 'House'.[7] Two Surrey cases, in

1662-3, both concern women.[8] A particularly determined effort was apparently made by the Middlesex authorities in 1639, when no fewer than twenty-two men were presented for being loose, idle fellows living out of service under pretence of coal heaving once or twice a month;[9] one later case is recorded, in 1665,[10] and quite a number of earlier ones, in the fifteen-seventies and eighties.[11] In Buckinghamshire instances occur in the sixteen-eighties at the rate of about one or two a year; altogether between 1679 and 1690 eighteen cases are recorded, of which five relate to women.[12] The justices of a Derbyshire wapentake, as we noticed before, reported in 1631 that there had been no presentments of this type;[13] but the Wiltshire magistrates, as we shall see later, provided a valuable clue – if one were needed – to the significance of 'living idly' in many cases, when in 1655 they made an order that no young men or maids fit to go to service (their parents not being of ability to keep them) should remain at home.[14] The Devonshire justices, in 1657, ordered all masterless persons to take masters within a month.[15]

The manuscript records examined throw additional light on the use of the justices' power in this matter. Devereux Edgar's diary shows a magistrate frequently acting on the complaint of individual inhabitants, the parish constable or the churchwardens and overseers. In the first place, they suggest that during the sixteen-thirties and forties special efforts were made to compel people to obtain services. The justices of Thetford (Norfolk), for instance, ordered in 1634 that all persons inhabiting the borough who were compellable to serve in husbandry yet lived at their own hands should be apprehended by warrant and sent to the workhouse, until they were lawfully retained in husbandry for a year at least.[16] On the first of May the following year they issued a further order that all fit to go to service should provide themselves with one before the first of June next, on pain of the workhouse.[17] The justices of Hertford were kept busy dealing with parents who kept great girls at home idly, and with lusty young fellows able to do good service who yet preferred to live idly about the town. If the parent promised to take the necessary steps, further proceedings were usually dropped – at a Month's Court held in April 1628, for example, 'Widow Watts did in open Court promise that her daughter be put out to service by Whit Sunday next'.[18] All parents were not equally repentant; however, some being rash enough to voice their indignation at the interference of the law in the hearing of the local constable or ill-disposed neighbours – Robert Simmonds, presented in 1636 for keeping two girls at home that were fit for service, was heard to boast that Mister

Mayor would place none of his.[19] Altogether, in the Hertford records that survive for the years 1627-41, fifty-seven cases (excluding where possible cases of 'not apprenticing', though the similarity of the offence and the loose use made of such terms as 'service' makes certainty impossible) are recorded, of which thirty-eight concern parents, and the remainder the people themselves. Sometimes there are as many as seven or eight instances brought up at one sessions, the peak years being 1629-30 and 1638-39. There are two cases additional to those mentioned, one in 1642 and one in 1645. Instances of roughly the same date are to be found in Norfolk[20] and Suffolk.[21]

Secondly, as one would expect, the normal punishment threatened or applied was the house of correction. Norwich, it is true, had a good deal of trouble in 1624-5 with feltmakers who lived at their own hands, and threats of severer punishment were used, but these people had no settlement there, and the object was to make them leave the city.[22] Thirdly, there was, of course, lack of uniformity in such matters as the time allowed for providing oneself with a service – it varied, in the records examined, from three months or so[23] to no time at all,[24] a fortnight being quite a usual period,[25] one father obtained the discharge of his daughter from Bridewell on promising that she should be retained in service within a week.[26] In other respects, too, discretion had to be exercised by the justices. The exceptional circumstances which might justify a relaxation of the law in this matter are well illustrated by cases in the Suffolk order books. Thus two children who had been presented for going at their own hands were discharged from their indictments on it appearing that they were not fit to go to service 'they being impotent and having scaldheads.'[27] This case, from other information given, apparently concerned apprenticeship: the criteria applied would however, be very similar. Another Suffolk case is worth giving in some detail. The inhabitants of a parish complained that a certain Elizabeth Nunn was fit to go to service notwithstanding the loss of one of her hands, but that she refused to serve anyone as a hired servant by the year. The court thereupon ordered the inhabitants to provide her with a fitting service before next sessions, but one 'that shall be approved and allowed by this Court'. If she refused to accept this service, she should be sent to Bridewell.[28] At a later sessions it was reported that she had been duly offered a service with a master of whom the court approved, but that 'she refused to accept him, and further said she would not accept any service but as she would provide for herself'. The court, however, taking into account the fact that she agreed to take this master on the Monday following the Saturday of her refusal (by which time he had obtained another servant), decided to extend the time-limit by another six months.[29] Here those most anxious to put the law in motion seem to have been the villagers, while the justices took a more lenient view of the case. On other occasions the magistrates, when their attention was drawn to disregard of the law, took special steps to enforce it. Thus at Norwich, on being informed by those concerned in the government of the trade of worsted weavers 'that it is a general practice for young boys and lads under the age of twenty-one years to take work from worsterers by the gross, and so will take and leave work at their pleasure, which this Court looks upon to be the same thing as if they did live at their own hands and without any legal retainer', instructions were issued to churchwardens and overseers to give an exact account every month of all such persons.[30]

Finally, there is additional evidence both in the Ipswich and Suffolk records in the seventeen-twenties, that the assessment of wages and the enforcement of the laws against living idly were, on occasion, very closely inter-related. Consideration of this aspect of the matter can, however, conveniently be postponed until a later stage.

Leaving the question of living out of service for the moment, we can go on to consider a group of offences of a rather similar type. Departing before the end of one's term, or leaving one's work unfinished was, after all, only a stage removed from living idly and refusing to go to service. The yearly contract of service which was compulsory in many occupations could only be broken by mutual consent and reasonable and sufficient cause shown to a justice (5 Eliz c 4, sec 4), and the servant wanting to depart in normal circumstances had to give one quarter's warning before the end of his term. In this case the justice's 'allowing' was essential. The penalty for unlawful departure before term was imprisonment (5 Eliz c 4, sec 6), and provision was made for apprehending servants who fled to other counties (5 Eliz c 4, sec 39). Similarly, artificers and labourers leaving the work they had undertaken to do before it was finished were to be imprisoned for one month without bail and to forfeit five pounds to the aggrieved party (5 Eliz c 4, sec 10); when this latter penalty, incidentally, was inflicted on an East Riding carpenter he was also required to pay those that set him on work 'such costs and damages as they shall be put unto recovery thereof'.[31] Instances of leaving before term are, as one might expect, to be found scattered throughout the North Riding records. Between 1605 and 1610 fourteen cases are recorded,[32] of which four were brought forward at one sessions in October 1608.[33] Thereafter instances are rarer – one in 1637 (when the offender was, the statutory penalty notwithstanding, fined ten shillings), one in 1642, another in 1655-6, and another in 1662.[34] A milner failed to appear at all after being hired in 1663,[35] a carpenter a year or two later did not stay and finish laying a barn floor,[36] while an employer accused of not paying his servant the wages due to him made the counter-accusation that the servant had left before his term.[37] Heaton, after a search of half-a-dozen West Riding indictments books, only found one case of this character, in 1648,[38] and none are to be found in the published West Yorkshire records; a colliery workman was, however, committed to Bridewell in 1681 for breaking his contract of service.[39] There are two East Riding instances in 1648.[40] The number of pages referred to in the index to the Kesteven minutes under 'work, refusing to perform' is deceptive, for thirteen of these prove to be concerned with only one instance. Actually there are only seven persons indicted, two in 1680[41] and five in 1683;[42] the offence is given in all cases as that of refusing to perform work undertaken. Lancashire provides a larger number of examples. Thus in 1600-1, 1603 and 1605[43] there are orders that the servants named shall serve out their term, the servant involved in the last order being required to accept a subsequent service at three-fourths of her salary; while in the published records of certain Manchester sessions eighteen cases occur in the period 1616-22.[44] Nottinghamshire[45] and Worcestershire[46] provide one or two early seventeenth-century instances, the former involving masons failing to finish their work. Hertfordshire examples are few – three in the seventeenth and three in the eighteenth century,[47] the latest being 1784[48] – but Middlesex provides even fewer (four, in 1565, 1628, 1686 and 1709-10[49]).

Other manuscript evidence does not suggest that this offence was common – or, more correctly, that it often formed the subject of Quarter Sessions presentments, indictments and orders. There are four Holland[50] and two Lindsey[51] cases in the sixteen-seventies, and one or two in the Norwich[52] and Suffolk[53] sessions records. There may, however, have been a good deal of activity, of which we know nothing, by justices acting out of sessions. From the diary of a Suffolk justice, Devereux Edgar, it would appear that the issuing of warrants in connection with the unlawful departure of servants was of fairly common occurrence – in the six years 1703 to 1708 this particular magistrate issued forty-six warrants in connection with failure to finish work, leaving before term, or not entering service after being hired. As to what, in addition, to such exceptional events as the death of one's master, tended to be regarded as reasonable and sufficient cause for not remaining the full term, it appears that the Suffolk justices, at least, were prepared to consider insufficient food and failure to pay wages as, on occasion, providing adequate justification. A servant who left her master because she did not get enough to eat was sent to her last place of lawful settlement, instead of being punished and sent back to her master, the court being of opinion that he was 'in no wise fit to keep a servant, by reason of disability in estate'.[54] Another servant was discharged of her service on it appearing that her master had detained her wages.[55] In one rather unusual Suffolk case a master complained that his servant had run away, but on examination of the servant it appeared that his master (who was a Dissenter) had tried to prevail on his servant by entreaty and threats to go to Dissenters' Meetings, and had found him work to do on Sundays in order to prevent his going to church. The master, on being threatened with further action if he did not humble himself, agreed to the discharge of his servant 'by mutual consent'.[56] Incidentally, it is perhaps worth noticing that the form of 'imprisonment' quite usually[57] employed for leaving one's work was a period in the house of correction – was this because those who had run away from their masters could conveniently be classed as idle or disorderly persons for whom, under the Statute of 1609-10 (7 Jac I/c 4),[58] Bridewells were to be provided, or did it mark the transition of these houses from workhouses to prisons?[59] It is clear, at least, that the justices were acting on instructions in sending 'dissolute or idle servants' to Bridewell.[60]

For the efficient working of the Elizabethan labour code it was, of course, essential that leaving one's work should be treated as an offence. For one thing, the enforcement of yearly hiring on many occupations would have lost much of its value if masters and servants were allowed to break contracts of service with impunity. For another thing, people not in regular employment were an evil example to those who had a taste for living idly, either at home or wandering abroad, and were likely, in the eyes of the authorities, to fall into evil ways. Again, departing at will led to all kinds of settlement difficulties. From the point of view of wage assessment in a narrow sense, however, one would be tempted to treat the prevalence of the offence in any locality at any time as evidence – if independent corroboration were possible – of a labour shortage. Yet in the records examined the volume of these cases is hardly at any point sufficient to suggest anything of this sort. It is of interest, therefore, to supplement these cases by examples of what is, in effect, the same offence committed by masters instead of servants. It will be remembered that the statute required that servants in husbandry and the 'enumerated occupations' should, on their lawful departure from the parish of their employment, obtain a testimonial[61] sealed by the constable and two householders certifying that their departure was in order (5 Eliz c 4, sec 7); and provided the penalty of being whipped and used as a vagabond for servants unable to produce such a testimonial within twenty-one days, and the penalty of a five-pound fine for masters retaining servants without requiring them to show their testimonials (5 Eliz c 4, sec 8). Instances of servants being indicted for not having testimonials are rare, probably because they were normally proceeded against under the 'unlawful departure' section, or because the particular form of their vagabondage was not given in the indictment (still less in the summary of the indictment in the sessions minutes), although at Norwich a number were sent to Bridewell or 'committed and punished'.[62] In a case in the North Riding a servant so offending is merely sent back to her former service. A later memorandum is perhaps significant – 'that there are presented ... diverse servantes who are departed from their maisters to other places without testimonialls therefore quere what shalbe done h'rin'.[63] That proceedings were taken against masters hiring servants without testimonials (or, which is from our point of view practically the same thing, hiring someone else's servant without his prior consent) is, however, amply borne out by sessions records printed and unprinted.

In the North Riding in the early seventeenth century the offence was very common. Although the abbreviated form in which some of the entries are given makes it difficult to be certain, there appear to have been fifty-nine[64] presentments between 1605 and 1611, of which twelve[65] were at the January 1606-7 sessions, and fifteen[66] at that of January 1608-9; at a 1616 sessions there were eleven further presentments.[67] Thereafter cases were less numerous – three in 1619, seven in the sixteen-twenties and thirties, one in 1640, 1655-6 and 1680-1.[68] The West Riding printed records, on the other hand, only yield two cases, in 1640 and 1641-2,[69] the latter being of interest as illustrating that, as a servant hired without a testimonial was not lawfully retained, the parish of her employment was not responsible for providing relief; there are three East Riding examples in 1648 and 1651.[70] The Kesteven minutes only provide one instance, where a man had taken a servant into his house and incited him to leave his old service[71] – an offence in many respects indistinguishable from those under consideration. The records of Ipswich and Norwich suggest that action was quite usually taken in the first half of the seventeenth century – in the former there were at least twenty-three cases between 1618 and 1640, 1621 and 1631 being the peak years, in the latter nine between ,615 and 1634. At Norwich, rather unusually, the emphasis was on punishing the servants rather than the masters; on one occasion, for instance, a master was given a fortnight to put away two male servants whom he had lately received from London without testimonials, on pain of the statutory penalty of ten pounds, but the two servants were to be committed and punished in any case.[72] By 1660 the requirement of testimonials from those seeking fresh employment had, a writer on the Middlesex records tells us, completely lapsed.[73] An attempt was, however, made to receive it, a Proclamation of 1684 (the only case in the printed Buckinghamshire records is of this date[74]) having that purpose in view; only one Middlesex indictment – ten years later – resulted, though there were apparently some indictments for retaining other people's servants.[75] The Gloucestershire justices made a belated attempt to enforce the practice – in 1731 a printed order relating to engaging servants without certificates was posted throughout the county.[76]

Action in this latter instance was, there is reason to believe, prompted by a desire to prevent an influx of those likely to become chargeable. Probably the tendency of the Norwich authorities to deal severely with servants so offending arose, in the same way, from a desire to dissuade those from other parts coming to settle in the city (reference, it will be remembered, was made earlier to their difficulties with 'foreign' feltmakers). Insistence on testimonials had, of course, a very direct connection with problems of chargeability and relief, since the information they contained was often instrumental in defining settlements. A further value of the testimonial system is suggested by a paragraph in Burn's *Justice of the peace,* where he remarks that its lapse is responsible for the dearness of labour, since the fixing of wages in one county simply induces servants to move elsewhere. In other words, where wage assessment was being used to keep wages down, insistence on testimonials was a natural and necessary corollary. It does not, of course, follow that this particular aspect was the main reason for its inclusion in the statute – the testimonial plan had many features to commend it. The 'memorandum' of 1573 gives as its justification, as one might expect, the prevention of thieving and other 'lewde Actes' by servants, for whom it is thereby made more difficult to depart with their masters' property and obtain other employment.[77] Masters who accepted servants without testimonials were, indeed, aiding and abetting servants in the desertion of their former masters, so that the two offences were, as suggested earlier, very close counterparts. In Devereux Edgar's diary, though nothing is said about testimonials, proceedings were taken against masters 'abetting and harbouring' servants who had run away. This is clearly brought out in a North Riding case where a certain William Eldridge was presented for refusing to serve Thomas Rowthe, and John Baines was presented at the same time for hiring Eldridge without a testimonial.[78] Where large number of servants are presented for departing unlawfully, and of masters for receiving servants without testimonials, there is naturally a presumption in favour of a labour shortage being the occasion of this law-breaking. In the North Riding in the years 1608-10, it will have been noticed, cases of offences of these two types appear alongside cases of paying or being paid more than the assessed rates. Insistence on testimonials coupled with failure to raise the assessed rates to the required level would, of course, aggravate a labour shortage. In practice, despite the express application of a testimonial requirement (in this case a 'temporary absence' certificate from a justice) to the case of harvesting in section sixteen, one would think it likely that even at its height, this requirement from persons entering was, in districts where labour was not too plentiful, relaxed. On the other hand, even a temporary relaxation might lead to an influx of undesirables and those likely to become chargeable, a consideration which may well have been uppermost in the minds of the Hertfordshire justices when, in 1656, they drew up an order requiring constables to take up all travellers coming out of their country to work at hay-time and harvest without testimonials.[79]

If the voluntary departure of servants sometimes indicated that labour was scarce, the putting-away of servants by masters must sometimes, one would think, have been associated with a situation in which labour was becoming more plentiful. Such putting-away, save in special circumstances, was illegal without the giving of a quarter's notice before the end of the term of hiring (5 Eliz c 4, sec 4), a forty-shilling fine being the penalty for infringement of this provision (5 Eliz c 4, sec 6). In the printed and manuscript material examined, however, instances hardly occur in sufficient numbers to suggest widespread action on the part of masters similarly affected by some change in the market position. Taking first straightforward cases, where no particular point of interest arises in connection with the entry, we find five in the North Riding between

1606 and 1616, one in each of the years 1635, 1669 and 1670, and two in 1682.[80] In Lincoln there was, in each of the three years 1658-60, an order requiring a master to take back a servant unlawfully put away;[81] there is a Lindsey instance in 1670,[82] a Holland case in 1676,[83] and three Kesteven cases in 1677, 1678 and 1692[84] respectively. There is a Norwich order requiring a master to take back a servant he had unlawfully turned away in 1656-7,[85] and two similar Suffolk orders in 1640-1 and 1641.[86] Suffolk provides a number of instances where it is not stated whether the servant ran away or was put away.[87] Some[88] of these cases arose, as might be expected, in connection with possible chargeability, the point then being not so much to determine whether master or servant was to blame, as to send the servant back for the unexpired part of his service and get him off your hands. The matter often[89] came before the court on complaint of the inhabitants of the parish to which the servant had gone after leaving, or as a result of a periodic 'diligent search' by constables for newcomers likely to become chargeable. Another common tendency was for cases of putting-away a servant to be combined with detaining wages. There are Suffolk examples in 1660,[90] 1702, 1703-4, 1705, 1710-11 and 1712,[91] while in Hertfordshire two cases in the seventeen-thirties show this dual character,[92] as does the only Surrey instance mentioned in the printed records.[93] There is a rather interesting Staffordshire case where turning-away without just cause was combined both with detaining wages and beating and wounding the servant. On this occasion the difference was, by consent of both parties, referred to Lady Littleton, but the master refused to abide by her award; the court, taking into consideration the poverty of the servant, which meant inability to bring suit against her master for recovery of her wages, ordered that Lady Littleton's award should stand and required the master to pay the wages detained, but apparently no action was taken against him in the matter of the assault or in that of his having turned away his servant without reasonable cause.[94] There is a Buckinghamshire case in 1685-6,[95] and Middlesex ones in 1683 and 1693 – the Brentford justices, we are told, 'were interesting themselves in the method of dismissal at this period'.[96]

Turning to the more interesting border-line cases, in which the master was able to put forward some justification for sending his servant away, we find that, as a rule, the justices were willing to allow employers to dispense with the services of servants who had become physically incapable of performing their duties. This was so, at least, when a lame servant in the North Riding could not do his work,[97] when a

Suffolk servant proved, after hiring, to be very infirm by reason of often being troubled with the falling sickness,[98] or another fell lunatic and lame.[99] Care had, however, to be taken that the business was done openly and in due legal form, as one Suffolk master found to his cost when, finding ten days after he hired a woman servant that she was so decrepit and sickly as to be unable to do her work, he complained to a justice, who sent her back by warrant to her previous place of settlement. The court found that this warrant was obtained surreptitiously, and ordered that the woman be taken back to serve out her time.[100] Another master sent a woman servant who fell sick back to her father but, as she was likely to become chargeable there, she was sent back to the parish where, by her retainer, she had a settlement.[101] In this instance it is not clear whether the overseers or her master provided for her. The statute, of course, expressly said that the party grieved should complain (5 Eliz c 4, sec 4), and those who took the law into their own hands must expect, unless the justices were in lenient mood, to be saddled with a physically unfit servant until the end of the term of hiring, even if – as usually seemed to happen – they escaped being fined. Even greater care had, one may assume, to be taken when pregnancy was the cause of the servant's inability to perform her duties, since suspicion might easily fall on the master. In an early seventeenth-century North Riding case, for instance, where the servant alleged that the master was the father of her child, the court imposed the fine of forty shillings for unlawfully putting her away.[102] Quite usually those discharging pregnant servants were ordered to take them back;[103] often 'until the time for which she was retained expires, or until one month after her delivery whichever is the sooner'.[104] Sometimes, however, it was deemed a sufficient and reasonable cause.[105]

The procedure envisaged in the act was, of course, that, instead of the servant departing or the master putting the servant away, the two of them should appear before a justice if any unforeseen difficulties arose, and should there by mutual consent (subject to his approval) bring their previous agreement to an end. Such discharges by mutual consent would seem, judging by a Suffolk magistrate's diary, to have been fairly common at the beginning of the eighteenth century. Sometimes a master, through ignorance or sympathy on the part of a justice, managed to obtain a discharge without his servant being consulted at all. When this was brought to the attention of the court, however, such proceedings were likely to be pronounced invalid. Thus in one case of this type, where the servant had not been brought before the justice of given her consent, 'the Court held Mr Hunt's discharge under hand and seal was not good, the parties not being before him or by writing to him having signified their agreement, and that putting his seal looked like a warrant or Judicial Act in him, whereas there is nothing required but a putting of the Justice's hand as an allowing'.[106]

As to the reason for taking proceedings against those unlawfully discharging servants, the position is in many respects similar to that of the other offences discussed in this chapter. The 1573 'memorandum' alleges that servants turned away destitute or ill fall into evil ways and that stubborn servants, who can only be cured by correction, become still more stubborn if merely put away.[107] Dowdell, on the basis of the post-Restoration Middlesex records, says that 'so far as there is any trace of a general object prompting the enforcement of annual contracts, it is the prevention of chargeability'.[108] Where wage assessment was in operation, however, there were other reasons for insisting on annual contracts; these will be examined in the course of the next chapter.

Disputes between masters and servants, over the amount of wages due and other matters, were of very common occurrence, if the evidence of sessions records is to be believed. If the servant were hired at a chief constable's petty sessions, the wage to be received would be on record, which must have tended to simplify matters considerably. Failing this, if the good advice offered by the Shropshire justices[109] were followed whereby the master was to reduce the terms of the agreement to writing in the presence of two witnesses, the same result would be achieved. However that may be, mention of wage disputes and of masters refusing to pay wages due is, on the whole, a great deal commoner than is mention of the other offences so far considered. Indeed, it is hardly possible to examine any book of sessions records without coming across material of this kind. This being so, any attempt to give a catalogue of cases of this type would be tedious, and all that need be done is to provide some indication of the nature of the information available.

Incidentally, a number of doubts exist as to the authority by which proceedings were taken by justices in this matter.[110] Where any statutory authority was given, it tended to be 5 Eliz c 4 as in Brown's *Advice*,[111] or in a West Riding case where, on an employer declaring 'that this Cort had no power to meddle with the wages of any servants or laborers', the matter was voted upon and 'the whole Cort, not one voice dissenting, were of opinion that by the course and practize of this Cort cases of a like nature were every sessions determined, and that the same were warranted by the statute 5 Eliz cap 4, and that the very same pointe being formerly questioned and afterwards debated att the Councell Board ... itt was approved as a legal proceeding'.[112] Justices were, of course, expressly authorized to adjudge disputes between masters and servants where the departure of one of the parties was involved (5 Eliz c 4, sec 5); very often the detaining of his wages by his master was given by a servant as the reason for his departure; and, by a natural extension of authority, justices may have come to regard other disputes, not involving departure, as coming within their jurisdiction. Alternatively, it might be held that, since the terms of the contract were in doubt, it must be assumed that the assessed rates were operative;[113] and that, if the master refused to pay these rates, he was in some way infringing the justices' scale. Burn quotes a judgement, 'tho' the statute gives them a power only to set the rate for wages, and not to order payment, yet grafting hereupon, they have also taken upon them to order payment, and the Courts of law are indulgent in remedies for wages'.[114] On one occasion the inability of one of the parties to sue the other for breach of contract at common law was even given by Quarter Sessions as justification – in view of the poverty of John Smith, he 'not being able to prosecute his suit at common law against the said Thomas Wells for his said wages, that the consideration hereof shall be referred to a justice';[115] similar justification (the poverty of the petitioner) was given in a Staffordshire case quoted earlier in this chapter.[116] None of these grounds seems altogether satisfactory, though the justices themselves might (and, when they gave as their authority 5 Elizabeth c 4, evidently did) regard them as adequate. Fortunately, however, Holdsworth has very recently explained how a case of 1598 (following precedents based on statutes repealed by 5 Elizabeth c 4), which 'laid it down that if a person was compelled to serve he could bring an action on the Statute for his wages, and was not driven to sue by action of debt', led to the view being taken that *if a person was compelled to serve in husbandry,* he could apply to a magistrate if his master detained his wages.[117] This, of course, explains why the justices' power to act in the matter was sometimes challenged on the ground that the wages in dispute were not for work in husbandry.[118] In the West Riding case we have noticed, however, the magistrates do not seem to have been any the less emphatic about their right to interfere because the wages involved were for charcoal carrying (perhaps this was counted as husbandry); while in Burn we find that 'orders have been held good, where it did not appear that the service was in husbandry, for the Court said they would intend it so, unless the contrary appeared'.[119] The majority of cases given in a Suffolk justice's diary relate to wages in husbandry, but warrants were occasionally issued in connection with the detaining of wages for work not coming within this category.[120] And the Middlesex magistrates, too, seem sometimes to have ignored the husbandry restriction.[121] At all events, the justices' activity seems (given the complaints) to have been spontaneous, in the sense, at least, that we do not know of pressure having been brought to bear on them from above in this connection. In the eighteenth century, more definite statutory authority was provided for recovery of wages; and, in legislation of that century applying assessment to particular trades, the mistake of omission made in the Statute of Artificers was not repeated, for special provision was made to deal with the detaining of wages.[122]

Turning to the cases themselves, the North Riding records, though not providing as many instances as might have been expected, illustrate the procedure often followed. Thus in January 1663-4 a New Malton yeoman was presented for refusing to pay three pounds to his servant for a year's service. The court ordered that the matter be referred to two justices, and at the next sessions we find an order that the master pay his servant two pounds in satisfaction of his wages.[123] North Riding cases appear to have been most numerous during the sixteen-fifties;[124] there is an East Riding instance in 1650 also.[125] In Holland and Kesteven, on the other hand (where records are, however, missing for earlier periods), the seventies and eighties provided cases at every sessions,[126] sometimes five or six at a time.[127] The records of Nottinghamshire,[128] Staffordshire,[129] Northamptonshire,[130] Suffolk,[131] Hertfordshire,[132] Buckinghamshire,[133] Middlesex,[134] Kent,[135] Surrey,[136] Worcester,[137] Wiltshire,[138] and Somerset[139] all contain examples, though not in as great quantity was the Lincolnshire records, but there were twenty one cases in Gloucestershire in 1716-91.[140] The astonishing number of cases recorded in Devereux Edgar's diary suggests that, if we had similar information regarding the activities of justices out of sessions in other parts of the country and for other periods, the issuing of warrants requiring masters to pay wages detained from their servants or else appear and show cause to the contrary, would prove to be one of the most important parts of a magistrate's business, and certainly much more important (in terms of number of cases dealt with) than any of the offences coming directly under the Statute of Artificers. The legal costs involved in obtaining redress must, of course, have meant that in many other cases of which we have no record, servants were unable to get the wages due to them.[141] That the authorities did not always ignore this difficulty is, however, to be inferred from a number of examples of attempts to overcome it in different parts of the country. Thus in Suffolk on one occasion, as it appeared to the court that a complainant had been at great expense both in fees to the clerk of the peace for orders and in payment for warrants, his master was ordered not merely to pay the wages due but also fourteen shillings extra;[142] while on two[143] later occasions the three shillings for the order was charged to the offending master, in one[144] case the servant being discharged of her service as well (there is another instance of this latter being done in the Buckinghamshire records[145]). In Buckinghamshire, indeed, steps of this kind seem to have been taken more often than elsewhere – the costs of appealing (amounting in one[146] case to £1 14s 4d) were usually[147] added to the wages to be paid, and masters were sometimes imprisoned[148] or fined[149] for disregarding orders, though when a magistrate, Sir Dennis Hampson, was at fault, the clerk of the peace was instructed[150] to write to him signifying the resentment of the court concerning his carriage in the matter – in relation, presumably, to the court, not his servant – this letter producing the desired effect.[151] A Warwickshire order of 1629 refers a wage dispute to a justice as, in view of the poverty of the claimant, he was not able 'to prosecute his suit at common law',[152] a Shropshire wages order of 1702 is to be paid for,[153] while a Somerset order of 1676 requires William Curry to pay to James Orchard a sum due to him for wages, plus twenty shillings for his expenses in recovering them, 'as the Court is informed that Curry has confessed the debt was due to Orchard, but said that he would not pay the same until he had put him to some expense'.[154]

A rather interesting instance illustrating the awareness of individual justices of the need for some effective method of recovery of wages without cost to the claimant is provided by a note in Devereux Edgar's diary. In this note he explains why, in the case of many of the complaints of servants 'against masters present and masters lately gone from, the first by misusage either in diet or beating and the latter from not paying of their wages when gone away' he has not granted warrants against the masters concerned. His main reason, he asserts, was a desire not to put complainants to any charge for warrants; with this end in view he tried as often as possible to adopt the method of sending a note to the master earnestly pressing him to take the matter into his serious consideration and do justice to his servant. Had he kept a clerk in his house as other justices did, the servant might, in his opinion, have been made to pay as much for the note as if it had been a warrant; but by dispensing with the services of a clerk, and adopting the note procedure, he claimed to be obtaining redress for servants in a large proportion of cases without any cost to them whatever. He adds, incidentally, that a further advantage of this procedure lay in the fact that only too often masters brought by warrants before justices had a grudge against complainants for bringing them into disgrace in this manner, and usually managed to obtain their revenge at some later date; by only using the method of warrants, therefore, as a last resort, this disadvantage was also got over.

As to the significance of the widespread failure of masters to pay wages due, and of the attempts to force them to do so, a satisfactory answer cannot yet be supplied. If the cases had, in any district, been mainly confined to one to two years, one might have guessed that masters who had taken on servants at high wages during a temporary labour shortage were reluctant to pay these wages when the time came, but an explanation of this kind will hardly meet this particular case. The editor of the printed Oxfordshire sessions records remarks 'on the much-argued question as to how far the wages rates that Quarter Sessions decreed were enforced, some light is thrown by entries [ordering payment of wages due to servants]'.[155] It is not, however, clear whether by this she means merely that the actual rates given in these orders are of interest for comparison with the assessed rates, or something more than this. I cannot help feeling myself that material relating to the non-payment of wages is less helpful, from the point of view of the assessment of wages, than the other types of case considered in this and the following chapter.

Notes

Chapter III

1 Gretton, *Oxfordshire JPs,* p x.

2 *NRQSR,* I, 220.

3 *NRQSR,* II, 213.

4 *NRQSR,* VI, 147.

5 See below pp 181-6.

6 Peyton, ed *Kesteven QS minutes,* p 417.

7 Kenyon, ed *Salop CR,* I, 119.

8 Dorothy L. Powell and Hilary Jenkinson, ed *Surrey Quarter Sessions records: order books and sessions rolls, 1559-1663* (Surrey Record Society, XIII, XIV, 1934-5), II, 150, 304.

9 Jeaffreson, ed *Middlesex CR,* III, 169-70.

10 Jeaffreson, ed *Middlesex CR,* III, 372-3.

11 Jeaffreson, ed *Middlesex CR,* I, 80, 131. A Chester case of about this date is given in Morris, *Chester,* p 358.

12 Le Hardy, ed *Bucks Sessions records,* I, 36, 74, 168, 177, 193, 234, 310, 319, 322, 328.

13 Bland, Brown and Tawney, *English economic history,* p 389.

14 *HMC Various,* I, 132; Bland, Brown and Tawney, *English economic history,* p 360.

15 Alexander H.A. Hamilton, *Quarter Sessions from Queen Elizabeth to Queen Anne* (Sampson Low, 1878), p 164.

16 Thetford court records, August 1634.

17 Thetford court records, Map 1635.

18 Hertford court records, April 1628.

19 Hertford court records, September 1636.

20 Eg Norwich court records, July 1630.

21 Eg Suffolk order books, October 1642.

22 Norwich court records.

23 Kenyon, ed *Salop CR*, I, 119.

24 Suffolk order books, January 1647-8.

25 Norwich court records, October 1659; Thetford court records, October 1751.

26 Norwich court records, August 1623.

27 Suffolk order books, Trinity 1659.

28 Suffolk order books, Hilary 1659.

29 Suffolk order books, Easter 1660.

30 Norwich court records, August 1668.

31 East Riding QS books, July 1649.

32 *NRQSR*, I, 11, 60, 68, 99, 131, 151, 156, 180, 202.

33 *NRQSR*, I, 131.

34 *NRQSR*, IV, 75, 232; V, 206; VI, 59.

35 *NRQSR*, VI, 75.

36 *NRQSR*, VI, 97.

37 *NRQSR*, VI, 174.

38 *EJ*, XXIV (1914), 231.

39 WRS order books, April 1681.

40 East Riding QS books, April, July 1648.

41 Peyton, ed *Kesteven QS minutes*, p 119.

42 Peyton, ed *Kesteven QS minutes*, pp 158, 162.

43 James Tait, ed *Lancashire Quarter Sessions records*, (Chetham Society, new series, LXXVII, 1917), I, 83, 192, 272.

44 Axon, ed *Manchester Sessions*, pp 3, 22 etc.

45 Copnall, ed *Notts CR*, p 68.

46 John W.W. Bund, ed *Worcestershire county records: calendar of the Quarter Sessions papers* (Worcester Historical Society, 1899-1900), pp 215, 273.

47 Hardy, ed *Hertford CR*, V, 407; I, 112; VI, 346; VII, 207; VIII, 96, 329.

48 Hardy, ed *Hertford CR*, VIII, 329.

49 Hardy, ed *Middlesex CR*, I, 54; III, 21; Dowdell, *QS*, p 147.

50 Holland QS minutes, 1674, 1676, 1677, 1678 (also one or two

later cases, eg 1682, 1684 and 1688).

51 Lindsey QS minutes, 1675, 1676 (also one earlier case, 1667).

52 Eg Norwich court records, November 1615.

53 Eg Suffolk order books, June 1642, January 1942-3.

54 Suffolk order books, Easter 1659.

55 Suffolk order books, Easter 1660. The circumstances of the case in *NRQSR,* VII, 237 are not altogether clear.

56 Devereux Edgar's diary, November 1702.

57 Eg *NRQSR,* VI, 59; Hardy, ed *Hertford CR,* VI, 346; Suffolk order books, June 1642; Norwich court records, November 1615.

58 This is implied in a case mentioned in *VCH Lincs,* II, 339.

59 Cf Gretton, *Oxfordshire JPs,* p lxxvii.

60 Axon, ed *Manchester Sessions,* p 58.

61 The form of words commonly used in these testimonials is also given in Ethel M. Hampson, *The treatment of poverty in Cambridgeshire, 1597-1834* (Cambridge UP, 1934), p 274. They cost twopence; 'some masters will give them that 2d againe' (*Rural economy in York, being the farming books of H. Best, 1641* (Surtees Society, XXXIII, 1857), p 134).

62 Eg Norwich court records, November 1615; August 1625; March 1631; April 1631.

63 *NRQSR,* I, 34, 222.

64 *NRQSR,* I, 2, 33, 41 etc.

65 *NRQSR,* I, 60-1.

66 *NRQSR,* I, 143-4.

67 *NRQSR,* II, 118.

68 *NRQSR,* II, 190, 197, 213, 239; III, 156 etc; IV, 181; V, 206; VII, 44.

69 Lister, ed *WRS records,* pp 218, 362.

70 East Riding QS books, April 1648, January 1650-1, April 1651.

71 Peyton, ed *Kesteven QS minutes,* p 138.

72 Norwich court records, August 1625. See also above p 130.

73 Dowdell, *QS,* p 147.

74 Le Hardy, ed *Bucks Sessions records,* I, 151, 159.

75 Dowdell, *QS,* p 148.

76 *EHR*, XLIII (1928), 403.

77 Tawney and Power, *Tudor economic documents*, I, 362.

78 *NRQSR*, II, 213.

79 Hardy, ed *Hertford CR*, I, 116.

80 *NRQSR*, I, 37, 143, 202, 227; II, 119; IV, 43; VI, 136, 148; VII, 54, 56.

81 Lincoln QS minutes.

82 Lindsey QS minutes.

83 Holland QS minutes.

84 Peyton, ed *Kesteven QS minutes*, pp 62, 92, 421. There is one mention in Axon, ed *Manchester Sessions*, p 106.

85 Norwich court records, February 1656-7.

86 Suffolk order books, January 1640-1, May 1641.

87 Eg Suffolk order books, June 1641, Hilary 1659.

88 Suffolk order books, June 1642, October 1644.

89 Suffolk order books, June 1645, Hilary 1658.

90 Suffolk order books, Easter 1660. Additional simple cases are to be found, October 1660 and April 1663.

91 Devereux Edgar's diary.

92 Le Hardy, ed *Hertford CR*, VII, 238, 274. There is no mention in Le Hardy, ed *Hertford CR*, VI, 270.

93 Powell and Jenkinson, ed *Surrey QS records*, II.

94 Staffs Sessions books, May 1621.

95 Le Hardy, ed *Bucks Sessions records*, I, 194.

96 Dowdell, *QS*, p 147. There is an earlier case in Jeaffreson, ed *Middlesex CR*, III, 34.

97 *NRQSR*, VII, 114.

98 Suffolk order books, January 1638-9.

99 Suffolk order books, January 1644-5.

100 Suffolk order books, Hilary 1658.

101 Sidney C. Ratcliffe and H.C. Johnson, ed *Warwick county records: Quarter Sessions order books, 1625-1674* (Warwick, 1935), I, 173.

102 *NRQSR*, I, 97.

103 *NRQSR*, III, 284; Suffolk order books, June 1650; Le Hardy,

ed *Hertford CR,* V, 441.

104 Suffolk order books, January 1642-3; *NRQSR,* II, 284.

105 Suffolk order books, January 1646-7.

106 Devereux Edgar's diary, January 1712-13.

107 Tawney and Power, *Tudor economic documents,* I, 361.

108 Dowdell, *QS,* p 146.

109 *EJ,* IV (1894), 517.

110 Dr Peyton very kindly supplied me with some of the material on which the following paragraph is based.

111 p 348.

112 *Yorkshire Archaeological and Geographical J,* V (1877-8), 372.

113 See below, pp 168-9.

114 Richard Burn, *The justice of the peace and the parish officer* (2nd ed London, 1756), p 625.

115 Ratcliff and Johnson, ed *Warwick CR,* I, 76.

116 See above, p 133.

117 William S. Holdsworth, *A history of English law* (Methuen, 1938), XI, 467-8.

118 Eg Burn, *JP,* p 625; *Justice's case law,* p 294.

119 Burn, *JP,* p 625.

120 Devereux Edgar's diary, March 1701-2, January 1702-3.

121 Dowdell, QS, p 153.

122 Holdsworth, *English law,* XI, 471, 473.

123 *NRQSR,* VI, 75-7.

124 Eg *NRQSR,* V, 137, 151, 175, 188.

125 East Riding QS books, July 1650.

126 Holland QS minutes from 1673; Peyton, ed *Kesteven QS minutes,* pp 9, 10, 14, 20 etc.

127 Eg Peyton, ed *Kesteven QS minutes,* pp 61-2, 119.

128 Copnall, ed *Notts CR,* p 67.

129 Eg Staffs Sessions books, 1626, 1628.

130 Joan Wake, ed *Quarter Sessions records of the county of Northampton, files for 6 Charles I and Commonwealth, (1630, 1657, 1657-8)* (Northampton Records Society, I, 1924),] 193.

131 Suffolk order books.

132 Le Hardy, ed *Hertford CR,* V, 107, 147 etc.

133 Le Hardy, ed *Bucks Sessions records,* I, 61.

134 Eg William Le Hardy, ed *Calendar to the [Middlesex] sessions records* (London, 1935), I, 8, 453.

135 *EHR,* XLIII (1928), 401-2.

136 Eg Powell and Jenkinson, ed *Surrey QS records,* II, 45.

137 Bund, ed *Worcs CR,* p 235.

138 *HMC Various,* I, 152.

139 Harbin and Dawes, ed *Somerset QS records,* IV, 4.

140 *EHR,* XLIII (1928), 401-2.

141 Cf Dowdell, *QS,* pp 153-4.

142 Suffolk order books, June 1645.

143 Suffolk order books, Easter 1660, October 1660.

144 Suffolk order books, Easter 1660.

145 Le Hardy, ed *Bucks Sessions records,* I, 201.

146 Le Hardy, ed *Bucks Sessions records,* I, 276.

147 Le Hardy, ed *Bucks Sessions records,* I, 4, 16, 57, 276.

148 Le Hardy, ed *Bucks Sessions records,* I, 52.

149 Le Hardy, ed *Bucks Sessions records,* I, 18.

150 Le Hardy, ed *Bucks Sessions records,* I, 471.

151 Le Hardy, ed *Bucks Sessions records,* I, 493.

152 Ratcliff and Johnson, ed *Warwick CR,* I, 76.

153 Kenyon, ed *Salop CR,* I, 199.

154 Harbin and Dawes, ed *Somerset QS records,* IV, 210.

155 Gretton, *Oxfordshire JPs,* pp 6-7.

IV Complementary parts of the policy: II

The information which was at the disposal of Quarter Sessions regarding the extent to which different sections of the Statute of Artificers were being observed did not, of course, any more than information connected with the operation of other statutes, come in altogether spontaneously. The presentments normally found in sessions records are, as is well known, of rather mixed origin, some being in effect answers to written questions, some being on the initiative of constables themselves, and some being matters within the grand jury's own knowledge. This being so, scarcity of cases connected with the assessment of wages may, where it is met with, be partly due to lack of interest on the part of the justices in enforcing these particular sections of the statute. We may, for instance, think it significant that none of the seventeen 'articles' to which Oxfordshire constables in the late seventeenth century were required to furnish answers[1] had anything to do with the subject of this study, since these articles represented a catalogue of those matters on which, at that time, the central government and the justices required their agents to exercise particular vigilance. On the other hand, the frequency with which wage assessments were accompanied by instructions,[2] which, in the West Riding, grew steadily longer,[3] to constables suggests that they were intended to be enforced (though one sometimes wonders whether the very inclusion of these instructions may have signified that constables were not as familiar with their functions under this as under other statutes). As against this, however, it has to be remembered that provision was made, both in the statute itself and subsequently, for additional assemblies to secure the smooth operation of the labour code, and that records of proceedings at these assemblies have not often come down to us. There were, to begin with, the chief constables' petty sessions, to be discussed shortly. Secondly, the justices in their several divisions were expected to meet twice a year to see that the act was duly executed (5 Eliz c 4, sec 30). Thirdly, instructions were issued in 1605[4] requiring that justices should assemble themselves together by divisions once (about mid-time) between every general sessions of the peace, to inquire of and see the due execution of, *inter alia,* the Statute of Artificers. Fourthly, the 'Book of Orders' issued in 1631,[5] directed justices to give monthly accounts of their proceedings to the sheriffs and to hold monthly meetings in their divisions in order to exercise a closer supervision over the administration of the poor laws; in all probability certain aspects of 5 Elizabeth c 4 were considered at these monthly meetings which Miss Hindmarsh found were regularly held in Hertfordshire, Sussex, Lancashire, Warwickshire, Nottinghamshire, Derbyshire, Staffordshire, Somerset and Worcestershire. There were, in addition, special arrangements in different counties which may, or may not, have represented attempts to comply with one or other of these provisions. These included the North Riding additional summer sessions to hear cases under the Act,[6] the Devonshire district sub-committees of the early seventeenth century,[7] and the Warwick sessions 'holden to enquire here and determyn causes towching Artificers laborers and Apprentices ... In wch chardge was given to the Jury to determyn and present matters contyned in crten artycles delivred to them';[8] while the Buckinghamshire 'governors of labourers' for every township, mentioned in the regulations following the wage assessment of 1561, were intended to ensure the execution of the statutes relating to labourers then in force.[9] When it is realised how much of this activity we have now no record of, it is clear that it would be unwise too hastily to assume that, at a given date in a given district, nothing was being done to secure the observance of the statute, unless strong corroborative evidence existed. It is, of course, true that – except in so far as they were additional general sessions held at a time other than the four regular dates – these meetings did not have the character of sessions, since petty sessions in any modern sense cannot (as the editor of the Oxfordshire Sessions records has recently adduced valuable additional evidence to show)[10] be regarded as having originated any earlier than the eighteenth century. Nevertheless, even a single justice could, *inter alia,* order the idle able-bodied to work, punish vagabonds, order committal to Bridewell, and adjudge controversies between servants and masters;[11] cases beyond the competence of one or two justices could be passed on to sessions; and the 'assemblies' possessed the added advantage that they provided the justices with additional means of getting to know, from chief and petty constables, how prevalent – short of the actual formulation of presentments – infringements of the statute were, and whether, for instance, some alteration in the justices' scale or the more vigorous application of the existing scale would best meet the case. One may, in fact, assume that causes of friction were quite usually eliminated in this way, so that it may often have been only a small percentage of the difficulties that appeared in the sessions records we know. Account should, at all events, be taken of the functions this additional machinery was intended to perform before finally attaching any special significance, for instance, to the complete absence of cases having to do with our aspect of the statute in the volume of Hampshire indictments and presentments 1646-1660,[12] or of 'prosecutions on any of the possible counts under the Statute of Apprentices'[13] in the Warwickshire records, or the finding of only one case relevant to this study (leaving before term) in a search of half-a-dozen volumes of West Riding indictment books.[14] Even in a case where ignorance of the procedure to be followed is found, as when the East Riding justices in 1647 instructed the clerk of the peace to certify the rates of wages up above and procure proclamations thereupon, there must have been rates to certify or the order would have had no meaning.[15]

One of these types of assembly would seem, because of its peculiar importance in the whole functioning of wage assessment, to demand separate treatment here, and that despite the admitted difficulty that, as one recent writer remarks, 'it was a Court with a history, but of which little is known'.[16] This type is, of course, the chief constable's petty or statute sessions. The commonest offence connected with statute sessions recorded in the North Riding sessions records is failure to appear. In one year, July 1608 to April 1609, no fewer than twenty petty constables were presented for not appearing at statute or petty sessions;[17] there had been nine such presentments earlier, and there was one later in 1609, followed by six in 1611,[18] (of whom one constable obstinately refused to make a presentment at a petty sessions, 'by reason he was to goe to a horse-race'). Thereafter, however, presentments were fewer in number – five in 1612-13, three in 1614, two in 1618 and two in 1619[19] – after which there would appear to be no further mention of the matter. In only two of the cases mentioned is there any doubt as to whether the person presented was a constable. At a midsummer sessions in Kesteven a constable was indicted for failing to deliver his bill of all servants at a statute sessions of the previous October,[20] while another North Riding case had involved a constable refusing to make presentment of the masters and servants and their wages.[21] It is fairly clear, therefore, that where statute sessions were in effective operation the attendance of petty constables was obligatory, and that the purpose of their presence there was to make presentment of those offending against 5 Elizabeth c 4 and certain other statutes, and to deliver their bills setting forth the names of masters and their servants and the wages they were paid in their several parishes. The North Riding justices issued instructions that those petty constables not appearing at the petty sessions to make presentments should themselves be presented by the high constables,[22] and there is reference on one occasion to 5s fines having been imposed,[23] though one man (who may not have been a constable) who submitted was only fined 6d.[24] Fines for negligence of this type seem to have varied widely. In the Great Grimsby court records we find constables being fined 10s for non-appearance at statute session in 1637 and 1638, 20s in 1645 and 1646, 2s 6d in 1650, 5s in 1653 ('for neglecting to return his bill at this sessions') and 10s in 1655 ('for neglecting of his office at this court'). Mere attendance was not in itself sufficient, for there is a case of a constable who appeared at a petty sessions but was presented for departing without leave, not having made any presentment;[25] while the 'bills' presented had to be complete.[26]

Failure of masters to appear might also, however, be treated as an offence. Thus no fewer than 120 people were presented at one Holland sessions for failure to appear at statute sessions to hear the assessed rates and hire their servants according to law,[27] two Northamptonshire yeomen and seven husbandmen were on one occasion presented for not appearing and recording their servants that they hired at statute sessions,[28] while an entry in the seventeen-twenties in a Suffolk book of precedents and indictments suggests that failure to attend at statute sessions and hire your servants there was still regarded as an offence.[29] Where the East Yorkshire practice was followed of having a roll call of masters,[30] offenders could easily be detected. In the same category, from our point of view, are the many Nottinghamshire presentments we are told of for hiring servants outside statute sessions, (including twenty-eight in July 1616 for retaining servants out of petty sessions and not recording them, and nineteen the following January for not recording the names of their servants in the books of the chief constable),[31] the presentment of three North Riding husbandmen for not recording the names and salaries of their servants before the chief constable at the time of hiring,[32] and the fining of two masters 1s 6d a piece at a Kesteven sessions in 1695 for failure to hire their servants at the chief constable's petty sessions.[33] Clearly, the master's legal duty was not performed merely by hiring his servants at the appropriate place and time; he had, in addition, to record the bargain in the chief constable's book which – taken in conjunction with the proclamation of the assessed rates, and the penalties for infringing them, at that assembly – would, it was hoped, ensure that no over-payment took place. On the other hand if, for some reason, a hiring did not take place at the appointed place and time, the master was expected to record the details with the authorities also, and was liable to be presented if he failed to do so. The periodic – in the West Riding, twice yearly[34] – visit of the petty constable to take a note of details regarding masters, servants and wages for entry in his 'bill' provided a final means of checking-up, as it were, those bargains which had somehow failed to be recorded elsewhere. We are probably justified in inferring from a North Yorkshire case, when a woman refused 'to give the names of her servants, nor tickets nor rates of her servants',[35] that these periodic visits were sometimes used to determine whether testimonials had been duly produced at the time of hiring. The Ipswich justices instructed constables in September 1575 to make what appears to have been a special search for all newcomers, and to certify to the bailiffs when and for what such servants were retained, and at what wages [36] Presentments for refusal to supply the necessary information are, in the North Riding in the early part of the century, fairly numerous. Two parishes were collectively presented for refusing to give the names of servants and their wages to the constables or the head constables[37] and, in the four years 1606-10, there were twelve cases of individuals being presented for this offence,[38] or for failing or refusing to register or record wages and names[39] (whether this latter referred to the periodic visits of the petty constable, or to statute sessions, is not clear). Failure to record details at statute sessions may sometimes have been due to the charge of a penny a servant made for this. The high constables in the West Riding, we are told, 'doe call in once or twice a year by warrantes all the servantes within their wapentackes, and comaund them to appeare before them to enter their names, their wages, there tearme for which they are hyred, and take a penny a piece for this of every servant'.[40] Whether the servants themselves paid in the West Riding or not, in the North Riding it is the masters who are presented for refusing to pay a penny to the head constable for entering servants' wages in their book according to the custom.[41] Henry Best's remarks on the hiring of servants in the East Riding throw additional light on this aspect of the matter; it would appear that the charge of one penny only applied where servants were hired for an additional year. At statute sessions 'if the master will not sette him att liberty, then the cheife constable is to lette them knowe what wages the statute will allowe, and to sette downe a reasonable and indifferent wage betwixt them, and hee is to have one peeny of the master for every servant that stayeth two yeares in a place, or is not sette att liberty, and this the pettie constables are to doe for him, viz: to sende in bills of the names of all such servants as stay with theire olde masters, and to gather the money, and sende it him'.[42] In any case, masters who proposed to pay servants more than the assessed rates would naturally be reluctant to have the details entered in the high constable's book; while one would probably be justified in guessing that failure to comply with the law in some respect (private hiring, overpayment, not requiring the production of a testimonial, or hiring for a shorter period than one year) was usually the reason for refusal to provide the petty constable on demand with names and other information regarding servants employed. There are a few[43] later North Riding cases of refusal to certify or record such information, but none of these is later than 1621.

To return, however, to a consideration of those whose attendance at statute sessions was obligatory, it naturally followed that, if masters were successfully persuaded to go there, servants' attendance would be required also. We have already seen that it was customary for the West Riding high constables to command servants to appear before them once or twice a year; there has to be added to this the presentment, in Northamptonshire in 1630, of seven labourers for not appearing at statute sessions[44] – the only case of its kind which appears to have survived. The attendance of justices at these sessions was not (except in some counties such as Nottinghamshire,[45] Grimsby,[46] and Suffolk[47]) essential. Where one or two of them did attend, the assembly presumably possessed the competence of a single justice. In Essex, however, a jury was appointed.[48] Cowell speaks of statute sessions as being for the debating of differences between masters and their servants, the rating of servants' wages and 'the bestowing of such people in Service, as being fit to serve, either refuse to seek, or cannot get Masters'; whether it was even possible to go as far as this without the presence of a justice is not, however, stated.

The purpose of all this is not a matter of doubt. Both the holding of statute sessions to which those concerned had to come, and the periodic visits of the petty constables to householders, were clearly intended, in the first place, to make private hiring, retaining servants without testimonials, paying more than the assessed rates, and so on more difficult. Secondly, they were intended to acquaint people who might genuinely be in doubt, with the rates in the justices' scale; thirdly, they were intended to provide the justices with information regarding the price that labour of different kinds was commanding, and the extent to which the statute was being observed; with, finally, the functions mentioned in the previous paragraph – adjusting the simpler differences between master and servant, and finding masters for those who were unable or unwilling to find them for themselves. Private hiring it was desirable to eliminate for a whole variety of reasons – it probably meant disregard of the assessed rates and of whether the servant had lawfully departed from his last master; it was liable to make disputes between the parties over the terms of hiring difficult to settle, it might lead to confusion later in appeals touching settlements.[49] How far it was possible to prevent such hiring is, however, doubtful. Despite such disadvantages as having no redress if your servant ran away,[50] private hiring seems to have been fairly common even at an early period, and to have been countenanced (at least in some districts) provided the details were recorded. Thus the Norwich records, for instance, contain entries regarding the retaining of servants on the following dates in 1615 – 3 May, 12 and 15 July, 11 November, and 9 December; again, in 1630 there were entries on 2 October, 13 November and 19 December.[51] On the other hand, a Hertfordshire draft order of 1656 suggests a more rigid interpretation of the statute. It is there provided that in case of death or other extraordinary occasion a servant may repair, along with the master wishing to retain him, to the high constable's register and obtain a certificate of hiring which is to be as effectual as if the hiring had been done at the set statute.[52]

The importance of retaining servants for a year is, of course, closely linked up with the considerations under discussion. Ideally, if one statute sessions were held in each district every year, and if all hiring were done there, idleness and vice would have been much reduced,[53] masters would have been able to get their servants at fair prices (in relation to the available supply), and infringements of the statute would have been at a minimum. In practice the holding of two statute sessions per hundred per year seems to have been quite a usual custom,[54] though there are signs that one a year became a commoner practice later on, as at Thetford during 1755-66 when it was held some time in September and in the East Riding in the 1720s, or two within a week or so of each other as in Nottinghamshire, on 16 and 26 October 1724,[55] and Suffolk.[56] Henry Best records that in East Yorkshire in the first half of the seventeenth century there are usually two, and sometimes three, sittinges or statute-dayes for every division, whereof the first is a weeke or more afore Martynmasse, and the next three or fower dayes after that'; the towns called to the earlier sitting had the best of this arrangement.[57] It rather looks, from the dates of petty sessions in the North Riding,[58] as though they were held in such a way as not to clash with each other – perhaps so that masterless men and servantless masters could have several opportunities of satisfying their needs; this was definitely not the case, however, in the East Riding in the eighteenth century, for the chief constables for the several divisions were ordered to hold their petty sessions on the same day.[59] The case of Holland is of considerable interest as giving us more clue to the reasons behind the insistence of the authorities on a particular number of statute sessions being held. In 1688, when confirming the existing assessed rates, the justices there ordered that privy sessions be kept only once a year.[60] In 1726, however, a petition of householders and other substantial persons was presented explaining that, although the original decision to hold statute sessions in each division only once a year had been intended to reduce the exorbitant demands of servants, this decision had had precisely the contrary effect – 'since the making of the said order servants were become more scarce and the same seemed rather to serve to enhance the rates and wages of servants'. Accordingly, the justices agreed that the earlier order should be rescinded and that 'the Chief Constables of each Division have liberty to hold Statutes as often as there shall be occasion for the service of the country, at such times and seasons in the year as the Law appoints and is customary for these purposes'; petty constables were particularly required to execute warrants in connection with the holding of such sessions, and to see 'that peace and order be duly observed during the same'.[61] Massingberd, while mentioning the first of these orders[62] omits all reference to the second and more interesting one. Local variations in all matters connected with statute sessions, which were older than the act, were expressly provided for in it (5 Eliz c 4, sec 40). Insistence on contracts being for a year, in the interest of stable and regular employment[63] and for reasons connected with chargeability,[64] or simply as a necessary corollary to statute sessions and wage assessment – for without annual contracts, private hiring and the arrangement of bargains not in conformity with the assessed rates would very probably have resulted – must usually, however, have taken the form of proceedings against servants leaving, or master putting-away before term, rather than proceedings against masters engaging servants (in husbandry and the enumerated occupations) for less than a year, for the latter are very rarely met with. The Suffolk justices were definitely of the opinion that the reason for the act's insistence on contracts being for a year was 'to prevent Clandestine settlements between Master and servant', and acted on this assumption when doubts arose as to whether a particular hiring had in fact been for a year.[65] The Ipswich justices, it is true, issued instructions in 1578 to constables that they should from time to time in their sessions and searches see that no servant was retained for less term than one whole year, a special search being undertaken forthwith for that purpose;[66] while there were, in Warwick in 1586, several presentments of glovers for retaining men to work with them by the day contrary to the statute,[67] and three tailors were in 1609 in North Yorkshire presented for taking wages by the day 'contrary to the Statute sett downe by the Justices';[68] but that is apparently all. Tailors were only included among those who must be hired for a year in the later stages of the bill's progress.[69] At Hedon, Yorkshire, it looks as though hiring for less than a year was allowed, provided the matter was put on record and the end of the term was Mayday or Martinmas, so that the same difficulty need not arise again; this, at least, would seem a reasonable interpretation of two entries on an otherwise blank page of a sessions book – '11 November 1663, M.B. hath hired herself to A.D. until Mayday next, twenty shillings wages, twelve-pence earnest penny: 31 December 1664, S.D. hired until Martinmas next, twenty-five shillings and twelve-pence earnest'.[70] Hiring for less than a year meant, of course (as in the case of private unrecorded hiring, or over-payment, or accepting a servant without a testimonial), that neither party had any redress if the other failed to carry out the terms of the agreement, since the contract was void from the beginning and carried with it the further disadvantage that the retainer, being void, did not confer a settlement. For example: 'X was never lawfully settled as a hired servant, but only did labour there with several inhabitants by the week'.[71]

This completes our survey of complementary parts of Elizabethan labour policy. Logically, of course, our net ought to have been cast sufficiently wide to include many other aspects of that policy, such as poor relief or action in regard to enclosures. Some may feel that, at the very least, an attempt should have been made to examine the extent to which the Statute 31 Elizabeth c 7, was enforced. How far, for instance, was the rule that cottages must, with certain exceptions, have four acres of land, used to prevent an influx of those likely to become chargeable as, for instance, in Chester in 1596;[72] or the provision against the taking of inmates by cottagers alternately relaxed and enforced according as a desire to relieve a labour scarcity or to keep down the poor rates predominated? Perhaps on another occasion it will prove possible to make such an attempt.

Notes

Chapter IV

1 Gretton, *Oxfordshire JPs*, p lxvi.

2 Eg *EHR*, LII (1937), 282, 285.

3 *EJ*, XXIV (1914), 229-30.

4 Gretton, *Oxfordshire JPs*, pp xxvi-xxvii.

5 Ratcliff and Johnson, ed *Warwick CR*, I, xxix.

6 *NRQSR*, I, 204.

7 Hewins, *Trade and finance*, p 85.

8 Thomas Kemp, ed *The book of John Fisher, town clerk and deputy recorder of Warwick, 1580-88* (Warwick, 1900), p 156.

9 Tawney and Power, *Tudor economic documents*, I, 336-7.

10 Gretton, *Oxfordshire JPs*, p lxxvi.

11 Gretton, *Oxfordshire JPs*, pp x-xi, quoting Michael Dalton, *The countrey justice* (London, 1697).

12 John S. Furley, *Quarter Sessions government in Hampshire in the seventeenth century* (Winchester: Warren, 1937), pp 106-7.

13 Ashby, *Poor law administration*, p 174.

14 *EJ*, XXIV (1914), 230-1.

15 East Riding QS books, October, 1647.

16 Peyton, ed *Kesteven QS minutes*, p xliv.

17 *NRQSR*, I, 112-13, 127, 131, 137, 142, 151-2.

18 *NRQSR*, I, 24, 33, 46, 56, 92, 112, 159, 212, 214, 232, 238.

19 *NRQSR*, II, 9, 42, 186, 209.

20 Peyton, ed *Kesteven QS minutes*, p 466.

21 *NRQSR*, I, 248.

22 *NRQSR*, II, 206-7.

23 *NRQSR*, I, 92.

24 *NRQSR*, I, 24.

25 *NRQSR*, I, 24.

26 *NRQSR*, VII, 41; Wake, ed *Northants QS records,* p 62.

27 Holland QS minutes, Midsummer 1676 (Spalding).

28 Wake, ed *Northants QS records*, p62.

29 Book of Precedents and Indictments, p 89.

30 *Rural economy in York*, p 135.

31 Copnall, ed *Notts CR*, p 66.

32 *NRQSR*, I, 27.

33 Peyton, ed *Kesteven QS minutes*, p 486.

34 *EJ*, XXIV (1914), 230.

35 *NRQSR*, I, 99.

36 Ipswich Court records, September 1575.

37 *NRQSR*, I, 60.

38 *NRQSR*, I, 60, 69, 99.

39 *NRQSR*, I, 71, 98, 105, 148, 163, 188.

40 Lister, ed *WRS records*, p 396.

41 Four instances, *NRQSR*, I, 60, 143.

42 *Rural economy in York*, p 135.

43 *NRQSR*, I, 207, 248-9; II, 13, 234; III, 111.

44 Wake, ed *Northants QS records,* p 62.

45 Copnall, ed *Notts CR*, p12.

46 Great Grimsby court records.

47 Devereux Edgar's diary.

48 Hindmarsh, 'Assessment of wages', p 122.

49 *EJ*, IV (1894), 517.

50 Le Hardy, ed *Hertford CR*, VI, 346.

51 Norwich court records.

52 Hardy, ed *Hertford CR*, I, 116.

53 Tawney and Power, *Tudor economic documents*, I, 360.

54 Ipswich court records, November 1578 – constables to keep petty sessions twice every year; Lister, ed *WRS records,* p 396.

55 *VCH Notts*, II, 295-6.

56 Devereux Edgar's diary.

57 *Rural economy in York*, pp 134-5.

58 Eg *NRQSR*, I, 24, 46, 92; II, 123.

59 East Riding order books, June 1722, October 1723.

60 Holland QS minutes, Easter 1688 (Kirton)

61 Holland QS minutes, Easter 1726 (Kirton)

62 *VCH Lincs*, II, 338.

63 See above, p 42.

64 Dowdell, *QS*, p 146.

65 Devereux Edgar's diary, January 1712-13.

66 Ipswich court records, November 1578.

67 Kemp, ed *Book of John Fisher*, p 161.

68 *NRQSR*, I, 148.

69 Tawney and Power, *Tudor economic documents*, I, 335.

70 Hedon sessions books. Cf Great Grimsby court books.

71 Suffolk order books, September 1650.

72 Morris, *Chester*, p 452.

V The cost-of-living aspect

As is well known, the Statute of Artificers contained, in its opening words, the justification for altering the existing law that the statutory rates of wages then in force had, owing to the advance of prices which had taken place since their enactment, become inapplicable; while, in the section (5 Eliz c 4, sec 11) dealing with the assessment of wages, it was expressly laid down that the justices should call to them such discreet and grave persons as they thought fit, and should confer together respecting the plenty or scarcity of the time and other circumstances. What light do the assessments themselves throw on the problem as to whether the justices did, in fact, make the cost of living a major factor in determining assessment?

There are, firstly, statements included in the actual wording of assessments as to the reason for altering the justices' rates. These, though not necessarily to be taken at their face value, can be accepted as evidence of a kind. (They are not to be confused, of course, with mere recitations of the opening words of the statute itself which nearly all the early, and some of the late, assessments contain). The earliest instances are to be found in the 1563 assessments. Thus in a rature for the city of Lincoln the prices of wheat, rye, malt, beans, pease and barley, mutton, veal, beef, eggs, butter and cheese are given at the outset as having been taken into account, together with other necessaries and victuals, being very dear,[1] while Holland and Rutland assessments of the same year speak of great prices and dearth.[2] A Chester assessment of 1570 mentions the *cheapness* of necessaries.[3] In the Canterbury rature of 1576 it is stated that 'the causes and concyd [erations] why the said Mayor, Aldermen, and Shyryffes, have rated and taxed the wages and rates above said, is onely the dearth of vitayles, cloth, and other necessaries, which at this pre [sent are] so scarce and deare within the sayde Citie, that poore men are not able at reasonable price to at [tayn t]heyr necessaries'.[4] Ten years later the Lord Mayor and certain London justices had 'an especiall consideracion and regard unto the high and verie chargeable prices of all kinde of victualls, fewell rayment and

CHANGES IN SOMERSET ASSESSED RATES (£ s d)

	1647	1648	reissue 1650	1651	1652	1653	1654
Menservants by the year		4- 0-0	4- 0-0	4- 6-8	4-10-0	4-10-0	4- 0-0
Maidservants by the year		2- 0-0	2- 0-0	2- 0-0	2- 0-0	2- 0-0	1-13-4
HAY HARVEST							
Mowers per diem, finding themselves	1-4	1-4	1-4	1-6	1-8	1-8	1-4
Mowers per diem, at meat and drink	8	8	8	9	9	10	8
Men making hay, finding themselves	10	1-0	1-0	1-0	1-0	1-0	10
Men making hay, at meat and drink	6	6	6	6	6	6	4
Women making hay, finding themselves	8	8	8	8	8	8	5
Women making hay, at meat and drink	4	4	4	4	4	4	3
CORN HARVEST							
Men at corn harvest, finding themselves	1-4	1-2	1-2	1-4	1-4	1-4	1-2
Men at corn harvest, at meat and drink	8	8	8	8	8	8	6
Women at corn harvest, finding themselves	1-0	1-0	1-0	1-0	1-0	1-0	8
Women at corn harvest, at meat and drink	6	6	6	6	6	6	4
Masons, carpenters and tilers from 15 Mar. to 15 Sep. finding themselves				1-2	1-2	1-2	1-0
Masons, carpenters and tilers from 15 Sep. to 15 Mar. finding themselves							
Masons, carpenters and tilers from 15 Mar. to 15 Sep. at meat and drink				8	8	8	6
Masons, carpenters and tilers from 15 Sep. to 15 Mar. at meat and drink							
Threshers and ditchers from 15 Mar. to 15 Sep. finding themselves				1-0	1-0	1-0	10
Threshers and ditchers from 15 Sep. to 15 Mar. finding themselves							
Threshers and ditchers from 15 Mar. to 15 Sep. at meat and drink				6	6	6	5
Threshers and ditchers from 15 Sep. to 15 Mar. at meat and drink							
PIECE WORK							
Mowing an acre of grass finding themselves							
Mowing an acre of grass to hay							
Mowing an acre of barley							
Cutting and binding an acre of wheat							
Mowing an acre of oats							
Cutting and binding an acre of beans							
Drawing an acre of hemp							

source: Harbin and Dawes, ed *Somerset QS Records*, III and IV.

1655	1666	1668	1669	1670 (reissue)	1671	1672	1673	1674 (reissue)	1675 (reissue)	1676	1677	1685
4- 0-0	4- 0-0	4- 0-0	4- 0-0	4- 0-0	4- 0-0	4- 0-0	4- 0-0	4- 0-0	4- 0-0	4- 0-0	4- 0-0	4-10-0
2- 0-0	2- 0-0	2- 0-0	2- 0-0	2- 0-0	2- 0-0	2- 0-0	2- 0-0	2- 0-0	2- 0-0	2- 0-0	2- 0-0	2-10-0
1-4	1-4	1-4	1-4	1-4	1-4	1-4	1-2	1-2	1-2	1-2	1-2	1-2
10	8	8	8	8	8	8	7	7	7	7	7	7
10	1-0	1-0	1-0	1-0	10	10	10	10	10	10	10	10
5	6	6	6	6	6	6	6	6	6	6	6	6
												7
												4
1-0	1-4	1-2	1-2	1-2	1-4	1-2	1-0	1-0	1-0	1-0		1-2
6	8	7	7	7	8	7	6	6	6	6		8
10	10	10	10	10	10	10	9	9	9	7	7	
4	6	5	5	5	6	6	5	5	5	5	5	
} 1-0	1-4	1-2	1-2	1-2	1-4	1-4	1-2	1-2	1-2	1-2	1-2	1-2
	1-2	1-0				1-2	1-0	1-0	1-0	1-0	1-0	1-0
} 6	8	7	6	6	6	8	7	7	7	7	7	7
	7	6				7	6	6	6			7
} 10	1-0	10	10	10	1-0	1-0	10	10	10	10	10	10
	10	9	9	9	10	10	8	8	8	8	8	8
} 5	6	5	5	5	6	6	5	5	5	5	5	5
	5	4	4	4	5	5	4	4	4	4	4	4
	1-2	1-2	1-4	1-4		1-2	1-2	1-2	1-2	1-2	1-2	1-2
	1-6	1-4			1-2	1-6	1-6	1-6	1-6	1-6	1-6	1-6
	10	10	10	10		10	10	10	10	10	10	1-1
	3-0	3-0	3-0	3-0	3-0	3-0	3-0	3-0	3-0	3-0	3-0	3-0
					10							
					2-0					2-0	2-0	2-0
										4-6		4-6

apparrell bothe linnen and wollen and alsoe of howsrente, and other especiall and accidentall charges' wherewith artificers and labourers living in the city were burdened,[5] In 1597 a Chester assessment referred to 'the great dearth and scarsitie of things at this present.'[6] The Somerset justices in the sixteen-forties asked the grand jury to present their opinions what wages they thought fit to be assessed, 'respect beinge hadd to the present tymes';[7] that this was not a mere form of words was suggested by the statement that, in 1648, the rates 'for such as find themselves are raised in regard to the greate price of all sortes of provision att this present.'[8] In fact, however, only one such rate was raised The Essex assessment of 1651 is said to have been made having a special regard to prices of victuals and apparel and other necessary charges 'wherewith artificers, labourers and servants have been grieviously charged with than in time past'.[9] (In Derbyshire, incidentally, we are told that during the years of the Commonwealth the justices were far fairer in their statute wages than at any other period).[10] In 1655 we get the first mention (apart from the Chester instance in 1570) of scaling wages downwards because of the cheapness of necessaries, both in Wiltshire and London. The justices of Wiltshire acted 'having considered together with respect to the present times and the cheapness of all sortes of provisions (praised be God for the same) with due consideration of all other circumstances necessary to be considered of';[11] while the Carpenters' Company had been requested to advise the Lord Mayor of London in the matter of 'the reducing of the excessive wages of Laborers and workemen in these times of great plenty'.[12] Tawney suggests that this scaling-down may explain the 'comparatively numerous assessments of the Restoration period'.[13] Scaling-up again is indicated by the wording 'more grieviously charged than in times past' in a Warwickshire assessment of 1672;[14] but the phrase 'having a special regard to the prices of provisions' in a 1738 rature for the same county is misleading, since the general increase in wages as compared with the scale of 1730 was not, in fact, accompanied by any substantial rise in prices.[15]

Information of this direct character being scanty, we have to fall back upon an attempt to decide whether there was any significant correlation between the justices' actions and the movement of prices. It is fairly clear, for instance, that the Chester authorities had changes in the cost of living particularly in mind when they reassessed wages in 1596 and the following year, for a comparison of the yearly rates without meat and drink set in 1593, 1596 and 1597 shows an increase in each of the

INDICES OF EXETER WHEAT ASSIZE PRICES
(Compiled from data kindly supplied by Sir William Beveridge)

Mean of 40 years 1640-79 taken as 100

1645	106	1655	105	1665	83	1675	73
1646	120	1656	106	1666	71	1676	73
1647	148	1657	113	1667	69	1677	102
1648	104	1658	103	1668	106	1678	93
1649	102	1659	107	1669	97	1679	75
1650	127	1660	120	1670	83	1680	76
1651	123	1661	138	1671	75	1681	96
1652	97	1662	100	1672	81	1682	90
1653	72	1663	93	1673	129	1683	86
1654	62	1664	87	1674	123	1684	85
						1685	59

later years in all of the thirty-nine categories; while of the daily rates *with* meat and drink, thirty-six show a fall, nine remain stationary, and only one shows a rise, in the four-year period.[16] I have not examined prices for Chester or district in these years, but the changes mentioned can hardly have had any other explanation than that given, while a substantial increase in wheat prices between 1593 and 1596 is, for what it is worth in this connection, shown by Thorold Roger's series.[17] The series of Somerset assessments in the seventeenth century enables us to examine the action taken by the justices there rather more closely. If we take as a basis for roughly measuring price movements the mean of wheat assize prices in Exeter for the forty-year period 1640-79, the first assessment to be dealt with – that of 1647 – was published (as can be seen from the table) at a time when prices were substantially above normal. As wages were assessed at Easter time, the prices for the *previous* harvest year will in each case be treated as those the justices had in mind. The following year's rature of 1648, claimed, as we have seen, to take into account high prices (they had been 48 per cent above normal in the previous year). Despite the statement that rates for such as find themselves were raised, however, the only increase of this character was one of 2d a day for men making hay. There was actually a corresponding *reduction,* moreover, for men at corn harvest finding themselves – harvest prospects were evidently good. These hopes were apparently justified, for prices that year were nearly back to normal, and remained so in 1649. 1650, however, saw a substantial rise in the cost of living (wheat prices were 27 per cent above normal) and in the 1651 rature some increases were sanctioned. Mowers finding themselves were to be allowed 2d a day extra, as were men at corn harvest finding themselves. There seems, too, to have been a slight shortage of male labour, for menservants' yearly rates were raised from £4 to £4 6s 8d, while the daily rate for mowers having meat and drink provided for them was raised by 1d. The cost of living remained high in 1651, and in the 1652 assessment mowers finding themselves were allotted a further 2d a day. Labour, too, seems still to have been scarce – the increase for mowers with meat and drink was maintained, while wages for menservants on a yearly basis were increased by a further 3s 4d. Prices fell to their normal level again in 1652, but no cut was made in the wages of those finding themselves, while a further increase of 3d a day was sanctioned for mowers with meat and drink. As prices continued to fall – they were 28 per cent below the mean in 1653 – rates for those finding themselves were, however, brought back to the level of 1650 or earlier. Thus of workers finding themselves the daily rate for mowers was reduced 4d; for men making hay 2d; for women making hay 3d; for women at corn harvest 4d (the first reduction, incidentally, to take place in these last two categories); men at corn harvest 2d. Similar reductions were made in the case of masons, carpenters, tilers, threshers and ditchers. In addition, however, the shortage of labour had apparently subsided. Menservants' yearly rates were brought back to the 1650 level and maidservants were temporarily reduced from £2 to £1 13s 4d (this latter reduction only operated for one year, the rate being subsequently brought back to £2 and kept there). Daily workers with meat and drink were affected in the same way. The mowers' increases of 3d and 1d were cancelled, men and women making hay had their rates reduced by 2d and 1d respectively, men and women at corn harvest suffered reductions of 2d each, masons and those in the categories following them in the list also had their wages with meat and drink reduced. Broadly speaking then, the 1654 assessment brought the rates of men finding themselves back to the 1647 level, while the rates of those at meat and drink, as well as those of women both finding themselves and at meat and drink, were reduced even below that level. In 1654 prices fell further. The only changes for those finding themselves in the assessment of 1655, however, were a reduction of 2d for men at corn harvest and an *increase* of 2d for women at corn harvest. The rates for mowers and men making hay at meat and drink were, however, increased by 2d and 1d respectively – evidently the cuts of the previous year had been too drastic, and difficulty was being experienced in obtaining labour.

An unfortunate gap in the sessions records deprives us of further information regarding the changes made in assessed rates until 1666. Though the assessment of that year followed two years of low prices – 13 and 17 per cent below the mean of 1664 and 1665 respectively – there were certain *increases* in rates for those finding themselves as compared with the 1655 position. Thus men making hay had an increase of 2d, men at corn harvest an increase of 4d and masons and those in the categories following them also experienced increases. There were increases in the rates for those at meat and drink as well – men making hay, men at corn harvest, women at corn harvest and the artificers. Mowers at meat and drink, however, who had, as we have seen, been the first amongst the daily workers to reflect a labour scarcity in the fifties, had their rate reduced by 2d. Yearly rates for menservants and maidservants remained absolutely stable for this and the following years (the first change of which we know from the printed records being an increase in 1685). 1666 saw a further fall of prices, which was maintained in 1667. The assessment of 1668 made some reductions – 2d a day in the rates of those finding themselves and also reductions of 1d a day in a number of rates including meat and drink. In 1668 prices recovered, and few changes were made in the 1669 assessment. This assessment was reissued unchanged in 1670, prices in 1669 being about average. There was a reduction in the cost of living in 1670, and in the 1671 assessment men making hay finding themselves were given 2d a day less. At the same time, however, certain other categories of workers finding themselves actually had their rates increased – men at corn harvest by 2d, masons, carpenters and tilers by 2d, and threshers and ditchers by similar amounts. A temporary scarcity of labour seems to have been the real reason for these increases, however, for quite a number of categories 'at meat and drink' show small increases also. There was a further fall of prices in 1671; and the 1672 assessment removed two of the increases of the previous year – men at corn harvest finding themselves had their increase of 2d a day cancelled, as well as the 1d a day increase for those not finding themselves. 1672, was another year of low prices, and the 1673 assessment, probably influenced by this and by a satisfactory labour market position, included reductions of 2d and 1d respectively for most categories of workers finding themselves and at meat and drink. There was a sharp rise in the cost of living in 1673, to 29 per cent above normal, but the low scale of 1673 was reissued in 1674 without alteration. In January 1673-4 the court had taken notice that badgers were enhancing prices and putting the poor to much trouble, and had ordered that no corn be bought in the market until the poor were served.[18] Peyton, commenting on this, observes that 'from the bare text, it is difficult to reconcile the justices' concern for the poor with the continuance of the low scale if the statute were strictly enforced'.[19] This scale was, moreover, reissued in 1675, though 1674 prices were still 23 per cent above the mean. Subsequent issues, with insignificant alterations, in 1676 and 1677 were, however, accompanied by a fall in prices in 1675 which was maintained in the following year. This is as far as the volumes of printed sessions records take us, but one further rature, for 1685, has been printed. It shows remarkably few alterations as compared with the last assessments we have considered. Men at corn harvest, however, had their rates increased, as did both yearly menservants and maid-servants.

What does this Somerset evidence, to which perhaps more attention than is justified has been given, suggest? It would appear, in the first place, that even here, where the justices, unlike those in most districts, were prepared to alter the scale at frequent intervals, the cost of living aspect was subordinate to the factor of labour scarcity. Particularly in the later part of the period covered by these ratures it will have been noticed how frequently changes in the rates of those finding themselves, which might at first sight have been taken to represent changes in living costs, are accompanied by corresponding changes in the rates for those at meat and drink. A second and closely related conclusion which may be put forward is that the justices were more often in this series attempting adjustments between different categories of worker than applying flat-rate increases or decreases throughout the scale. Both these conclusions, incidentally, contrast strongly with the Chester situation in the fifteen-nineties when, as we have seen, rates even for the widely different crafts covered by the assessments, tended to be altered *en bloc.* The first of these conclusions is, it will be noticed, in line with Tawney's experience, for though he found a rough parallelism in the rise of wheat prices and wages in one or two instances, he more often found there seemed to be no correspondence at all. Two factors which he advanced to explain this were the need for a 'differential' to ensure a supply of agricultural labour, and the circumstance that the justices themselves belonged to a class which felt a rise in prices severely, as their copyhold and freehold tenants' rents were fixed.[20] I cannot altogether agree, however, with another conclusion of Tawney's when he says that 'if movements in wages had been adjusted with any accuracy to movements in prices, it would have been necessary for them to take place not only from year to year, but from month to month, and, indeed, almost from day to day'.[21] The Somerset material we have just examined seems to me to suggest, not so much that it was impossible for a year-to-year adjustment to cost of living changes to be achieved, as that, although this was done on occasion, the factor of labour scarcity had also to be taken into account and tended increasingly to become the dominant consideration. It is admitted, of course, that for such an adjustment frequent alteration in the scale, as was actually done in Somerset, was necessary; and that where the practice of reissue without alteration, except when factors of major importance supervened, obtained, the attempt had obviously been abandoned. To admit that the justices were not as a rule prepared to take the trouble, however, or that they did not wish to secure this yearly adjustment, is not to admit that it could not have been achieved if desired, particularly as the central authority obviously thought of the annual nature of assessment as making it possible to provide just such an adjustment. The regulation of markets and the fixing of prices of food supplies was, it is true, a policy which the central government invariably brought to the attention of local authorities at times of scarcity. That this latter policy was regarded by the Council as making the annual adjustment of wages to changes in the cost of living unnecessary, however, is not, I think, proved. The evidence would seem to suggest that the two were regarded as complementary – after all, the smaller the proportion of people coming wholly within the categories in wage assessments, the more necessary regulation of markets and of grain supplies and prices obviously was. If the justices tended to prefer the latter policy to the former, it was no doubt because it was in their interests to do so, rather than because the machinery of wage assessment was totally unfitted for one of the purposes for which it had been, ostensibly at least, devised.

For the same reasons, I cannot subscribe to one of the propositions advanced by Miss Hindmarsh in this connection. Her contention is that assessments were never intended for those entirely dependent upon their wages, but for a population which was hardly affected by fluctuations in the prices of food.[22] While freely admitting that, in point of numbers, the class of landless labourers was not a large one, and had to be augmented as a labour force by those with land, it seems to me that the modification of assessed rates to meet increases in the cost of living was indeed, *inter alia,* to dissuade this landless class from adopting the alternative policy of leaving work and squatting on the waste.[23] In this sense employers of agricultural labour who increasingly gave wages with board or with allowances in kind, and the central government recommending the revision of official scale in times of high prices, were tackling the same problem in slightly different ways – if the former expedient appealed to employers more than the latter, this constitutes no proof that the rating of wages was not devised partly to meet such a situation or that it could not, given the co-operation of those charged with its execution, have succeeded. Moreover, a clear distinction could not always be drawn between changes in the cost of living incidental to monetary factors (which the act was surely intended to provide for) and those arising from other factors.

There remain to be considered additional means whereby pressure was, at different times, brought to bear on the justices to alter or enforce the assessed rates so that wage-earners might be able to obtain a living. So far in this study we have spoken of the Statute of Artificers as providing for the assessment of *maximum* rates. There is evidence, however, that the justices sometimes regarded them as *minimum* rates, a point mentioned in a previous chapter in connection with compelling masters to pay wages due. At a Holland sessions in 1667, for instance, a certain John Brassey was indicted for refusing to pay John Clark, firstly for hay making and secondly for diking, *according to the assessed rates.*[24] Miss Hindmarsh records that in 1625 the Sussex justices circumvented an attempt on the part of the King's Purveyors to pay workers in that county less than the assessed rates,[25] though in this case it seems to me possible that all that was involved was an undertaking to pay the rates current in the district – an obligation not necessarily applying to *other* employers. Again, a 1724 Nottinghamshire wage assessment contains the phrase 'where less wages have been given than are hereby appointed within one year past, that such less wages shall be given and taken still',[26] the implication being that, but for this permission, the assessed rates would have been treated as legal minima; while a Warwickshire assessment of 1657 declares that the rates 'shall be such and no more',[27] and similar wording is found in a few other assessments. Moreover, there are occasional passages in the textbooks used by justices which would have supported their adopting an attitude of this kind. There is such a passage in Burn's *Justice of the peace* – 'in order to intitle the servant to wages he needed not to prove how much his master had agreed to pay him, *for that was fixed by the justices,*[28] but only how long he had served, and then the wages followed of course'.[29] Dalton, more reasonably, seems to apply such reasoning only to cases where master and servant had not mentioned the matter of wages; 'If a man retainest a laborer or servant, to serve him according to the Statute, though no wages be spoken of upon the retainer, yet the retainer is good, and they shall have such wages as are assessed and appointed by Proclamation, for that wages are certain'.[30] This probably explains the Kent justices' procedure.[31] It is interesting to note, also, a case in which, in certain circumstances, local opinion seems to have compelled the payment of the statutory rates as minima. Amongst the customs of the township of Weeton, East Yorkshire, put into writing in November 1669, the third contains a clause to the effect that if certain fences are out of repair the byelawmen shall give twenty-four hours notice to the owners or occupiers concerned and, should the latter not put matters right, shall set workmen to make the fence right, and if the owners or occupiers 'refuse to pay within 24 hours after the work be Dun such wages for such work as ye statute will allow then it shall be lawfull to distreine praise and sell ... deducting reasonable charges'.[32] When these customs were again committed to writing in 1714, this particular one was repeated. In a loose way, of course, the desire expressed in the statute (5 Eliz c 4) to afford the hired person both in time of scarcity and in time of plenty a 'convenient proportion' of wages might be taken as implying the idea of wages not falling below a standard, and letter from the Privy Council (as, for instance, the one quoted later in this chapter)[33] sometimes use wording of the same type. As is well known, however, the only definite statutory justification for treating the justices' rates as minima was restricted to the clothing industries – 'if any clothier or other ... shall not pay so much or so great wages to their weavers, spinsters, workmen or workwomen as shall be so ... rated ... every clothier ... so offending shall forfeit and lose for every such offence, to the party aggrieved, ten shillings'; and clothiers who happened to be justices were not to take part in the assessment of wages for clothing workers (1 Jac I c 6). Not only the state but also the town authorities tended to apply a minimum to this industry, probably because the early emergence of clothiers as entrepreneurs necessitated action of this kind.[34]

As to the extent to which the justices carried out their statutory obligations in this matter, we know that in June 1614, as a result of a petition from the poor craftsmen of Wiltshire, a letter was sent from the Privy Council to the justices there which included the following paragraph. 'And whereas it is understood that many of those poore craftsmen are for the most parte weavers and belonging unto the mistery of cloathing, and doe cheifely complaine on the small wadges gyven them by the clothier, being no more then what was accustomed to be payde 40 yeres past, notwithstanding that the prises of all kinde of victuall are almost doubled from what they were, it is also thought fitting that, having called the clothiers before you, you examine the truthe of this complaint, and finding it to be as is informed, to use your best endevors for the proportioning of their wadges unto the state of these present tymes, as in all other trades is it observed'.[35] The earlier part of this letter had ordered the justices to restrain maltsters, millers, badgers and drivers who enhanced the market, or to diminish their number. At the summer sessions that year the justices duly took steps of this latter type;[36] but whether they did anything in the matter of the wages paid by clothiers we cannot, from what has been printed, say. In 1623, however, the weavers and spinners petitioned the justices, asking them 'to appoint certain grave and discreete persons to view the straitnes of workes, to assease rates for wages according to the desert of their workes, now especially in this great dearth of corne'.[37] The justices accordingly ordered the workers and employers concerned 'to be at the Devizes the Thursday in the next Whitson weeke, to conferr with us hereabouts'.[38] The order resulting from that meeting was to the effect that the general table of wages should continue as formerly assessed, and that the wages fixed for those connected with clothing should be published on the next market day 'in order that workmasters and workmen alike may take notice thereof, and that the workmen who desire that the same rates may stand may be the better satisfied'.[39] Apparently, therefore, the workers' request for a re-assessment of wages was not met, the existing rates being proclaimed afresh.

In the years 1629-31 the Council, as those concerned with the history of poor relief have noticed, seems to have been particularly active in this matter. To begin with, in 1629 the Essex authorities were told that the weavers of baize in the Bocking and Braintree district should be remunerated on a just and reasonable basis.[40] In February of the following year the textile workers of Sudbury petitioned that their wages had been abated, notwithstanding the present state of scarcity and dearth.[41] Commissioners were accordingly appointed to inquire into the matter and, as a result of their investigations, the Essex justices made a special order setting forth the piece-rates that the saymakers of Sudbury were to pay.[42] This particular matter does not, however, seem to have been satisfactorily adjusted until some years later.[43] In the meantime, the Council had, in September 1630, sent letters to Cambridge, Essex, Suffolk, Norfolk and Norwich, pointing out that the hard and necessitous times being experienced formed a clear case for the putting into execution of the statutes 5 Elizabeth c 4, and 1 James I c 6, so that 'the poore should not be pinched in theise times of scarcitie and dearth'.[44] (The Suffolk justices had already, apparently without previous pressure of this kind, re-assessed wages the previous April).[45] The statement by Hampson that 'the towns of Bury St Edmunds and Norwich, which had received similar communications from the Council, definitely did draw up new assessments as a consequence' apparently overlooks this difference in dates.[46] It has not, of course, escaped notice that it was to the cloth-working districts that these letters were sent.[47] For other counties a more general letter,[48] dated June 1630 and sent to all cities and counties, detailing measures to be taken to keep down the price and maintain the supply of bread and grain for poor people, later supplemented by a Book of Orders,[49] was deemed sufficient. Wage assessment as a means of alleviating hardship in an emergency of this kind was, apparently, thought of by the Council as mainly applicable to clothworking counties.

It is by no means certain that appropriate action was taken by the justices on receipt of the letter reminding them of the acts of 1562-3 and 1603-4. A report of the justices of some of the Cambridgeshire hundreds in 1632 (which was not, however, intended as a reply to this particular letter) included the statement that they had taken the statute and questions relating to retaining of servants and ordering of wages into their consideration, 'but have perfected nothinge, the care of the poore and putting forth of apprentices hath imployed so much of our tyme'.[50] The reply of the Norwich justices, in December 1630, seems at first sight, it is true, to be favourable, and has been generally accepted as meaning that a new assessment was drawn up. 'And we have accordinge to the Statute appointed the wages of servants, laborers and workemen at such Rates as will conveniently recompence their paynes and yeld unto them competent maintenunce'.[51] This could, however, merely mean that the old rates, which the justices considered to be still adequate, had been confirmed, and a close examination of the Norwich records rather suggests that the latter interpretation is the correct one. For not only is there no hint in the court records of a new assessment having been drawn up at this time (and both the Quarter Sessions and the Mayor's Court Books normally refer to this particular question); but there is definite record of wages being continued on 10 August 1629, and again continued in 5 Charles 1, the day and month being, unfortunately, eaten away.[52] Furthermore it is significant that their letter of December 1630 to the Council was intended mainly as an answer to the latter's general letter dated 13 June; this is made perfectly clear by the entries in the Norwich court records in connection with the reply – no mention is made of the inclusion of any reference to wages, which looks very much as if it was an afterthought. However, justices of certain counties which did not, to our knowledge, receive special instructions in the matter, beyond the references to 5 Elizabeth c 4, in the Book of Orders 1631, took steps which must, one would think, have represented an attempt to bring the assessed rates into line with the sharp rise in the cost of living. Thus the justices of at least two divisions of Hertfordshire drew up an assessment in 1631,[53] which included a section for clothing workers. Spinsters' and weavers' piece-rates, it may be mentioned, were, unlike any other piece-rates in the assessment, given without the qualifying phrase 'not above'; while the yearly rates for weavers' servants were distinguished from other yearly rates in the same way. (Incidentally in the Suffolk assessment of 1630, where similar rates appear together, the qualification 'not above' is also omitted in the sections on husbandry probably due to carelessness).[54] Again, the Gloucester[55] and Herefordshire[56] justices drew up new assessments in 1632. Finally, amongst the justices' reports on the execution of the 1631 Book of Orders (which was, of course, more concerned with other statutes, but naturally referred to the 'poor law' aspects of 5 Elizabeth c 4)[57] there was one from the mayor of Guildford which spoke of causing the Statute of Labourers to be put in execution,[58] one from certain Cambridgeshire hundreds (which we have noticed already),[59] and one from the justices of a Derbyshire wapentake reporting 'that the Statute for Labourers and for the ordering of wages was carried out, and that none were presented to them for refusing to work at reasonable wages'.[60]

When this Privy Council supervision – which Tawney ascribes in part to 'a desire to prevent agitation by removing the material causes of discontent, and incidentally to put pressure on the middle and upper classes, who were the stronghold of religious and constitutional opposition'[61] – was relaxed, it was not to be expected that the justices would constantly keep the cost-of-living aspect of wage regulation in mind. If we ignore presentments such as the following – 'all clothiers and serge makers who do put work to any spinsters by the bundle or any other term than the just pound of 16 ounces',[62] there continued to be a significant absence of cases, in Quarter Sessions records, of clothiers being accused of not paying the assessed rates. The later Hertfordshire assessments[63] omit any mention of piece-rates for clothworkers although they do give yearly rates for journeymen, while the 1647 West Riding assessment treats clothworkers on the same basis as other workers – they shall not take for their wages above so much per day or per year[64] – and, from 1671 onwards, the West Riding justices apparently ceased to assess wages for such workers altogether.[65] The Devonshire justices, while continuing to include rates for spinners in their assessments, renewed the 1679 rates without change up to 1790.[66] We are probably justified in concluding that, by 1640,[67] the attempt to provide a minimum for clothworkers was at an end, the Gloucestershire dispute of 1756-7[68] merely serving to show that, though the existing law was on the side of the workers, the arguments used by the clothiers had a stronger appeal to the legislature. One cannot be equally definite about it, but the evidence strongly suggests that, from the latter part of the seventeenth century, the cost of living ceased to be a major consideration in assessment. The general trend of prices was, it is true, downward for some time thereafter; but there were individual years of scarcity which would have justified changes in assessments. Henceforth the emphasis was on another aspect of wage regulation, to be discussed in the following chapter.

Note: In support of the argument advanced on pages 167-8, it may be pointed out that the framers of the 1563 policy were, in one respect, merely returning to the practice laid down in a statute of 1389-90[69] – the non-employment of the 'statutory limit' arrangement in force before and after the latter date was deliberate, and must surely have been due as much as anything else to a desire to give *local* conditions (both in respect of food and labour scarcity) greater weight.

Notes

Chapter V

1 *VCH Lincs*, II, 330.

2 Robert R. Steele, ed *Tudor and Stuart proclamations, 1485-1714* (Oxford, 1910), I, 61.

3 Hindmarsh, 'Assessment of wages', p 158.

4 Steele, ed *Tudor and Stuart proclamations*, I, 75.

5 Tawney and Power, *Tudor economic documents*, I, 366.

6 Morris, *Chester*, p 367.

7 Harbin and Dawes, ed *Somerset QS records*, III, 40.

8 Harbin and Dawes, ed *Somerset QS records*, III, 67.

9 Rogers, *History*, VI, 694.

10 John C. Cox, *Three centuries of Derbyshire annals as illustrated by the records of the Quarter Sessions of the county of Derby from Queen Elizabeth to Queen Victoria* (London and Derby, 1890), II, 242.

11 Cunnington, ed *Wilts CR*, p 290.

12 *EJ*, X (1895), 406.

13 See above, p 54.

14 Ashby, *Poor law administration*, pp 171-2.

15 Ashby, *Poor law administration*, p 175.

16 The assessments are printed in Morris, *Chester*, pp 367-8.

17 Rogers, *History*, V, 268.

18 Harbin and Dawes, ed *Somerset QS records*, IV, 147.

19 Peyton, ed *Kesteven QS minutes*, p cxii.

20 See above, pp 81-2.

21 See above, p 61.

22 Hindmarsh, 'Assessment of wages', p 147.

23 See note on p 173.

24 Holland QS minutes, Michaelmas 1677.

25 Hindmarsh, 'Assessment of wages', p 142.

26 Copnall, ed *Notts CR*, p 65.

27 Ashby, *Poor law adminstration,* p 170.

28 My italics.

29 Burn, *JP,* p 626.

30 Dalton, *Countrey justice,* p 127.

31 *EHR,* XLIII (1928), 401.

32 Welwick byelawmen's and miscellaneous accounts book.

33 See below, pp 69-70.

34 See above, pp 43-5, 69-72.

35 *Acts of the Privy Council, 1613-14,* p 458.

36 *HMC Various,* I, 87.

37 *HMC Various*, I, 94; Bland, Brown and Tawney, *English economic history,* pp 356-7.

38 Bland, Brown and Tawney, *English economic history,* pp 356-7.

39 *HMC Various,* I, 94.

40 Ellen M. Leonard, *The early history of English poor relief* (Cambridge UP, 1900), p 160.

41 Bland, Brown and Tawney, *English economic history,* p 358.

42 Bland, Brown and Tawney, *English economic history,* pp 359-60.

43 Leonard, *Poor relief,* p 161.

44 *EHR*, XIII (1898), 91.

45 *EHR*, XII (1897), 307-11.

46 Hampson, *Poverty in Cambridgeshire,* p 48.

47 See above, pp 76.

48 Privy Council register, 13 June 1630.

49 Privy Council register, 9 September 1630.

50 Hampson, *Poverty in Cambridgeshire,* p 48.

51 Leonard, *Poor relief,* p 163.

52 Norwich court records. The illegible entry is on a page which has been rebound, so its position provides no clue as to the month.

53 See Appendix A, pp 206-35.

54 *EHR*, XII (1897), 307-11.

55 Rogers, *History,* VI, 694.

56 *HMC Portland,* III, 31.

57 Leonard, *Poor relief,* p 343.

58 Leonard, *Poor relief*, p 358.

59 See above, p 171.

60 *VCH Derbyshire*, II, 182.

61 See above, p 75.

62 Harbin and Dawes, ed *Somerset QS records*, IV, 224.

63 Hardy, ed *Hertford CR*, I, 292; VI, 400.

64 *EJ*, XXIV (1914), 223-5.

65 *EJ*, XXIV (1914), 228-9.

66 Hoskins, *Industry and trade*, p 130.

67 See above, p 57.

68 Fully dealt with in Lipson, *Economic history*, III, 266-70.

69 *EcHR*, I (1927), 138.

VI The 'excessive exactions' aspect

One of the first things likely to strike anyone about the wage assessment provision of the Statute of Artificers was that, providing as it did for a legal maximum wage, it was not in the interests of the wage-earner. Previous legislation of this type had been intended, in part, to keep wages down, while Cecil's preliminary draft of the bill alluded to the unreasonable wages demanded by servants in husbandry.[1] Not unnaturally, therefore, Thorold Rogers looked with suspicion on the claim made in the act that it was intended to ensure a convenient proportion of wages both in plenty and in scarcity. 'I contend that from 1563 to 1824', he declared, 'a conspiracy ... was entered into to cheat the English workman of his wages, to tie him to the soil, to deprive him of hope, and to degrade him into irremediable poverty'.[2] Other writers of the same period came, after examination of Quarter Sessions material, to the same conclusion. Cox, for instance, speaks of 'this odious Act ... the results of which were so momentous and delivered English labour, tied and bound, into the hands of the most interested capitalists for nearly three centuries'.[3] Even those who saw good in the statute could not deny that it had potentialities of this character. Stress could, of course, he laid – as, for instance, by Cunningham[4] – on the significance of the amending act providing a minimum for clothworkers; but, as we have seen, both the application of this minimum and emphasis on the cost of living in assessment depended on a considerable measure of central supervision. There remained, it is true, the faint possibility that the grave and discreet persons whose advice was, by the terms of the statute (5 Eliz c 4, sec 11), to be obtained, might have the interests of artificers and labourers and servants at heart. Where, as happened in a few counties, the grand jury presented their opinion as to the rates they thought suitable, the cost of living aspect might occasionally be stressed – this happened, for instance, in Somerset in 1647-50,[5] and in Staffordshire,[6] while the Essex grand jury recommended increases in 1599 and 1611;[7] from what we know of the composition of such juries, however, it is not surprising to find one in Worcestershire making the following presentment, which has caught the attention of most writers on the subject – 'we desire that servants' wages may be rated according to the statute, for we find the unreasonableness of servants' wages a great grievance so that servants are grown [so] proud and idle [that the master cannot be known from the servant, except it be because the servant wears better clothes than his master]'.[8] It seems probable that where advice was taken at all, the grand jury was used for this purpose; it is just possible, however, that the time at which the committee of justices charged with the rating of wages in the East Riding was directed to meet – six o'clock in the evening – may indicate that some attempt was made to choose a time convenient for the appearance of wage-receivers whose advice might be asked, particularly as the times of meeting of other committees seem almost invariably to have been earlier in the day than this.[9] On at least one occasion the London magistrates sought the advice of the Carpenters' Company, the latter co-operating with them 'for the reducing of the excessive wages of laborers and workemen in these times of great plenty';[10] and the Lindsey justices may possibly have taken the advice of the chief constables – 'the rates of wages to continue for the year following confirmed under the hands of the Chief Constables'.[11] What little evidence we have on the question of advice taken does not, therefore, materially alter the position. Moreover when, after the Great Fire of London, it was desired to prevent workmen taking advantage of the demand for building labour to force up its price, (or, as the act put it, making 'the common Calamity a Pretence to extort unreasonable ... wages') the assessment of wages was the method chosen; the act of 1666 (19 Chas II c 3) was for the express purpose of preventing 'excessive exactions'.

The assessment of wages, then, had as one of its purposes that of keeping wages below the level they would otherwise have reached, of preventing the exploitation of a labour scarcity situation by those who stood to benefit by it, of maintaining the traditional and therefore natural rate of wages as against what laisser-faire economists later came to describe as the 'natural' rate. It will be clear from what has been said earlier that wage assessment was only one among a number of expedients which separately or in conjunction according to circumstances, could be employed for this purpose. Of these expedients, proceedings against those living idly or at their own hands, or refusing to work for reasonable wages, were naturally often used instead of (or along with) wage assessment to combat the excessive exactions of workers. Thus a West Riding order of 1641 mentioned 'a general complaint of the inhabitants of these parts that servants refuse to work for reasonable wages, and cannot be hired for competent allowance as formerly, making advantage of the much business of the times';[12] while a well-known Wiltshire order of 1655 aptly illustrates the close relationship between assessment and other parts of the policy. The assessed rates had duly been proclaimed 'but young people both men and maids, fitting for service, will not go abroad to service without they may have excessive wages, but will rather work at home at their own hands, whereby the rating of wages will take little effect; therefore no young men or maids fitting to go abroad to service (their parents not being of ability to keep them) shall remain at home, but shall with all convenient speed betake themselves to service for the wages aforesaid, which if they refuse to do the justices shall proceed against them'.[13] Refusing to go to service, and living at one's own hands must, indeed, as Tawney has suggested, often have been used as a lever for raising wages; a further means to the same end was, as he points out, provided by the existence of waste land[14] which in this respect had much the same effect as did, at a later date, the American frontier, in its influence on the wages of those who did not migrate. Another weapon available to the worker – for preventing the use of which the Statute, as we have seen, did not fail to provide – was that of leaving before term, or before a piece of work was finished. The Council might upbraid justices who failed to assess wages in times of scarcity, but was itself quite capable of condemning attempts of labourers to exploit a scarcity situation – 'we are informed that it is a thing usuall amongst workemen employed in such labours to exact great prises and high rates, when the worke growes to any perfection or finishing, then either take their owne unreasonable demandes, or to desert the worke, and so put the work maister to some extraordinaries'.[15] Much the same complaint is made by the Hertfordshire justices in assessing wages in 1687. 'Whereas the licentious humours of some servants have prevailed so far upon the Lenity and good nature of their masters, that they have advanced the charge of their wages and the expence of their diet above the rents of their Master's farms; and to highten this grievance they have been soe exorbitant in their severall services, that they will not work but at such times, and in such manner as they please; and when their work is most necessary, they often-times leave the same, if not their services'.[16] Another 'unreasonable and unlawful doing' is hinted at on the same occasion for, in the list of offences and penalties attached to the assessment, the £10 fine for conspiring together to advance wages is included.[17] We have already noticed that a petition of householders and other substantial persons presented to the Holland justices gave as the reason for the holding of petty sessions only once a year the reduction of the exorbitant demands of servants, and suggested a return to the older practice of holding more frequent statute sessions because the 'one session' arrangement had served to enhance the rates and wages of servants, who had tended to become more scarce since that procedure was put in operation; the justices, by complying with this request, clearly indicated that they were in sympathy with the attitude of these petitioners.[18]

It would, of course, be wrong to suppose that the justices invariably reacted to a labour scarcity situation by enforcing the assessed rates that had previously obtained, and compelling those living at home or at their own hands to go to service. Sometimes they merely raised the assessed rates and, so far as we know, took no special measures by way of compulsion – this, at least, is suggested by a comparison of the Warwickshire assessments of 1730 and 1738.[19] Sometimes the county justices, interested in maintaining the supply of agricultural, as distinct from other labour, sought to achieve this by advances in the assessed rates for agricultural work, accompanied by no change, or a decline, in the assessed rates for other categories. This, in Tawney's opinion, was happening in Wiltshire in 1635 and in Warwickshire in 1672.[20] Sometimes labour would be accepted from other districts without insistence on a 'settlement certificate' by way of indemnification against chargeability. Thus Chambers points out that in the printed records of Nottingham for the period 1700-60 there is not a single allusion to the settlement system, suggesting deliberate relaxation of the normal requirements of the time on entry.[21] Such a relaxation was, indeed, expressly provided for by the Somerset justices on one occasion in 1676. 'The Court declares that healthy single persons may go to any place to serve for one year, upon any legal retainer, such masters ... (being payers to poor rates and other usual taxes) as are qualified in the judgement of the nearest justice to receive them: without any discharges being given to indemnify any parish to which they shall go from being chargeable by reason of their settling in service there'.[22]

No doubt it would be equally wrong to assume too readily that the rating of wages, coupled with the enforcement of the assessed rates and compelling the idle to work, always signified a labour shortage. Cunningham suggested, for instance, that the Shropshire justices, faced with an unemployment problem, in 1732 assessed rates of wages at which men might be compelled to work,[23] (though this interpretation is not altogether satisfactory). Nevertheless, sufficient evidence exists to show that, faced with a labour shortage, the justices quite often took action on these lines. Thus Miss Hampson shows how the severe scarcity of agricultural labour in parts of Cambridgeshire was reflected by the activity of the county magistrates during the Restoration period in such matters as compelling the idle to work, enforcing public hiring, and insisting on testimonials.[24] Again, there is the case of Suffolk in the seventeen-twenties. In April 1723 an order was issued to the high constables requiring them to issue out their warrants to the overseers to bring in lists 'of the several persons of the meaner sort with the names and ages of their respective children that the justices may judge who are fit to be bound out apprentices and who to go to service'. Both in this and the following year numerous cases of living idly appear in the Ipswich records; while in 1724 – for the first time, judging by the silence of minute and order books, for over half a century – a Suffolk wage assessment was drawn up.[25] There is evidence, too, that efforts were made to enforce it. For in a little note-book drawn up just about this time, marked 'Precedents and Indictments', where samples of what appear to be actual cases are given (presumably as a guide), there is an instance of a master overpaying his servant, whom he had hired outside statute sessions;[26] even if this case were imaginary – which, in view of the names and details given, seems unlikely – it still provides evidence that the question of overpayment was liable to arise at this time, for the number of types illustrated in the book is not large. A final example – that of the justices of East and North Yorkshire in the early sixteen-eighties – deserves rather fuller treatment because it is possible to reconstruct the whole episode fairly satisfactorily. The justices were, in effect, faced with a temporary shortage of labour as a result of an epidemic.

The least interesting aspect of the situation – the evidence regarding the existence of an epidemic likely to bring about a temporary scarcity of labour – can be summarised quite shortly. According to my original plan in this case, a fairly extensive sample of parishes in the area under review was taken, and the recorded burials in the three years 1679-81 were compared with the mean of six years (the three preceding and the three following). Although this method suggested that an epidemic affecting most of East and North Yorkshire must have taken place at this time, it was open to the objection that the years chosen for comparison might not be representative – that the number of deaths in this six-year period might be below normal. In order to meet this objection, fuller information was obtained about a smaller sample. Twenty-four of the parishes in the original sample provided burial figures for the whole of the thirty-year period 1664-1693. Taking these twenty-four as a new sample, it was found that in twenty-one of them the number of recorded burials in 1679 and 1680 was the largest for the thirty-year period. In the remaining three parishes, 1682 was the year with the highest number of recorded burials, 1680 being the second highest. Taking this sample as a whole, the highest years of twenty-one parishes and the second highest of three parishes exceeded the mean of the thirty years by 121 per cent. It can hardly be doubted that such a situation would, in a large agricultural area, be likely to lead to a temporary shortage of yearly farm servants, particularly as, in most of the parishes examined, several years of high mortality followed one another. So far as the epidemic is concerned, it is true that evidence other than that of parish registers is lacking; but Creighton, on the basis of contemporary London material, records an influenza in 1679, and epidemic agues extending over three seasons 1678-80.[27]

What policy did the justices adopt? Taking the East Riding first, although unfortunately both rolls and minutes are missing for the period under review, something can be learnt from two recently discovered wage assessments; as these have already been printed, it will be sufficient to indicate their bearing on this particular inquiry.[28] The assessments are for 1669 and 1679 respectively, and while the first relates to the whole of the Riding, the second would appear to apply merely to the Ouse and Derwent Division. The first relevant point seems to be that later assessment is prefaced, in the petty constable's memoranda book where it was found, by a set of rules summarizing the duties of masters, servants and constables as contained in the Statute of Artificers. We are, perhaps, justified in assuming that it was not an accident that these rules should accompany the second rather than the first assessment; for if the justices proposed to attempt wage regulation under rather abnormal circumstances, it would be natural to provide a 'refresher course' for those to whom unfamiliar duties would fall. A second point of interest is that the 1679 rature contains yearly wages only. This fits in very well with the circumstance (to which attention will be drawn in a moment) that all the North Riding presentments for over-payment were in connection with yearly wages. It would have been foolish to disturb the existing daily- and piece-rates for farm work and village crafts because of a temporary labour shortage; such a shortage would naturally show itself first in the hiring of yearly servants where, in any case, latitude had always to be allowed for differences in experience and efficiency. Corroboration of the nature of the situation with which the justices had to deal is, it may be suggested, provided by the absence of daily- and piece-rates in the 1679 assessment. A third point of significance is that the increases sanctioned were for yearly rates *with board.* These increases, as compared with the rates drawn up ten years previously, ranged from twenty to sixty-seven per cent, the mean increase being thirty-six per cent.[29] As these changes in rates include board, they cannot well have been necessitated by a rise in the cost of living. There is, moreover, no reason to suppose that any substantial change in the demand for labour took place in these ten years. A change in the supply curve of labour, connected with factors other than the cost of living, would provide a reason; and the only factor likely to lead to such a change in this area at this time is, it would seem, increased mortality due to sickness. Concerted action by workers to raise wages would, quite apart from the legal obstacles involved, be unlikely in a large agricultural area; while migration on the necessary scale would have created problems elsewhere of which we should expect to have heard.

Our information regarding action taken by the North Riding justices is, of course, fuller. Action was first taken on 20 April 1680, when a new wage assessment for the whole of the Riding was drawn up; at the same time chief constables were ordered for the future to keep their statute sessions according to law, to inquire into offences against the Elizabethan labour code, and present them at the next sessions.[30] At the sessions held the following July, further steps were taken. The chief constables of the Western Division of the Riding were ordered to issue out their warrants to the petty constables requiring them to make their returns in writing, at the next statute sessions, of the usual details regarding masters and servants in their parishes (names, wages, and when contracts of service would terminate) as well as the names of masters and servants refusing to furnish the information required.[31] At the next sessions (in October) a similar order, relating to chief constables in the *Eastern* Division of the Riding, was made; and warrants were to be issued out against petty constables in the Western Division who had made imperfect returns, or had failed to make returns.[32] Then, in the following January, we find the first results of all this activity – presentments, evidently arising from the statute sessions of the previous Martinmas. One of these related to an employer receiving a servant who had departed from her former master without permission.[33] The other relevant presentments relate to masters and servants agreeing to wages above the rates assessed the previous Easter. The way in which these presentments are recorded in the minutes, quite apart from their number, is of some interest.[34] Instead of merely stating that the following presentments were concerned with paying and receiving more than the allowed rates, as in previous instances in these minutes, and in similar instances elsewhere, the more elaborate method is adopted of giving one case in detail, and then adding a list giving the status and parish of other masters offending in this way, possibly to add emphasis or make the nature of the offence clearer. Thus we are told that twenty-six masters overpaid their maidservants, and twenty-seven their menservants in husbandry, and in one instance in each class the exact extent of the overpayment is noted.

There was an adjournment to Bedale a few days later, when five further presentments relating to overpayment of servants are recorded.[35] The justices evidently felt, however, that they must not confine their attention solely to raising the assessed rates and preventing these new rates from being exceeded; but that something should also be done to render the shortage itself less acute. When reminding the chief constables of the Western Division of their previous instructions, they therefore took the opportunity of ordering them also to issue out their warrants to the petty constables to make returns of all servants who, though able to work, remained at home, so that such action might be taken by the justices as the law directed.[36] The following Easter there were seven further presentments in which overpayment was the offence; the degree of overpayment, if we are to judge by the 'sample' case given on each occasion, was steadily falling, however, either owing to an improvement in the labour position, or to the increasing success of the justices' policy. At subsequent sessions, indeed, nothing is heard of overpayment, though in July the petty constables of the Western Division are once more exhorted to deliver returns at the next statute sessions of all the names and ages of men and women servants remaining at home and not going to service.[37] By the following year the labour shortage has evidently ceased to be acute, for we find two presentments involving dismissal without legal cause.[38] It may be assumed that, apart altogether from a reduction of deaths, migration of farm labour into the North Riding had taken place, in response to higher wages, from adjacent districts not so seriously affected, and was by this time making itself felt.

At no point, it may be observed, is it expressly stated in the minutes that a labour shortage existed – the announcement that wages have been reassessed is not accompanied by any explanation of this action, and the subsequent orders and presentments we have discussed are also recorded without explanatory comment. This, while explaining why the special significance of the episode has hitherto passed unnoticed does not, however, cast any very serious doubts upon the existence of the labour shortage which is here treated as being a clue to the justices' policy. For the presentments relating to overpayment are more numerous than any recorded in the North Riding or elsewhere for such a short period. Only thirty other cases of overpayment are, as already noticed, recorded in the North Riding minutes for the whole period 1605-1716. And it also happens that the employers concerned in these presentments are drawn, in the main, from two small areas represented in our burial register sample by parishes with abnormally high mortality for the three years 1679-81.

What conclusions regarding the working of wage assessment machinery under abnormal conditions can be drawn from the episode? It is clear that emphasis must, in the first place, be laid on the delays inherent in the whole procedure of assessment and enforcement. It had originally been laid down, as we have seen, that wages were to be rated at Easter Sessions, or at a sessions held within six weeks after Easter. Where this rule was still adhered to, and where statute sessions were held only once a year, it might, therefore, in the absence of additional sessions, be anything from nine months to a year and a half after an emergency had arisen before a new wage policy could be put into operation and the first batch of those defying that policy proceeded against. Some of the delays might have been reduced had it been the practice to require petty constables to bring their bills of masters and servants before the justices, either at Quarter Sessions or 'assemblies', instead of having to wait until Martinmas for this necessary information. No hint is, however, contained in the minutes that, on this occasion, any such attempt to short-circuit normal procedure was made. Had statute sessions been held twice a year, too, greater speed in execution might have been achieved. A second conclusion suggested by the evidence is that delays incidental to the observing of customary seasons for assessment and hiring were, as one would except, amplified by the failure of the officers concerned to carry out their instructions. The chief constables had to be reminded, after the original orders had been issued, to take steps to bring negligent petty constables into line; they themselves, to judge by the wording of the order at Easter Sessions 1680, had been lax in the holding of their statute sessions. The presentments which finally emerged were, as we have seen, highly localised in character, presumably partly because the tendency towards overpayment was stronger in some areas, but probably partly also because of wide variations in the attention paid by different officers to the instructions they received. If adequate records of wage bargains were kept at statute sessions, of course, a partial check on the correctness and completeness of petty constables' bills was provided This would depend for its value, however, upon the extent to which private unrecorded bargains were entered into. As we have seen, there seems to have been fairly general evasion of the master's duty to attend statute sessions in Holland about this time; so that hiring outside the statutes may have been quite common in North Yorkshire. There are obvious *a priori* reasons for supposing that, in the peculiar conditions of the years under review, private bargains would be increasingly resorted to; and the repeated insistence of the justices on the return of bills by the petty constables is, therefore, understandable. Delays of some of these types were, in the third place, made more serious in their effects by the fact that the justices had, in setting their assessment, to make certain assumptions both regarding future supplies and regarding present supplies; the more serious the delays in determining the extent of non-observance, the slower the discovery of errors in these assumptions, and hence in the assessed rates, was bound to be. The volume of North Riding presentments, coupled with the sanctioning of apparently larger increases in the East Riding rature of 1679, suggests that the North Riding justices had underestimated the extent of the labour shortage; but by the time this was made clear, the emergency itself had almost passed. Altogether, therefore, this Yorkshire episode would seem to show that the machinery of wage assessment was not well adapted to meet short-period fluctuations in labour supply. That the justices should have made the attempt is not, however, surprising, since assessment was, after all, an accepted method of combating 'excessive exactions'.

In conclusion, it must be emphasised that to admit that the 'excessive exactions' aspect of wage assessment was in line with the ideas of the town bourgeoisie and of employers of agricultural labour, and that the justices, as members of these classes, applied assessment in this spirit, is *not* necessarily to admit the justice of the strictures of Thorold Rogers and Cox. For, on the one side, the seventeenth-century wage-earner was not (outside industries such as clothmaking where, in some cases, what American scholars call the dependent phase of the wholesale handicraft stage had been reached) normally solely dependent on wages for his livelihood but could, within limits, offer or withdraw his labour as market conditions warranted. While on the other side, the seventeenth-century employer was not, with the same qualifications, normally a capitalist operating on a large scale, but was often not far removed, in social status and yearly income, from the man he employed. In these circumstances the employer, with wage assessment and other sections of the statute as his main weapons, was not altogether unequally matched with the worker, whose ability, in fact if not in law, to withdraw his labour or not offer his services or strike a private bargain, provided a formidable defence. In Tawney's words, 'the object ... of assessing wages was not to benefit a privileged oligarchy of employers at the expense of the vast majority of workers, but to protect one class of workers against another'.[39]

Notes

Chapter VI

1 See above, p 51.

2 James E. Thorold Rogers, *Six centuries of work and wages: the history of English labour* (10th ed T. Fisher Unwin, 1909), p 398.

3 Cox, *Derbyshire annals,* II, 237.

4 *EJ,* IV (1894), 515.

5 Harbin and Dawes, ed *Somerset QS records,* III, 40, 67, 121.

6 Staffordshire sessions books, April 1656.

7 Hindmarsh, 'Assessment of wages', p 49.

8 *HMC Various*, I, 322; Bland, Brown and Tawney, *English economic history,* p 361. The portions in square brackets were crossed out in the original.

9 East Riding Order Books, Easter 1722.

10 *EJ*, X (1900), 406.

11 Lindsey QS minutes, April 1666.

12 Lister, ed *WRS records,* p 333.

13 *HMC Various,* I, 131; Bland Brown and Tawney, *English economic history,* p 360.

14 See above, pp 67-8.

15 *Acts of the Privy Council, 1625-6,* pp 27-8.

16 Le Hardy, ed *Hertford CR,* VI, 405.

17 Le Hardy, ed *Hertford CR,* VI, 406.

18 Holland QS minutes, Easter 1726 (Kirton).

19 Ashby, *Poor law administration,* p 175.

20 See above, p82.

21 Chambers, *Nottinghamshire,* p 271.

22 Harbin and Dawes, ed *Somerset QS records,* IV, 190-1.

23 *EJ*, IV (1894), 514.

24 Hampson, *Poverty in Cambridgeshire,* pp 54-7.

25 Suffolk order books, Easter 1727 (Beccles).

26 Book of Precedents and Indictments, p 89.

27 Charles Creighton, *A history of epidemics in Britain from AD 604 to the extinction of the plague* Cambridge UP, 1891), pp 328-35.

28 *EHR*, LII (1937), 283-9.

29 Due to an unfortunate arithmetical slip, these three percentages were wrongly given in *EHR*, LII (1937), 287; they are the only percentages affected by this slip however.

30 *NRQSR*, VII, 34.

31 *NRQSR*, VII, 38.

32 *NRQSR*, VII, 41.

33 *NRQSR*, VII, 44.

34 *NRQSR*, VII, 45.

35 *NRQSR*, VII, 47.

36 *NRQSR*, VII, 48.

37 *NRQSR,* VII, 51.

38 *NRQSR*, VII, 54, 56.

39 See above, p 65.

VII The decay of the system

It would be possible to produce evidence of a sort to prove either the cessation of wage assessment in the last quarter of the seventeenth century, or its continuation into the second half of the eighteenth. On the one hand, the general impression which an examination of sessions books leaves on one is very definitely that wage assessment was not a 'live issue' in the eighteenth century; for if it was in effective operation, how is the absence of proceedings against those infringing the ratures to be explained? Thus Hewins long ago advanced the view that the period during which the act was effective even to a limited extent practically terminated with the fall of the Stuart monarchy;[1] while, more recently, Heaton gave it as his opinion that, for three quarters of a century before its removal from the statute book, it had been a shadow without substance.[2] On the other hand, in some counties the practice of assessing wages showed remarkable tenacity of life. In the East Riding a new assessment was drawn up in 1722, and there was a reissue as late as 1757.[3] In Warwickshire reissues continued until 1773, the last reassessment of rates having been in 1738.[4] In Devonshire there were actually new scale of wages drawn up in 1732, 1750 and 1778,[5] while reissues of rates for spinners apparently continued until 1790.[6] In Shropshire the reassessment of 1732 (which Cunningham, as we have seen, thought was a revival of the practice to meet special circumstances)[7] was reissued in the three following years;[8] in 1738 the wording is doubtful ('order under 5th of Elizabeth'),[9] followed by a reissue[10] and then no further mention. In Suffolk, after silence on the matter in the records since 1667, a new assessment was, as we have seen, apparently issued in 1724;[11] furthermore, proceedings against those infringing these rates were either taken or contemplated,[12] while the rates themselves were not merely reissued until 1764,[13] but the reprinting and distributing of the scale – which would surely not have been indulged in had reissue been a mere formality – was undertaken at least up to 1748.[14] Middlesex reissues continued until 1725, though Dowdell thinks these were largely a formality,[15] as were, in Heaton's view, the

West Riding reissues up to 1812.[16] There were reassessments of Gloucestershire wages in 1728[17] and 1732,[18] while the episode of 1756-7 could almost equally well be advanced as proof of the vitality of the system,[19] or of its decay. Kent wages were rated afresh in 1724 and possibly also in 1732, and one or other of these scales would appear to have been officially in force as late as 1740.[20] There are also reassessments, dating from the seventeen-twenties or later, for Nottinghamshire, Lancashire, Westmorland, Holland, where a reissue as late as 1746 is recorded in the Quarter Sessions minutes, and Buckinghamshire.[21] Faced with known activity of this character, Tawney was led to remark that the view formerly held – that the wage assessment clauses of the act had become a dead letter by the eighteenth century – was at least not proven.[22]

What are we to make of this somewhat contradictory evidence, of the silence of sessions records in one part of the country accompanied by rating and reissue in another? It is at least clear that there was little uniformity of practice. Even in those districts just reviewed, however, I rather think the vitality of the system in the eighteenth century is disproved by a number of considerations. The first of these is the absence (except in Suffolk) of recorded proceedings against those infringing the assessed rates. By itself this would not, of course, be conclusive, but it is accompanied in the second place by a marked tendency (which was examined at an earlier stage in this study)[23] for eighteenth century assessed and actual rates of wages to diverge from one another. In Middlesex, for instance, though the court in 1694 took notice of widespread disregard of the assessed rates, not a single case of indictment for overpayment or accepting wages higher than those rates was found in the century 1660-1760.[24] In the third place, there is sometimes evidence that essential complementary parts of the wage assessment policy had fallen into disuse. It is hard to believe, for instance, that attendance at statute sessions was still being enforced in Shropshire when the justices in 1732 stressed the daily inconveniences in connection with settlement and other disputes arising from private contracts, and merely recommended that the terms of the agreement be reduced into writing in the presence of witnesses;[25] otherwise they would surely simply have stated the law – that hirings outside statute sessions were, save in exceptional circumstances, void. Or that they were fulfilling their functions adequately in Thetford, where 'none hired' was recorded at the statute sessions held in 1760, 1761, 1763, 1765, and 1766; or in Grimsby, where the number of hirings at statute sessions had notably diminished by the end of the seventeenth and the beginning of the eighteenth centuries. Attendance of petty constables with their 'bills' seems to have varied very much even within the same county – in the East Riding the Millington constables regularly recorded in their accounts their charges for attending the chief constable with the servants' bill in the seventeen-forties and fifties, but no mention of such activity is to be found in the Weeton constables' accounts[26] of the thirties and forties. We have definite knowledge, moreover, that difficulties were being experienced in keeping statute sessions alive in the East Riding in the seventeen-thirties. 'A motion being made by Mr Recorder of York that notice should be ordered to be given to all the inhabitants of this Riding that they conform themselves to the Laws in being in their hiring of servants for the year ensuing, ordered that the Clerk of this Court at the next Session recommend to the Bench to consider of proper means to hinder the Petty Sessions held by the Chief Constables according to Law from being disused'.[27] There is no evidence, however, of any further action having been taken in the matter. Clearly, unless the machinery of statute sessions was in effective operation, the assessment at least of yearly wages could hardly be working altogether satisfactorily since the two, as we have seen, were necessary complements to one another. Insistence on testimonials seems too, to have been less emphasised in the later period in many parts of the country; though this is less significant than the decay of petty sessions. Finally, contemporary opinion can be advanced to support the view that wage assessment had fallen into disuse – both Dowdell and Lipson point out, for instance, that Fielding (who, as a Middlesex magistrate, is a valuable witness) commented on the utter neglect of the rating of wages in the middle of the eighteenth century.[28]

Turning to the reasons for this development, it cannot, I think, be attributed to the removal of the strong hand of the Council. No doubt, as we have seen, the establishment of minimum rates for clothworkers, and the emphasis on the cost-of-living factor in assessment generally, depended to a large extent on central supervision; but there is no reason to suppose that the rating of wages as a means of preventing excessive exactions conflicted in any way with the views of justices. Why, then, should it have been neglected? Three lines of argument would seem to be possible. Of these the easiest to establish is the first, to the effect that legal obstacles were put in the way of assessment. Holdsworth points out how, by legal decisions of the sixteen-eighties and nineties, a restrictive construction was put upon the statutes, which were now held to apply only to workers hired by the year;[29] while a better-known decision some years later limited wage assessment to husbandry,[30] and the passing of legislation applying assessment to particular trades[31] must have seemed to confirm this. It is true that, in spite of this, some of the ratures of the later period cover daily wages outside husbandry, as, for example, those discussed by Mrs Gilboy, but it seems highly improbable that these sections were, or could have been, enforced. Support is, moreover, lent to the view that legal obstacles were deterring the justices from making and enforcing assessments, by some new, but unfortunately incomplete, manuscript evidence. The East Riding justices, as we have seen, revived the practice of assessment in 1722.[32] Two years later[33] the court requested their chairman to apply in their names to the Custos Rotulorum, asking him if possible to procure an act of parliament to enable them the better to execute the powers given them under 5 Elizabeth c 4, 'and that he would also transmit to the Custos Rotulorum a Copy of the Heads of Difficulties in that case touched upon and agreed on at the Sessions held after Michaelmas 1723'. Clearly the justices were experiencing difficulties; there is, however, no further mention of them, and a search for a copy of the 'heads of difficulties' proved fruitless.

In the second place, it may be suggested that the labour situation with which the justices had to deal was undergoing profound modification. Enclosure, and the contraction of the range of by-employments formerly available, were making it more and more difficult to live at one's own hands. Gradually deprived of this possibility as the eighteenth century advanced, wage-earners both agricultural and otherwise found themselves in a weaker bargaining position, and the danger of excessive exactions was materially lessened; though when they tried to raise their wages by combination, the existence of assessed rates which they had conspired to infringe could always be assumed in taking proceedings against them. If this line of argument is adopted, the paradoxical position is reached that, just when wage assessment could, in theory, have been effectively applied to an increasingly large proportion of the occupied population (because of their increasing dependence on wages) it was discarded as unnecessary. Yet, looked at in one way, this situation is not as paradoxical as it appears at first sight. For if the assessment of wages and the complementary parts of the policy were employed to neutralize the advantages which workers who had opportunities of squatting on the waste or living at their own hands in a variety of ways possessed, then their loss of these advantages would naturally render these special provisions obsolete. Or, putting it in a slightly different way, workers who no longer had the same opportunities of what the authorities were pleased to call 'living idly' were led to adopt other forms of resistance, to meet which those in authority had to adopt other means than those provided in the Statute of Artificers. It was not merely that the small class of landless persons was greatly augmented by eighteenth-century developments for, in my view, wage assessment had been devised with that class, amongst others, in mind; but rather that those without land were both larger in numbers and lacked, in large part, even the limited opportunities open to their predecessors. And this, it seems to me, is exactly what happened. Nor does the fact that the legislature applied assessment to certain specified trades in the eighteenth century, capitalistic forms had yet developed far enough to from a national or a local standpoint, be need for special measures in particular occupations, even when the *general* need for such measures was no longer felt.

For economic historians concerned with general rather than special problems, however, it is necessary to bring the decay of wage assessment into line with general economic and social trends. Viewed from this standpoint, it is not difficult to suggest that, as the rise of a class of business leaders and the adequate performance of the entrepreneur function meant the sweeping away of hindrances to freedom of contract, the rating of wages had to go. The language used by the clothiers in the course of the 1756 Gloucestershire dispute was, as Lipson pointed out,[34] significant. And though it is worth remembering that this language was employed when the use of assessment to deprive clothiers of their freedom to scale wages *downwards* was involved, it is clear that the fixing of maxima, too, was a curb on the activities of entrepreneurs who must, if they were to make full use of their talents, be free to offer higher rates then their competitors, for labour as for anything else, when the occasion arose. It seems to me, however, that a generalised argument on these lines is highly dangerous. The question at issue, after all, was the rating of wages in a small range of occupations which, except for the clothing group, did not include trades in which, in the eighteenth century, capitalistic forms had yet developed far enough to make the employers involved feel that their activities were unduly circumscribed by the imposition of maximum wages which could be adjusted from year to year as required. If the legislature, as Lipson has warned us,[35] was not sufficiently conscious of the need for freedom in economic relationships to refrain from applying wage assessment to a variety of trades by different eighteenth-century statutes, it is hardly to be supposed that the justices up and down the country abandoned this procedure as being out of conformity with the necessities of an expanding economy. Had they felt the need for wage assessment and its corollaries, they would not have been deterred from revising it by anything less concrete than legal decisions limiting the scope of their activities. Presumably, therefore, they were either impeded by these legal obstacles or, as suggested above, wages could now be kept at the required level without the aid of the machinery of assessment.

There remains, it is true, the awkward problem as to what lay behind these legal decisions. One eminent authority has recently said that the courts 'having regard to the prevailing economic conditions and the current of economic opinion, construed the Statutes [relating to wage assessment] restrictively'.[36] To subscribe to this proposition would seem, however, to involve giving an affirmative answer to at least three questions. Did prevailing economic conditions at the time of the decisions demand as restrictive an interpretation as the courts gave? Was the current of economic opinion at that time so definitely set towards complete freedom in economic relationships? Were the courts more likely to be influenced by such factors than the local magistrates or the central legislature? Each of these questions would have to be examined separately in the light of the available evidence, it seems to me, before the proposition could be regarded as finally established. Moreover, any explanation of the cases under consideration which did not, with suitable adaptation, explain also the 1598 decision (whereby, despite 5 Elizabeth c4, a remedy was provided for workers in husbandry whose masters detained their wages) *and* the nineteenth and early twentieth-century animus of the courts against trade unions, would be unsatisfactory. It might be possible to show that all these decisions were in line with the economic interests of those charged with the administration and interpretation of the law in the different periods involved. Here, as in so many other instances, the need for co-operation between research workers in legal and economic history is self-evident.

Notes

Chapter VII

1 *EJ,* VIII (1898), 345.
2 *EJ,* XXIV (1914), 232.
3 East Riding Sessions books, June 1722, April 1757.
4 Ashby, *Poor law administration,* pp 175, 176.
5 Gilboy, *Wages,* p 88.
6 Hoskins, *Industry and trade,* p 130.
7 *EJ,* IV (1894), 514.
8 Kenyon, ed *Salop CR,* II, 82, 85, 87.
9 Kenyon, ed *Salop CR,* II, 95.
10 Kenyon, ed *Salop CR,* II, 98.
11 Suffolk order books, Easter 1727 (Beccles).
12 Books of Precedents and Indictments, p 89.
13 Suffolk order books, April 1764.
14 Suffolk order books, April 1748 (Ipswich).
15 Dowdell, *QS,* p 150.
16 *EJ,* XXIV (1914), 232.
17 Lipson, *Economic history,* III, 266.
18 Rogers, *History,* VII, 623.
19 *EHR,* XLIII (1928), 402.
20 *EHR,* XLIII (1928), 400-1.
21 See Appendix A, pp 206-35.
22 See above, p 61.
23 See above, pp 115-19.
24 Dowdell, *QS,* p 150.
25 *EJ,* IV (1894), 517.

26 Welwick byelawmen's and miscellaneous accounts books.

27 East Riding order book, November 1731.

28 Dowdell, *QS,* p 151; Lipson, *Economic history,* III, 264.

29 Holdsworth, *English law,* XI, 467.

30 Lipson, *Economic history,* III, 263-4.

31 Holdsworth, *English law,* XI, 467.

32 East Riding order books, April and June 1722.

33 East Riding order books, October 1724.

34 Lipson, *Economic history,* III, 268-9.

35 Lipson, *Economic history,* III, 270.

36 Holdsworth, *English law,* XI, 467.

CENTURY OF WAGE ASSESSMENT IN HEREFORDSHIRE 1666-1762

R. KEITH KELSALL
(1942)

Introductory

So thoroughly have the records of most counties and boroughs been searched with this object in view, that the finding of even one new wage assessment is by now a comparatively rare event. It was therefore surprising recently to find, in the Herefordshire Sessions records, practically a complete set of such assessments for the period 1666 to 1762.[1] The practice of the clerks concerned was the rather unusual one of entering the agreed wage schedules in full in the minute books. As a result Hereford, which has up till now been represented in comparative studies of wage regulation under the Statute of Artificers by only one assessment, that of 1632,[2] is now better represented than most counties.

During the period covered the assessed wages were altered in some respect on twenty occasions, the old rates were re-issued without alteration fifty-nine times, and for only eighteen years out of the ninety-seven have we no information at all. It seemed best to present this material in tabular form, with the inclusion, for purposes of comparison, of some of the rates given in the 1632 schedule.

What light does this new material shed on the main questions at issue regarding the use by the justices of the powers given to them under the Statute of Artificers, 1563? There would appear to be several problems to the elucidation of which the Hereford evidence can contribute something.

Firstly, was the cost of living a major consideration in determining the changes that were made? Even without reference to particular grain price series, it is clear that this was not so. The comparative stability of the assessed rates 'without diet' up to 1732, and of assessed rates of all types thereafter, must be taken as meaning that, in this area and at this period, the justices were not endeavouring conscientiously to apply the Elizabethan instruction that one of the considerations affecting their rating of wages should be the plenty or scarcity of the time. They were obviously more concerned with the scarcity of labour aspect of wage regulation including, as the yearly rates in the table show, both the short-term variations in the relative scarcities of different types of farm labour, and the longer-period general tendency for the demand for agricultural labour as a whole to outrun supply. Such a conclusion fits in well with what we know of the seventeenth-century practice of the Somerset justices, one of the other main sources of information on this question.[3] It may even be that only in the early years of the statute's operation was the cost-of-living aspect of wage assessment given the intended weight, though such a suggestion can still not be completely substantiated, owing to the relative paucity of connected series of assessments as well as prices. Yet it does seem significant that the only clear case of *continuous* alteration in the assessed rates to meet increases in prices is to be found in Chester in the latter part of the sixteenth century.[4]

Secondly, the change in the form of the Hereford assessment in 1732 lends support to the view that assessments tended as a rule to become more, rather than less, detailed. This was already known to be true in several other cases, from a comparison of Kent assessments for 1563 and 1724, of Hull ratings for 1570 and 1721, of Holland schedules for 1563 and 1680, and of Hertfordshire scales for 1631 and 1678 or 1687. The precise reasons for the change in form are, as in the other instances mentioned, difficult to determine. It will, however, be noticed that in the present instance the change allows of a greater degree of differentiation as between workers of different ages, of varying degrees of responsibility, and of different sex: whilst at the same time less differentiation is provided for in respect of seasons of the year.

The change in form is important in at least one further respect, as having a bearing on a *third* problem, namely, whether or not the effective regulation of wages by the justices died a natural death at least a century before its final repeal by the legislature. For, clearly, if the Hereford magistrates thought it worth while completely to alter the form in which assessments for that county had for a very long time previously been drawn – the change in 1684 was a relatively minor one – they must have thought that their activities had some bearing on the current labour situation, or there would have been no point in going to this trouble. To that extent the new Hereford evidence suggests that the older view (held, for instance, by Hewins) regarding the early decay of the practice of assessment was true, at most, of certain limited areas, and did not apply generally. We already know that new assessments were drawn up for at least twelve other counties in the seventeen-twenties or later.[5] As against this, however, it has to be admitted that, once the new Hereford form had been devised, little use seems to have been made of the types of differentiation which it made possible. A glance at the accompanying table is sufficient to show that, in the period 1732 to 1763, remarkably few changes of any kind are recorded in the rates by comparison with the changes before 1732. Moreover, it is highly probable that after 1763, when the schedule of wages is replaced in the sessions minutes by the phrase 'carriers and servants wages ordered as usual', reissue became a mere matter of form, though by that time there is general agreement that decay had set in in most areas. Contradictory though the Herefordshire evidence may appear to be on this particular question, it at least does not run counter to a suggestion made above that two factors – the lessening need for the weapon of wage assessment, and legal impediments to its employment – were primarily responsible for the justices' failure in the eighteenth century to make the same use as formerly of their powers in this respect.[6]

On other matters of interest these new schedules give little help. Of themselves, for example, they tell us nothing regarding the relation between the assessed rates and market rates of wages, nor do the sessions records contain examples of proceedings against those infringing the provisions of the statute in regard to wages. And as it seems probable that the inmobility of the eighteenth-century daily rates of pay is connected with assessment issues rather than reflecting market conditions, no support is lent by this Hereford material to the theory advanced by an American scholar that wages in the west of England, as distinct from those in the north and in the metropolitan area, showed abnormal stability in the eighteenth century.[7]

CHANGES IN HEREFORDSHIRE ASSESSED RATES (£ s d)

	1632	1666	1667	1668-1670	1671-1673	1674-1677, 1681-1682	1684, 1687, 1690, 1694-1700	1702	1703-1706	1707	1708-1710	1711	1712-1719	1720-1722	1723	1724-1728	1730-
Every bailiff in husbandry, per annum and with diet	2-13-4	3- 0-0	3- 0-0	3- 0-0	3- 0-0	3- 0-0	3-10-0	3-10-0	3-10-0	3-10-0	3-10-0	3-10-0	3-10-0	4-10-0	3-10-0	4- 0-0	4-10-0
Common servants, per annum and with diet	2- 0-0	2- 0-0	2- 0-0	2- 0-0	2- 0-0	2- 0-0	2-10-0	2-10-0	2-10-0	2-10-0	2-10-0	2-10-0	2-10-0	3-10-0	2-10-0	3- 0-0	3- 0-0
Driving boys, per annum and with diet		1- 5-0	1- 5-0	1- 5-0	1-10-0	1- 5-0	1- 5-0	1- 5-0	1- 5-0	1- 5-0	1- 5-0	1- 5-0	1- 5-0	1- 5-0	1- 5-0	1-10-0	1-10-0
Servant maids, per annum and with diet	1- 0-0	1-10-0	1-10-0	1-10-0	1-10-0	1-10-0	1-10-0	1-10-0	1-10-0	1-10-0	1-10-0	1-10-0	1-10-0	1-10-0	1-10-0	1-15-0	2- 0-0
Carpenters, masons, plasterers, and other artificers, and also mowers and reapers, in harvest time at their own diet per diem	1-0	1-0	2-0	1-0	1-0	1-0	1-0	1-0	1-0	1-0	1-0	1-0	1-0	1-0	1-0	1-0	1-0
do and with diet	6	6	6	6	6	6	6	6	6	6	6	6	6	6	6	6	
Labourers to artificers and in husbandry, at their own diet per diem	8	7	8	7	7	7											
do and with diet	4	3	3	3	3	3											
Every day labourer, from Lady Day to Michaelmas, per diem without diet							8	8	8	8	8	8	8	8	8	8	8
do with diet							3	3	3	3	3	3	3	3	3	3	3
do from Michaelmas to All Saints, per diem without diet							7	8	7	7	7	7	7	7	7	7	7
do with diet							3	3	3	3	3	3	3	3	3	3	3
do from All Saints to Candlemas, per diem without diet	6						6	6	6	6	6	6	6	6	6	6	6
do with diet	3						3	3	3	3	3	3	3	3	3	3	3
do from Candlemas to Lady Day, per diem without diet	8						7	7	7	6	7	6	7	7	7	7	7
do with diet	4						3	3	3	3	3	3	3	3	3	3	3

CHANGES IN HEREFORDSHIRE ASSESSED RATES (£ s d)

	1732	1733	1734	1735-1737	1738, 1741-1751, 1753-1762
Every head servant, waggoner or bailiff in husbandry	4-10-0	4-10-0	4-10-0	4-10-0	4-10-0
Every second servant in husbandry	3-10-0	3-10-0	3-10-0	3-10-0	3-10-0
Every servant boy from 11 to 14 years of age	1- 0-0	1- 0-0	1- 0-0	1- 0-0	1- 0-0
Every servant boy from 14 to 18 years of age	1-10-0	1-10-0	1-10-0	1-10-0	1-10-0
Every head servant maid in dairy or cookery	2-10-0	2-10-0	2-10-0	2-10-0	2-10-0
Every second servant maid	2- 0-0	2- 0-0	2- 0-0	2- 0-0	2- 0-0
Labourers from Michaelmas to Lady Day	8	8	8	8	8
Labourers from Lady Day to harvest and after harvest to Michaelmas	9	8	8	8	8
Labourers with diet by the day	4	4	4	4	4
Every mower and reaper in hay and corn harvest, with drink	1-0	1-0	1-0	1-0	1-0
do without drink	1-2	1-2	1-2	1-2	1-2
Weeders of corn, with drink	4	5	4	4	4
do without drink	5	6	5	5	5
Every woman in corn harvest, with drink	5	5	5	5	5
do without drink	6	6	6	6	6
Every woman in haymaking, setting beans, or picking fruit, with drink	5	4	4	5	4
do without drink	6	5	5	6	5
Every carpenter, wheelwright, plasterer, mason, thatcher, winter and summer, with drink	1-0	1-0	1-0	1-0	1-0
do without drink	1-2	1-2	1-2	1-2	1-2

1 The work of finding this and other material was greatly helped by a Leverhulme Research Grant towards the expenses entailed in a larger project of which this forms a part.

2 *HMC Portland*, III, 31.

3 See above, pp 159-76.

4 Rupert H. Morris, *Chester in the Plantagenet and Tudor reigns* (Chester, 1893), pp367-8.

5 See above, pp 190-1.

6 See above, pp 192-5.

7 Elizabeth W. Gilboy, *Wages in eighteenth century England* (Cambridge, Mass, Harvard UP, 1934).

Appendix A
List of wage assessments

This list of wage assessments made under the Statute of Artificers (5 Elizabeth c 4) is compiled from the list which appeared in Professor Kelsall's book when it was first published (corrected where necessary),[1] the London assessments which he excluded,[2] assessments which have come to light since Professor Kelsall's book was published, together with a note of all known reissues. The conventions which applied to Professor Kelsall's list when it was originally published have largely been retained.[3]

1 Assessments and reassessments are indicated by the place name in capitals, eg LINCOLN. Reissues without alteration have, as far as possible, been excluded from this category, though some probably still remain.

2 Assessments in square brackets, eg [ESSEX], were mentioned in Dr Hindmarsh's thesis and are based on evidence which Professor Kelsall did not see. As the definition of a reissue differed, an unknown proportion of these may in fact be reissues.

3 Assessments printed with the place name in italic capitals, eg *NORWICH,* are taken from the lists in Ephraim Lipson, *Economic history of England, III: the age of mercantilism* (Black, 1931), pp 256-7, 260, 262-3. Professor Kelsall was in some doubt whether these assessments were reassessments or reissues.

A reasonably complete and accurate copy of the rates is shown by the word 'full' and a shortened version by the word 'partial'. Where no printed version is known to exist, an owner or custodian is given, if the actual assessment is known to have been in existence within the past century or so.[4] Some assessments are included in categories 1-3 of which no copy now survives ('evidence only'), but only where there is reason to believe that reassessment, and not merely reissue, was involved.

4 To Professor Kelsall's list which comprises categories 1-3 has been added a note of all assessments which have subsequently been discovered and all reissues. These are indicated by italic entries thus: *Exeter.* In this category also some are included of which there is 'evidence only'.

Every effort has been made to indicate where a printed version of each assessment may be found and the following abbreviations have been used:

CR	County records
CRO	County Record Office
EJ	*Economic Journal*
EHR	*English Historical Review*
Hindmarsh	Nora Hindmarsh, 'The assessment of wages by the justices of the peace', PhD thesis, University of London, 1932
H & L	Paul L. Hughes and James F. Larkin, ed *Tudor royal proclamations* (New Haven, Conn: Yale UP, 1969)
HMC	*Historical Manuscripts Commission*
NRQSR	John C. Atkinson, ed *North Riding Quarter Sessions records, 1605-1786* (North Riding Record Society, old series, I-IX, 1884-1892)
QS	Quarter Sessions
RO	Record Office
SPD	*State Papers Domestic*
Steele	Robert R. Steele, ed *Tudor and Stuart proclamations, 1485-1714* (Oxford, 1910)
VCH	*Victoria County History*

1563 [COVENTRY] Rates in Hindmarsh, p 164

EXETER Exeter City RO (preamble only): H & L, II, 218; *HMC Exeter,* p 50

KENT *Archaeologia Cantiana,* XXII (1897), 316-19 (full); *EHR,* XLI (1926), 270-3 (full); H & L, II, 215-18 (full).[5] Reissued until 1589

LINCOLN (city) H & L, II, 225-7 (full); *VCH Lincs,* II, 330 (full); James W.F. Hill, *Tudor and Stuart Lincoln* (Cambridge UP, 1956), pp 220-1 (full)

LINCOLNSHIRE Copy of proclamation at Queen's College, Oxford (Sel B 230, 77-9); H & L, II, 221-3 (full); *HMC Lincoln (Fourteenth report, Appendix VIII),* pp 55-6

London H & L, II, 233-5 (full)

New Windsor H & L, II, 219-20 (full)

RUTLAND James E. Thorold Rogers, *A History of agriculture and prices in England* (Oxford: Clarendon P, 1882-1902), IV, 120-3 (full); H & L, II, 210-14, (full). The assessment that William Cunningham, *The growth of English industry and commerce* (Cambridge UP, 1882, 1907), p 894, dated 1564 is apparently this one wrongly dated – he gives a Bodleian reference (Arch F c 11) and this is the only Rutland assessment of the period in their possession (Arch G c 6 (86-7))

SOUTHAMPTON (town and county) Copy of proclamation (preamble only) in Bodleian Library (Arch G c 6 (88b)). Cunningham, *Growth of English industry* p 895 gives 1564 as date and a different Bodleian reference; they only have this one however. Steele, I, no 576; H & L, II, 228

Winchester Tom Atkinson, *Elizabethan Winchester* (Faber & Faber, 1963), pp 201-2

York Angelo Raine, *York civic records* (Yorkshire Archaeological Society, Record series, XCVIII–, 1939-), VI, 56-60; H & L, II, 223-4 (full)

1564 EXETER *HMC Exeter,* pp 50-1 (full); H & L, II, 251

London H & L, II, 256 (reissue)

Southampton (incomplete) Hindmarsh, p xix

1564-97 *Leicester* Leicester Museum and Art Gallery (evidence only)

1564- *Coventry* Hindmarsh, p xix (evidence only)

1565 *London* H & L, II, 265 (reissue)

New Romney and Lydd H & L, II, 265-70 (full)

1566 *Exeter* *HMC Exeter,* pp 50-1; H & L, II, 283-5 (full) (reissue)

London H & L, II, 283 (reissue)

Northamptonshire H & L, II, 285-7 (full)

1567 *Exeter* Printed notice, Exeter City RO

1568 *London* H & L, II, 294 (reissue)

1569-81 *Bath* Hindmarsh, p xix (evidence only)

1570 CHESTER Rupert H. Morris, *Chester in the Plantagenet and Tudor reigns* (Chester, 1893), pp 367-8 (partial); H & L, II, 339

HULL Copy of proclamation in British Museum copy of Humphrey Dyson, *A booke containing all such proclamations as were published during the raigne of the late Queen Elizabeth* (London, 1618), f 77; Steele, I, no 654; H & L, II, 337-9 (full)

London H & L, II, 335 (reissue)

1571 *Chester* British Museum Harleian Mss 2054 (9); Hindmarsh, pp xix, xxv

1573 *London* H & L, II, 372-4 (full)

1575 *Chester* *Cheshire Sheaf,* 3rd series, LVIII (1963), 21, 22; H & L, II, 392-3

1576 CANTERBURY Steele, I, no 703; H & L, II, 405-7 (full)

Chester Morris, *Chester,* p 409; H & L, II, 409 (full)

London H & L, II, 401-3 (full)

1577 *Doncaster* W.J. Hardy, *Calendar to the records of the borough of Doncaster* (Doncaster, 1899-1903), III, 210; H & L, II, 419

1578 [CAMBRIDGESHIRE] Mentioned in Hindmarsh, p xxvii

London H & L, II, 422-5 (full)

Rochester Hindmarsh, p xix (evidence only)

1580 [HERTFORDSHIRE] Mentioned in Hindmarsh, p 57

London H & L, II, 471-3 (full)

1581 *Hertfordshire* Hindmarsh, p 57

1583 *Colchester* H & L, II, 499-501 (full)

London H & L, II, 502 (reissue)

1584 *London* H & L, II, 503-5 (full)

1585 *London* H & L, II, 512-14 (full)

1586 *London* H & L, II, 522-4 (full); Richard H. Tawney and Eileen Power, *Tudor economic documents* (Longmans, Green, 1924), I, 363

Warwick Hindmarsh, p xix

1587 *London* H & L, II, 536-9 (full)

St Albans Arthur E. Gibbs, *The Corporation records of St Albans* (St Albans, 1890), p 17 (reissue)

1588 *Exeter* *HMC Exeter,* pp 50-1; H & L, III, 1819 (full) (reissue)

London H & L, III, 22-5 (full)

St Albans Gibbs, *Corporation records of St Albans,* p 25 (reissue)

1589 *Hertfordshire* *Guide to the Hertfordshire Record Office, part I* (Hertford, 1961), pp 15-19

Kent H & L, III, 36-8 (full)

London H & L, III, 40-2 (full)

1590 *Hertfordshire* Hertfordshire CRO

London Hindmarsh, p 166; H & L, III, 59 (reissue)

1591 *Hertfordshire* H& L, III, 74-7 (full); *VCH Herts,* IV, 227

1592 HERTFORDSHIRE William J. Hardy, ed *Hertford County records* (Hertford, 1905), I, 8-12 (full). Reissued 1593-6, Hertfordshire CRO

Liverpool James A. Picton, *Selections from the municipal archives and records from the 13th to the 17th century inclusive* (Liverpool, 1883-6), I, 114; J.A. Twemlow, *Liverpool town books: proceedings of assemblies, common councils, portmoot courts &c, 1550-1862* (Liverpool UP, 1918-35), II, 637

1593 CHESTER Both Rogers, *History,* VI, 685-6 (incorrectly headed 1591) and Frederick M. Eden, *The state of the poor or an history of the labouring classes in England from the conquest to the present period* (London, 1797), III, xciii, print this assessment but in each case there are serious errors and omissions. Morris, *Chester,* pp 367-8 (full) and H & L, III, 117-18 (full) are more reliable

Essex Hindmarsh, p 51

Hertfordshire Hindmarsh, p 61

Liverpool Twemlow, *Liverpool town books,* II, 656 (reissues)

Sussex Hindmarsh, p 66

YORKSHIRE EAST RIDING Rogers, *History,* VI, 686-9 (full); H & L, III, 122-5 (full). One or two minor discrepancies between these and Steele, I, 96 (partial); Eden, *State of the poor,* III, xc-xcii

1594 CANTERBURY Steele, I, no 868 (partial); H & L, III, 138-41 (full); Civis (William Welfitt), *Minutes collected from the ancient records and accounts in the Chamber of Canterbury of transactions in that city* (Canterbury, 1800-1)

Cardiganshire Hindmarsh, p 59

Chester Rogers, *History,* VI, 685; Hindmarsh, between pp 164-5

DEVONSHIRE Alexander H.A. Hamilton, *Quarter sessions from Queen Elizabeth to Queen Anne* (Sampson Low, 1878), pp 12-13 (full); H & L, III, 136; Hindmarsh, pp 59, 61

Hertfordshire Hindmarsh, p 59

Lancashire Hindmarsh, p 59

Liverpool Picton, *Municipal archives,* I, 114; Twemlow, *Liverpool town books,* II, 678 (reissue)

Yorkshire East Riding Hindmarsh, p 59

1594-1639 *Essex* Sidney and Beatrice Webb, *English local government: the parish and the county* (Longmans, 1924), p 455, note 2 (evidence only); Hindmarsh, pp 49, 61-3, xiv; *HMC County of Essex (Tenth report, Appendix IV),* p 491

1595 CARDIGANSHIRE Steele, I, no. 875 (full); Dyson, *Proclamations,* f 331b (full)

Devonshire H & L, III, 150-1 (full)

Exeter H & L, III, 143-5 (full)

HIGHAM FERRERS (Northants) Copy of proclamation in Society of Antiquaries Library, London (Collection of Broadsides, Ely, no 102); Steele, I, no 877; H & L, III, 145-7 (full)

LANCASHIRE Steele, I, no 876 (partial); Rogers, *History,* VI, 689-91 (full); H & L, III, 149-50 (full)

NEW SARUM (Salisbury) Copy of proclamation in Queen's College, Oxford (Sel b 20, f 331b); Steele, I, no 878 (partial); H & L, III, 147-8 (full)

1596 *Barnstaple* Hindmarsh, p xix

CHESTER Eden, *State of the poor,* III, xciv-xcv (full); Rogers, *History,* VI, 685-6 (incorrectly headed 1594 and with errors and omissions); Morris, *Chester,* pp 367-8 (full); H & L, III, 158-9 (full)

1597 CHESTER Morris, *Chester,* pp 367-8 (full); H & L, III, 173-4 (full); Eden, *State of the poor,* III, xciv

Hertfordshire Hertfordshire CRO. Reissued 1599

1598 *Chester* Hindmarsh, between pp 164-5

1600 *Hertfordshire* Hertfordshire CRO. Reissued 1601-3

1601 *Merionethshire* Walter Davies, *General view of the agriculture and domestic economy of north Wales* (London 1813), pp 500-1

1602 WILTSHIRE *HMC Various,* I, 162-7 (full). Proposed by weavers and clothiers and confirmed by justices

1603 WILTSHIRE *HMC Various,* I, 162-7 (full); A.E. Bland, P.A. Brown and R.H. Tawney, *English economic history: select documents* (Bell, 1914), pp 345-50, wrongly headed 1604

Yorkshire West Riding Hindmarsh, p xiv

1604 *Hertfordshire* Hardy, ed *Hertford CR,* I, 35; Hindmarsh, pp xiv, xxviii

Somerset Somerset CRO

1605 *Wiltshire* *HMC Various,* I, 167-9. 'The annual orders (in which the years 1621, 1627-32, 1642-3 and 1645-6 are wanting) appear to continue the same rates unaltered up to the year 1654, except that in 1635 there are alterations in the husbandry wages, on the recommendation of the Grand Jury' (p 161)

York York Corporation House Book in City Library, York

1606 *Somerset* Somerset CRO

Staffordshire Sambrooke A.H. Burne, ed *The Staffordshire Quarter Sessions Rolls,* V (Kendal: Staffordshire Record Society, 1940), pp 324-6

Sussex Hindmarsh, p 64

1607 *Hertfordshire* Hertfordshire CRO

[STAFFORDSHIRE] Rates given in Hindmarsh, pp 61-3

	York York Corporation House Book in City Library, York
1608	*Middlesex* Greater London RO (Middlesex Records) (MJ/SBR/1/p13) (reissue). Eric G. Dowdell, *A hundred years of Quarter Sessions: the government of Middlesex from 1660 to 1760* (Cambridge UP, 1932), p 149 incorrectly gives this date as 1610. A similar order is entered into the sessions registers or books for almost every Easter Sessions from 1608 to 1725
	Sussex Hindmarsh, p 64
1609	*York* York Corporation House Book in City Library, York
1610[6]	*Norfolk* *EHR,* XIII (1898), 522-7; Hindmarsh, pp 62-3
	OAKHAM (Rutland) Rogers, *History,* VI, 691-3 (full); Eden, *State of the poor,* III, xcv-xcvii; Hindmarsh, p 63; *Archaeologia,* XI (1794) 200-7
	York York Corporation House Book in City Library, York
1611-13	*Somerset* Somerset CRO
1613	*Norfolk* Norfolk and Norwich RO
1615	*Sussex* Hindmarsh, p 64
1616	*Hertfordshire* Hertfordshire CRO
1617	*Hertfordshire* Hertfordshire CRO
	Sussex Hindmarsh, pp 45, 64
	Tenterden (Kent) Hindmarsh, p xix. Reissued most years (45) until 1667
1617-18	*Somerset* Somerset CRO
1618	*Derbyshire* Hindmarsh, p xiv
	Hertfordshire Hertfordshire CRO
1619	*Derbyshire* 'a bundle of servants rates in existence', Hindmarsh, p 47

KESTEVEN In possession of Duke of Rutland at Belvoir Castle in 1888 according to *HMC Rutland,* I, 455. Rates given in Hindmarsh, p 64

1620 *Manchester* Hindmarsh, p xix

Somerset Somerset CRO

[STAFFORDSHIRE] Mentioned in Hindmarsh, p 47

1621 FAVERSHAM *Archaeologia Cantiana,* XVI (1886), 270 (full)

KESTEVEN *HMC Rutland,* I, 460-2 (full)

[STAFFORDSHIRE] Mentioned in Hindmarsh, pp 50, xiv. Reissued until 1640.

1623 *Somerset* Somerset CRO

Wiltshire Hindmarsh, p xiv

1625 *Sussex* Hindmarsh, p 64

1625-6 *Somerset* Somerset CRO

1625-8 *Hampshire* Hindmarsh, p 51

1625-8 *Hertfordshire* Hindmarsh, p xiv (reissue)

1627 *Sussex* Hindmarsh, pp 64, 68

1628 *Shrewsbury* *Transactions of the Salop Archaeological Society,* LVII (1956), 136-42

Sussex Hindmarsh, pp 64, 66, 68

1629 *Northamptonshire* Northamptonshire CRO (Isham (Lamport) papers)

Somerset Somerset CRO

Wiltshire Benjamin H. Cunnington, ed *Records of the county of Wilts being extracts from the Quarter Sessions great rolls of the seventeenth century* (Devizes: G. Simpson, 1932), p 93 (reissue)

1630 NORWICH Evidence only (improbable, see text); *SPD 1629-1631,* p 396. Reissued 1631-3 (see p 106)

SUFFOLK (Bury division only?) *EHR,* XII (1897), 307-11 (full)

Wiltshire Cunnington, ed *Wilts CR,* pp 94 (reissue)

1631 *Arundel, (Sussex)* Hindmarsh, p vi (evidence only)

HERTFORDSHIRE (one division?) *HMC Hertford (Fourteenth report, Appendix VIII),* p 160. Previously given as for Hertford but is probably for one division of Hertfordshire

Somerset Somerset CRO; Hindmarsh, pp 47, xiv

ST ALBANS Robert Clutterbuck, *The history and antiquities of the county of Hertford,* I (London, 1815), pp xxii-xxiv (full). Lipson, *Economic history,* III, 257, following *VCH Herts,* IV, 227-8; Gibbs, ed *Corporation records of St Albans,* pp 280-2 (where an unreliable summary is given) wrongly dates this assessment 1632

Surrey Hindmarsh, p vi (evidence only)

1631-3 *Norwich* see above p 106 (reissues)

1631-46 *Ipswich* see above, p 106 (reissues)

1632 *Dorset* Hindmarsh, pp 51, xiv (reissue)

GLOUCESTERSHIRE Rogers, *History,* VI, 694 (full)

HEREFORDSHIRE *HMC Portland,* III, 31 (full)

Shrewsbury *Transactions of the Salop Archaeological Society,* LVII (1956), 136-42

St Albans Hindmarsh, p xiv

1633 DORSET George Roberts, *The social history of the people of the southern counties of England in past centuries* (Longmans, 1856), pp 207-10 (full); *Sussex Archaeological Collections,* I (1848), 75 note

1634 DERBYSHIRE *VCH Derbyshire,* II, 183 (partial); John C. Cox, *Three centuries of Derbyshire annals* (London and Derby, 1890), II, 239-40

[DORSET] Rates given in Hindmarsh, pp 66-8

	NORWICH Norwich Sessions Records (Norfolk and Norwich RO) (evidence only). Reissued 1635, 1637-9
1635	*Dorset* Hindmarsh, pp 51, xvi (reissue)
	Somerset Somerset CRO
	WILTSHIRE *HMC Various,* I, 169 (full)
1636	[NOTTINGHAMSHIRE] Mentioned in Hindmarsh, p 47
	Sussex Hindmarsh, pp 66, 68
1637	*Dorset* Hindmarsh, p 51. Reissued 1638-9 (Hindmarsh, pp 51, xiv)
	Sussex Hindmarsh, p 68
1638	*Somerset* Somerset CRO
	Sussex Hindmarsh, p 68
1639	*Shrewsbury* *Transactions of the Salop Archaeological Society,* LVII (1956) 136-42
	Sussex Hindmarsh, p 68
1639-41	*Middlesex* Hindmarsh, p 51
1640	NORWICH Norwich Sessions Records (Norfolk and Norwich RO) (evidence only). Reissued 1641-7
	Shrewsbury *Transactions of the Salop Archaeological Society,* LVII (1956), 136-42
	Somerset Somerset CRO
	Sussex Hindmarsh, p 68
1641	STAFFORDSHIRE Staffordshire Sessions books, Easter 1641 (evidence only); Hindmarsh, p 50
	Yorkshire West Riding Hindmarsh, pp 223, xv; *EJ,* XXIV (1914), 220
1641-1700	*Sussex* Hindmarsh, pp xvi, xxx
1642	PORTSMOUTH Robert East, ed *Portsmouth records: extracts from records in the possession of the municipal corporation of the borough of Portsmouth* (Portsmouth, 1891), pp 161-2 (rates not given)

1643 *Norfolk* see above, p 106; also Hindmarsh, p xvi (reissue)

Staffordshire Hindmarsh, p xvi (reissue)

1643-4 *Middlesex* Hindmarsh, p xvi (reissues)

1645 *Essex* Hindmarsh, p xv

1646 *Somerset* Hindmarsh, pp 227, xxx

1646-7 *Middlesex* Hindmarsh, p xvi (reissues)

1647 SOMERSET Edward H.B. Harbin and M.C.B. Dawes, ed *Somerset Quarter Sessions records* (Somerset Record Society, XXIII, XXIV, XXVIII, XXXIV, 1907-19), III, 40 (full)

YORKSHIRE WEST RIDING *EJ,* XXIV (1914) 221-4 (full)

1647-8 *Staffordshire* Hindmarsh, p xvi (reissues)

1648 DERBYSHIRE *VCH Derbyshire,* II, 183 (partial); Cox, *Derbyshire annals,* II, 240-2 (full)

NOTTINGHAMSHIRE Norman Penney, ed *Journal of George Fox ... eighth (bi-centenary) edition ... with revised and enlarged indexes* (Friends' Tract Association, 1901), I, 65-6 (evidence only)

SOMERSET Harbin and Dawes, ed *Somerset QS records,* III, 66-7 (full)

1648 or 1649 STAFFORDSHIRE Staffordshire Sessions books, Easter 1648 (or 1649); Harbin and Dawes, ed *Somerset QS Records*, III, 67, (evidence only)

1648-9 Ipswich see above p 106 (reissues)

1648-61 *Yorkshire West Riding* Hindmarsh, p xvi (reissues)

1649 *Norfolk* Hindmarsh, p xvi (reissue)

1650 NORWICH Norwich Sessions records (evidence only)

Somerset Harbin and Dawes, ed *Somerset QS records,* III, 121

1650-2 *Middlesex* Hindmarsh, p xvi (reissues)

1650-1 *Suffolk* see above p 106 (reissues)

1650-4 *Norfolk* see above p 106; Hindmarsh, p xvi (reissues)

1651 ESSEX Rogers, *History,* VI, 694-7 (full); Eden, *State of the poor,* III, xcviii-ci (full); *Essex Review,* XLIII (1934) 10-11 (partial) – minor discrepancies in rates between these three –; *The particular rates of wages* (British Museum, 816 m 15 44)

SOMERSET Harbin and Dawes, ed *Somerset QS records,* III, 150-1 (full)

Suffolk Hindmarsh, p xvi (reissue)

1652 SOMERSET Harbin and Dawes, ed *Somerset QS records,* III, 176-7 (full)

Yorkshire North Riding Hindmarsh, p xv

1652-3 *Ipswich* see above p 106 (reissues)

1652-4 *Shropshire* Hindmarsh, p xvi (reissues)

1652-6 *Norwich* see above p 106; also Hindmarsh, p xx (reissues)

1653 SOMERSET Harbin and Dawes, ed *Somerset QS records,* III, 211 (full)

1653-5 *Suffolk* Hindmarsh, p xvi (reissues)

1654 DEVON Hamilton, *QS,* pp 163-5 (full)

SOMERSET Harbin and Dawes, ed *Somerset QS records,* III, 236 (full)

1654-6 *Middlesex* Hindmarsh, p xvi (reissues)

1655 GLOUCESTERSHIRE Rogers, *History,* VI, 694 (full)

London *EHR,* XV (1900), 455

SOMERSET Harbin and Dawes, ed *Somerset QS records,* III, 263 (full)

WILTSHIRE *HMC Various,* I, 169-73 (full); some of the rates given differ from Cunnington, ed *Wilts CR,* pp 290-4 (full). Reissued until 1684

1655-6 *Kent* Hindmarsh, p xvi (evidence only)

1656 *Shropshire* Hindmarsh, p xvi (reissue)

STAFFORDSHIRE Staffordshire Sessions books, Easter 1656 (full)

[SUFFOLK] Mentioned in Hindmarsh, p 223

1656-84 *Wiltshire* Hindmarsh, p xvi (reissues)

1657 NORWICH see above, p 104. Reissued until 1697

WARWICKSHIRE Arthur W. Ashby, *One hundred years of poor law administration in a Warwickshire village* (Oxford: Clarendon P, 1912), pp 170-1 (full); Sidney C. Ratcliffe and H.C. Johnson, ed *Warwick county records: Quarter Sessions order books, 1625-1674* (Warwick, 1935), IV, 11

1657-9 *Somerset* Hindmarsh, p xxx

1657-61 *Suffolk* Hindmarsh, p xvi (reissues)

1658 *Middlesex* Hindmarsh, p xvi (reissue)

YORKSHIRE NORTH RIDING *NRQSR,* VI, 3-5 (full); Eleanor Trotter, *Seventeenth century life in the country parish with special reference to local government* (Cambridge UP, 1919), pp 161-2

1658-9 *Kent* Hindmarsh, p xv

1658-9 *Shropshire* Hindmarsh, p xvi (reissues)

1660 *Staffordshire* Hindmarsh, p xvi (reissue)

1661 ESSEX Rogers, *History,* VI, 697-8 (full); Eden, *State of the poor,* III, cii

NORFOLK Norfolk QS minutes say wages were 'pub-increased

Worcestershire *HMC Various,* I, 282; Hindmarsh, pp 223, xv

1661-2 *Middlesex* Hindmarsh, p xvi (reissues)

1662 NORFOLK Norfolk QS minutes say wages were published and made'. Reissued 1663

Yorkshire West Riding *EJ,* XXIV (1914); Hindmarsh, p xxxi

1663 WORCESTERSHIRE *HMC Various,* I, 323 (full)

1663-6 *Suffolk* Hindmarsh, p xvi (reissues)

1663-7 *Kent* Hindmarsh, p xvi (evidence only)

1664-7 *Middlesex* Hindmarsh, p xvi (reissues)

1665 *Bedfordshire* Bedfordshire CRO (Renhold parish records)

1665-9 *Shropshire* Hindmarsh, p xvi (reissues)

1666 *Dorset* Hindmarsh, p xv

HEREFORDSHIRE *EHR,* LVII (1942), 115-19

Norfolk Hindmarsh, p xvi (reissue)

SOMERSET Harbin and Dawes, ed *Somerset QS records,* IV, 13 (full)

1666-72 *Herefordshire* see above pp 200-5

1667 NORTHAMPTONSHIRE *EcHR,* I (1917-28), 133-4 (full)

1668 HOLLAND (for the hundreds of Elloe, Kirton and Skirbeck only) *VCH Lincs*, II, 336 (partial). This assessment was first published in full by Pishey Thompson, *The history and antiquities of Boston* (Boston, 1856), pp 761-6, who dated it 1680 but it was drawn up at Quarter Sessions held on Thursday and Friday, 2 and 3 April 20 Charles II. Thus its correct date is 1668 (Thomas S. Willan, 'A Bedfordshire wage assessment of 1684', *Bedfordshire Historical Record Society Publications, XXV. Miscellaneous Records* (1947), 130)

SOMERSET Harbin and Dawes, ed *Somerset QS records* IV, 43 (full)

Worcestershire Hindmarsh, p xv

1669 HULL In custody of Town Clerk, Hull

[KENT] Mentioned in Hindmarsh, p xxviii

LINDSEY (all divisions) Lindsey QS minutes (Lincolnshire RO): definite evidence – 'new rates of wages agreed upon and confirmed at this session for the whole parts of Lindsey' – but no assessment has survived

SOMERSET Harbin and Dawes, ed *Somerset QS records,* IV, 61 (full)

YORKSHIRE EAST RIDING *EHR,* LII (1937), 283-9 (full)

166- MIDDLESEX Cunningham, *Growth of English industry,* III, 887-93 (full)

1669-1701 *Norwich* Hindmarsh, pp xx, xxi (reissues)

1669-73 *Middlesex* Hindmarsh, p xvi (reissues)

1670 *Caernarvonshire* Caernarvonshire RO (QS records)

Somerset Harbin and Dawes, ed *Somerset QS records,* IV, 84 (reissue)

1670-2 *Kent* Hindmarsh, p xvi (evidence only)

1671 SOMERSET Harbin and Dawes, ed *Somerset QS records,* IV, 99 (full)

1671 or 1672 YORKSHIRE WEST RIDING *EJ,* XXIV (1914), 229 (partial)

1671-5 *Dorset* Hindmarsh, p xv

1672 [CO DURHAM] Mentioned in Hindmarsh, p xxviii

Hertfordshire Hindmarsh, p xv

SOMERSET Harbin and Dawes, ed *Somerset QS records,* IV, 116 (full)

WARWICKSHIRE Ashby, *Poor law administration,* pp 172-3 (full); Ratcliffe and Johnson, ed *Warwick CR,* V, 183-4. Reissued 1764

Yorkshire East Riding Herbert Heaton, *The Yorkshire woollen and worsted industries* (Oxford UP, 1920), p 313

1673 *Blackburn (Lancs)* Charles Hardwick, *History of the borough of Preston and its environs in the county of Lancaster* (Preston, 1857), pp 405-6

BUCKINGHAMSHIRE William Le Hardy, ed *Buckinghamshire Sessions records* (Aylesbury, 1933), I, 149-50: doubtful evidence

Lincolnshire Hindmarsh, p xvi (reissue)

[NORTHAMPTONSHIRE] Mentioned in Hindmarsh, p xxvix

SOMERSET Harbin and Dawes, ed *Somerset QS records,* IV, 134 (full)

Warwickshire Ratcliffe and Johnson, ed *Warwick CR,* VI, 209-10

1674 [CO DURHAM] Mentioned in Hindmarsh, p xxviii

Hampshire Hindmarsh, p xv

Somerset Harbin and Dawes, ed *Somerset QS records,* IV, 159 (reissue)

Warwickshire Hindmarsh, p xxxi; Ratcliffe and Johnson, ed *Warwick CR,* VII, 7

1675 [NORTHAMPTONSHIRE] Mentioned in Hindmarsh, p xxvix

Somerset Harbin and Dawes, ed *Somerset QS records,* IV, 173 (reissue)

1676 BUCKINGHAMSHIRE Le Hardy, ed *Bucks Sessions records,* I, 29, 52, 71, 121 (evidence only)

[CO DURHAM] Mentioned in Hindmarsh, p xxviii

HOLLAND (work on sewers) Copy in parish chest, Sutterton

SOMERSET Harbin and Dawes, ed *Somerset QS records,* IV, 202 (full)

1676-90 *Middlesex* Hindmarsh, p xvi (reissues)

1677 BURY ST EDMUNDS (Suffolk) *East Anglian Miscellany*, I (1907), 87 (full)

[CO DURHAM] Mentioned in Hindmarsh, p xxviii

Hertfordshire *VCH Herts,* IV, 228

SOMERSET Harbin and Dawes, ed *Somerset QS records,* IV, 224 (full)

1678 [CO DURHAM] Mentioned in Hindmarsh, p xxviii

Dorset Hindmarsh, p xv

HERTFORDSHIRE Hardy, ed *Hertford CR,* I, 292 (full)

Nottinghamshire Henry Hampton Copnall, ed *Nottinghamshire county records: notes and extracts from the Nottinghamshire county records of the 17th century* (Nottingham, 1915), p 65 (reissue)

1679 *Bury St Edmunds (Suffolk)* Bury St Edmunds and West Suffolk RO

DEVONSHIRE Mentioned in William G. Hoskins, *Industry and trade in Exeter 1688-1800* (Manchester UP, 1935; University of Exeter, 1968), p 130

[CO DURHAM] Mentioned in Hindmarsh, pp xv, xxviii

NORTHAMPTONSHIRE Hindmarsh, p xvi (reissue)

YORKSHIRE EAST RIDING (Ouse and Derwent division only?) *EHR,* LII (1937), 283-9 (full)

1679-84 *Buckinghamshire* Le Hardy, ed *Bucks Sessions records,* 1, 29, 52, 71, 95, 121, 149 (reissues)

1680 *Lincolnshire* Hindmarsh, pp 223, xxix

YORKSHIRE NORTH RIDING *NRQSR,* VII, 45 (partial: 4 rates only): original missing

1681 *Hertfordshire* William Le Hardy, ed *Hertford county records, V-VIII 1619-1799* (Hertford, 1928-35), VI, 337; Hindmarsh, p xvi (reissue)

1682 BURY ST EDMUNDS (or SUFFOLK, Bury Division) Rogers, *History,* VI, 698-9 (full); Eden, *State of the poor,* III, ciii

Yorkshire North Riding Hindmarsh, p xvi (evidence only)

1683 *Hertfordshire* Hindmarsh, p xvi (evidence only)

HULL (may be for 1678 however) In custody of Town Clerk, Hull

Kent Hindmarsh, p xvi (evidence only)

Staffordshire Staffordshire CRO (QS rolls)

Surrey Hindmarsh, p xvi (evidence only)

1683-4 *Suffolk* Hindmarsh, p xvi (reissues)

1684 *Bedfordshire* *Bedfordshire Historical Record Society Publications, XXV. Miscellaneous Records* (1947), 129-37

Hertfordshire Hindmarsh, p xv

[NORTHAMPTONSHIRE] Mentioned in Hindmarsh, p xxvix

WARWICKSHIRE Rogers, *History,* VI, 699-700 (full); Ratcliff and Johnson, ed *Warwick CR,* VIII, 92-3; Eden, *State of the poor,* III, civ-cv. Almost certainly a reissue; rates are the same as the 1672 assessment except for those for the chief hind and shepherd which, as given by Rogers, seem highly improbable. Reissued 1685

Winchester Hindmarsh, p xx

YORKSHIRE WEST RIDING *EJ,* XXIV (1915), 229 (partial)

1685 *Leicester* Hindmarsh, p xx

Northamptonshire Hindmarsh, p xvi (reissue)

SOMERSET *HMC Seventh report* (1879), Appendix, pp 698-9 (full)

[STAFFORDSHIRE] Mentioned in Hindmarsh, p xv

Warwickshire *Archaeologia,* XI (1794), 208-11; Ashby, *Poor law administration,* p 173; Eden, *State of the poor,* III, civ-cv (reissue)

WILTSHIRE *HMC Various,* I, 174-5 (full); one of the rates given differs from Cunnington, ed *Wilts CR,* pp 294-6 (full). 'The same scale appears to be re-enacted up to 8 Will III [1796]' *(HMC Various,* I, 175)

1685-6 *Hertfordshire* Hindmarsh, p xvi (reissues)

1686 [KENT] Mentioned in Hindmarsh, p xxviii

Northumberland Hindmarsh, p xv

Nottinghamshire Copnall, ed *Notts CR,* p 65 (reissue)

Shropshire Hindmarsh, p xvi (reissue)

[STAFFORDSHIRE] Mentioned in Hindmarsh, p xxx

Worcestershire *HMC Various,* I, 282; Hindmarsh, p 223

1686-97 *Wiltshire* Hindmarsh, p xvi (reissue)

1687 BUCKINGHAMSHIRE Le Hardy, ed *Bucks Sessions records,* I, 227-9 (full). The summary given in *VCH Bucks,* II, 70-1 differs in some rates

HERTFORDSHIRE Le Hardy, ed *Hertford CR,* VI, 400-4 (full). Reissued 1688

[KENT] Mentioned in Hindmarsh, p xvi

OXFORDSHIRE May S. Gretton, *Oxfordshire justices of the peace in the seventeenth century* (Oxfordshire Record Society, XVI, 1934), pp lxiii-lxiv (full). Mention is made in Hindmarsh of assessments for eight of the last nine years of the century

1687-8 *Northamptonshire* Hindmarsh, p xvi (reissues)

1688 BUCKINGHAMSHIRE Le Hardy, ed *Bucks Sessions records*, I, 262 (full); Hamilton, *QS*, p 249

Lincolnshire Hindmarsh, pp 223, xv

1689 *Hertfordshire* Hindmarsh, p xvi (reissue)

Lincolnshire Hindmarsh, p xvi (reissue)

[STAFFORDSHIRE] Mentioned in Hindmarsh, p xv

1690 BUCKINGHAMSHIRE Hardy, ed *Bucks Sessions records,* I, 337 (full)

Gloucestershire Hindmarsh, p xvi (evidence only)

KESTEVEN Sidney A. Peyton, ed *Minutes of proceedings in Quarter Sessions held for the parts of Kesteven in the county of Lincoln, 1674-1695* (Lincoln Record Society, XXV, XXVI, 1931), pp 364, 376 (evidence only)

Shropshire Hindmarsh, p xvi (reissue)

1691 *Hertfordshire* Hertfordshire CRO; Le Hardy, ed *Hertford CR,* VI, 442

1691-2 *Yorkshire North Riding* see above, pp 58-9; *NRQSR,* VII, 7

1691-6 *Buckinghamshire* Le Hardy, ed *Bucks Sessions records,* I, 386, 425, 465, 504; II, 44, 87 (reissues)

1691-1701 *Oxfordshire* Oxfordshire CRO; Hindmarsh, p xxx

1692 *Bedfordshire* Bedfordshire CRO (Renhold parish records)

Hertfordshire Hertfordshire CRO; Le Hardy, ed *Hertford CR,* VI, 448

Middlesex Hindmarsh, p xvi (reissue)

Shropshire Hindmarsh, p xvi (reissue)

1692-3 *Kent* Hindmarsh, p xvi (reissues)

1692-5 *Northamptonshire* Hindmarsh, p xvi (reissues)

1693 HERTFORDSHIRE Le Hardy, ed *Hertford CR,* VI, 460 (full)

Yorkshire West Riding Hindmarsh, p xvi (reissue)

1694 *Cambridgeshire* Hindmarsh, p xvi (evidence only)

Hertfordshire Le Hardy, ed *Hertford CR,* VI, 470 (reissue)

Nottinghamshire Copnall, ed *Notts CR,* p 65; Hindmarsh, p xv

	Surrey Hindmarsh, p xv
1694-7	*Shropshire* Hindmarsh, p xvi (reissues)
1694-1700	*Middlesex* Hindmarsh, p xvi (reissues)
1695	*Hertfordshire* Hertfordshire CRO; Le Hardy, ed *Hertford CR,* VI, 476, 486, 493-4. Reissued 1696-7
	[KENT] Mentioned in Hindmarsh, p xvi
	YORKSHIRE WEST RIDING *EJ,* XXIV (1914) 229 (partial)
1695-6	*Warwickshire* Hindmarsh, p xvi (reissues)
1696-7	*Hertfordshire* Hindmarsh, p xvi (reissue)
1697	[BUCKINGHAMSHIRE] Mentioned in Hindmarsh, p xxvii; Le Hardy, ed *Bucks Sessions records,* II, 125. Reissued 1698-1700 (Le Hardy, ed *Bucks Sessions records,* II, 173, 204, 247)
1697-8	*Northamptonshire* Hindmarsh, p xvi (reissues)
1698	*Kent* Hindmarsh, p xvi (evidence only)
1699	*Cambridgeshire* Hindmarsh, p xvi (evidence only)
	Warwickshire Hindmarsh, p xvi (reissue)
	[WORCESTERSHIRE] Mentioned in Hindmarsh, p xxxi
1699-1708	*Shropshire* Hindmarsh, pp xvi, xvii (reissues)
1700	*Devonshire* Elizabeth W. Gilboy, *Wages in eighteenth century England* (Cambridge, Mass: Harvard UP, 1934), p 88
	Surrey Hindmarsh, p xv
	Yorkshire West Riding 'Pontefract QS order books; Hindmarsh, p xxxi
1700-6	*Hertfordshire* Hertfordshire CRO; Le Hardy, ed *Hertford CR,* VII, 3, 14, 26, 36, 48, 58, 68; Hindmarsh, p xvii
1701	DEVONSHIRE Gilboy, *Wages,* pp 88-9, 110-11 (partial). Reissued to 1704

	OXFORDSHIRE Gilboy, *Wages,* p 89 (partial)
	Surrey Hindmarsh, p xvii (reissue)
1701-8	*Cambridgeshire* Hindmarsh, p xviii (evidence only)
1701-8	*Northamptonshire* Hindmarsh, p xvii (reissues)
1701-10	*Buckinghamshire* Le Hardy, ed *Bucks Sessions records,* II, 288, 325, 383, 422; III, 11, 51, 94, 132, 165, 216, (reissues)
1702	*Gloucestershire* Hindmarsh, p xvii (reissue)
	Suffolk Hindmarsh, p xviii (evidence only)
1702-3	*Kent* Kent CRO
1702-11	*Middlesex* Hindmarsh, p xvii (reissues)
1703	*Suffolk* Hindmarsh, p xvii (reissue)
1703-8	*YORKSHIRE WEST RIDING* Rogers, *History,* VII, 610-14 (full) (reissues, see *EJ,* XXIV (1914) 229, 232). Reissued almost every year until 1733
1704	*Oxford* Hindmarsh, p xvii (reissue)
1705	*Worcestershire* Hindmarsh, p xvii (reissue)
1706-13	*Suffolk* Hindmarsh, p xvi (reissues)
1707	*Nottinghamshire* Kenneth T. Meaby, *Nottinghamshire: extracts from the county records of the eighteenth century* (Nottingham: Thomas Forman, 1947), p 232 (reissue)
	Worcestershire Hindmarsh, p xvii (reissue)
1708	HERTFORDSHIRE Le Hardy, ed *Hertford CR,* VII, 85 (full); Gilboy, *Wages,* p 89
	Kent Kent CRO
1708-25	*Sussex* Hindmarsh, p dxviii (evidence only)
1710	WARWICKSHIRE *VCH Warwickshire,* II, 180 (full). Only two rates differ from the 1672 assessment
1710-11	*Cambridgeshire* Hindmarsh, p xviii (evidence only)

1710-12 *Shropshire* *EJ,* IV (1894), 514

1712 *Devonshire* Gilboy, *Wages,* p 88 (reissue)

1712-24 *Northamptonshire* Hindmarsh, p xvii (reissues)

1713 DEVONSHIRE Hamilton, *QS,* p 273 (full). Probably a reissue: see Gilboy, *Wages,* p 88. Wrongly given as 1712 in Cunningham, *Growth of English industry,* p 896

1713-17 *Middlesex* Hindmarsh, p xvii (reissues)

1713-31 *Cambridgeshire* Hindmarsh, p xviii (evidence only)

1714 *Devonshire* Rogers, *History,* VII

HOLLAND Holland QS minutes (Lincolnshire CRO), Easter 1714 (full)

Norfolk Hindmarsh, p xvii (reissue)

1715-16 *Herefordshire* Hindmarsh, p xviii (evidence only)

1715-17 *Suffolk* Hindmarsh, p xvii (reissues)

1716 *Bedfordshire* Hindmarsh, p xvii

1716-22 *Devonshire* Gilboy, *Wages,* p 88 (reissues)

1717-19 *Norfolk* Hindmarsh, p xvii (reissues)

1719 KENDAL *Ars Quatuor Coronatorum,* X, 32-3 (full); *EcHR,* III (1931-2), 358 (partial)

1719-21 *Middlesex* Hindmarsh, p xvii (reissues)

1721 HULL In custody of Town Clerk, Hull

1722 *Kent* Kent CRO

YORKSHIRE EAST RIDING Definite evidence in East Riding order book

YORKSHIRE WEST RIDING Rogers, *History,* VII, 614 (merely a reissue, see *EJ,* XXIV (1914) 232)

1723 *Suffolk* Hindmarsh, p xvii (reissue)

1723-5 *Middlesex* Hindmarsh, p xvii (reissues)

1723-32 NOTTINGHAMSHIRE Jonathan D. Chambers, *Nottinghamshire in the eighteenth century* (P.S. King, 1932), pp 281-3 (partial); Meaby, *Notts CR*, pp 232-4

1724 KENT *EHR*, XLIII (1928), 405-8 (full)

NOTTINGHAMSHIRE *VCH Notts*, II, 295 (partial). Apparently not a reissue of the assessment discussed by Chambers as some of the rates given differ

NOTTINGHAMSHIRE Copnall, *Notts CR*, p 65. A different assessment from that given in *VCH Notts*, II, 295 (possibly for a different division)

SUFFOLK Evidence in Suffolk QS order book, April 1727. Reissued until 1764

1724-6 *Devonshire* Gilboy, *Wages*, p 88 (reissues)

1725 LANCASHIRE *Annals of Agriculture*, XXV (1796), 305-16 (full); Eden, *State of the poor*, III, cvi-cx; Hardwick, *Preston*, pp 410-11

Northamptonshire Printed assessment in Northamptonshire RO. Reissued until 1753

1726 *Gloucestershire* Hindmarsh, p xvii (reissue)

1727 [DORSET] Mentioned in Hindmarsh, p xxvii. Reissued 1728

Gloucestershire Hindmarsh, p xxviii

Somerset Somerset CRO

1727-8 *Kent* Kent CRO

1728 GLOUCESTERSHIRE *House of Commons Journal*, XXVII, 503, 730; *VCH Glos*, II, 161; Lipson, *Economic history*, III, 266 discusses but does not give rates; William A.S. Hewins, *English trade and finance chiefly in the seventeenth century* (Methuen, 1892), p 160 prints weavers' assessed rates for 1727; should this be 1728?

1728-9 *Norfolk* Hindmarsh, p xvii (reissues)

1728-33 *Devonshire* Gilboy, *Wages*, p 88 (reissues)

1729 [DORSET] Mentioned in Hindmarsh, p xxvii. Reissued until 1737

Kent Hindmarsh, p xvii

1730 [OXFORDSHIRE] Mentioned in Hindmarsh, p xxx but not in Gilboy, *Wages*

WARWICKSHIRE Ashby, *Poor law administration,* p 174 (full)

1730-1 *Kent* Kent CRO

1731 HOLLAND Holland QS minutes, May 1731 (evidence only)

1732 DEVONSHIRE Gilboy, *Wages,* pp 88-9, 110-11 (partial). Reissued 1733

GLOUCESTERSHIRE Rogers, *History,* VII, 623 (full)

KENT Rogers, *History,* VII, 623 (full); rates doubtful; see *EHR,* XLIII (1928) 400-1

Maidstone Kent CRO

SHROPSHIRE *EJ,* IV (1894), 516-18 (full): differs slightly from the assessment printed in R.L. Kenyon, ed. *Shropshire county records: orders of the Shropshire Quarter Sessions,* II, 79, probably due to errors in the latter. Reissued 1733-5, 1738-9

1732-7 *Canterbury* Kent CRO

1733 *Yorkshire West Riding* see above pp 190-1. Reissued until 1812

1733-9 *Cambridgeshire* Hindmarsh, p xviii (evidence only)

1734 *Maidstone* Kent CRO

1736-7 *Maidstone* Kent CRO

1738 [DORSET] Mentioned in Hindmarsh, p xxvii. Reissued until 1756

	WARWICKSHIRE Ashby, *Poor law*, p 175 (full); Bland, Brown and Tawney, *English economic history*, pp 546-7 (full). Reissued until 1755
1739	*Shropshire* see above p 190 (reissue)
1740-1	Devonshire Gilboy, *Wages*, p 88 (reissue)
1741-2	*Cambridgeshire* Hindmarsh, p xviii (evidence only)
1742	*Canterbury* Kent CRO
	Sussex Hindmarsh, pp xvii, xxx
1742-3	*Maidstone* Kent CRO
1743	*Norfolk* Hindmarsh, p xvii (reissue)
1745	*Maidstone* Kent CRO
1746	*Holland* see above 191 (reissue)
1750	DEVONSHIRE Gilboy, *Wages*, pp 88-9, 110-11 (partial)
	WESTMORLAND Westmorland CRO (Rydal manuscripts)
1752	*Canterbury* Kent CRO
1752-3	*Devonshire* Gilboy, *Wages*, p 88 (reissues)
1754	LINCOLNSHIRE Thompson, *Boston*, pp 766-7 (partial); *VCH Lincs*, II 346
1755-87	*East Sussex* East Sussex CRO
1756	GLOUCESTERSHIRE *House of Commons Journals*, XXVII, 732 (full); *VCH Glos*, II, 161
	Warwickshire Hindmarsh, p xvii
1757	[DORSET] Mentioned in Hindmarsh, p xxvii; Edward Boswell, *The civil division of the county of Dorset* (Sherborne, 1795), pp 100-1
	Yorkshire East Riding see above p 190 (reissue)
1757-72	*West Sussex* West Sussex CRO
1762-3	*Warwickshire* Hindmarsh, p xvii (reissues)

1764 *Lincoln* James W. Francis Hill, *Georgian Lincoln* (Cambridge UP, 1966), p 107

1765 BUCKINGHAMSHIRE *VCH Bucks,* II, 84 (partial)

Warwickshire *VCH Warwick,* II, 181

1777-9 Warwickshire Philip Styles, *Development of county administration in the late XVIIIth and early XIXth centuries, illustrated by the records of Warwickshire Court of Quarter Sessions, 1773-1837* (Oxford: Dugdale Society, 1934), p 7

1778 DEVONSHIRE Gilboy, *Wages,* pp 88-9, 110-11 (partial)

1779 *Monmouthshire* Monmouthshire CRO

1 *Wage regulation under the Statute of Artificers.*

2 In B.L. Hutchins, 'The regulation of wages by gilds and town authorities', *EJ,* X (1900), 404-11 and Ellen A. MacArthur, 'The regulation of wages in the seventeenth century', *EHR,* XV (1900), 445-55.

3. It has not been thought necessary in this list to mark with an asterisk, as Professor Kelsall did originally, those assessments which were not mentioned in Lipson, *Economic history,* III.

4 An updated version of Professor Kelsall's original statement made in 1938, 'within the last fifty years or so'.

5 Lipson has pointed out that the Kent and Maidstone assessments of 1563 are identical *(Economic history,* III, 515*)*.

6 The twelfth assessment in Douglas Knoop and Gwilym P. Jones, *The medieval mason* (Manchester UP, 1933), p 239 is a misprint: nothing is known of a Surrey assessment of this date and the reference they give is to the Oakham assessment of 1610.

Appendix B
Summary of the Statute of Artificers
(5 Elizabeth c.4)

Summary of the relevant sections of 5 Elizabeth c 4.

I Previous laws limiting wages have been rendered out-of-date by the advancement of prices. If the principles of such of these laws as are meet to be continued are brought together in one law, this should 'banish idleness, advance husbandry, and yield unto the hired person both in the time of scarcity and in the time of plenty a convenient proportion of wages'. All previous statutes of the hiring, departing, working, and wages of servants are therefore repealed.

II No-one to be retained for less than one whole year in any of certain enumerated occupations.

III Every person unmarried, and everyone under thirty, who has been brought up or has engaged for three years or more, in one of these occupations, and who does not fulfil a minimum property qualification and is not already retained shall, upon request, serve anyone requiring them to do so in that occupation.

IV No person to put away a servant and no servant to depart before the end of his term unless it be for some reasonable cause to be allowed before a justice, to whom any of the parties grieved shall complain. No putting away or departing at the end of term without one quarter warning given.

V Everyone between twelve and sixty not otherwise lawfully retained or coming under various exemptions is compellable to serve in husbandry by the year.

VI	Penalty on masters unduly dismissing servants, 40s; on servants unduly departing or refusing to serve, imprisonment.
VII	No servant to depart out of the parish where he was last retained without a testimonial under the seal of the constable and two other honest householders, declaring his lawful departure. This testimonial to be delivered to the servant and registered by the parson.
VIII	Penalty on a servant departing without such testimonial, imprisonment or whipping; on anyone hiring him, £5.
IX	Hours of work for day labourers laid down.
X	Penalty on artificers etc breaking contracts with employers, imprisonment and fine of £5.
XI	Justices, mayor, etc to rate wages of any workers on a time- or piece-rate basis at every general sessions within six weeks after Easter, calling unto them such discreet and grave persons as they shall think meet, and conferring together respecting the plenty or scarcity of the time and other circumstances necessary to be considered. Provisions regarding certifying of such assessments into Chancery and the proclaiming of the rates locally, as well as for reissue in lieu of reassessment.
XII	Penalty on justices absent from sessions for rating wages, £5.
XIII	Penalty for giving wages higher than the rate, ten days' imprisonment and fine of £5; for receiving the same, twenty-one days' imprisonment.
XV	At harvest time justices or constables may cause all such artificers and persons as be meet to labour to do daily harvest work. Penalty for persons refusing, imprisonment in the stocks.
XVI	Those going harvesting in other counties must have a 'temporary absence' certificate from a justice.
XVII	Mayor or two justices may compel any unmarried woman between twelve and forty not already in service to do any suitable work.

XXX Justices in their divisions to meet twice yearly to see to the execution of the statute.

XXXI Justices at such sessions to be allowed 5s per day.

Bibliography

I Manuscript sources

BEVERLEY: East Riding County Record Office
East Riding Sessions books 1647-51 and 1708 onwards
Miscellaneous Beverley Sessions papers, seventeenth and eighteenth centuries
Miscellaneous Hedon Sessions papers for some parts of the seventeenth century
Philip Constable's account book 1672-92 (Maxwell Constable papers)
Captain Bosseville's account book (relating to Penistone, West Riding) (Bosvile-Macdonald papers)

CHICHESTER: West Sussex County Record Office
Sussex QS records 1614-1772

DORCESTER: Dorset County Record Office
QS records

GLOUCESTER: County Records Office
QS records

GRIMSBY: Central Library
Miscellaneous Sessions papers covering most of the period under review

HERTFORD: County Record Office
QS records

HERTFORD: Town Clerk
Miscellaneous Sessions papers 1627 onwards

HULL: University Library
Welwick (East Riding) byelawmen's and miscellaneous accounts book 1651-1764

HULL: City Record Office
Hull Sessions books eighteenth century
Wage assessments separately filed

IPSWICH: Ipswich and East Suffolk Record Office
Suffolk QS minute books 1650-67 and 1674 onwards
Suffolk QS order books 1639-51 and 1658 onwards
Books of Precedents and Indictments (a justice's note book of the early eighteenth century)
Session rolls sampled
Miscellaneous Aldeburgh Sessions papers, late sixteenth and early seventeenth centuries
Ipswich Sessions books covering practically the whole of the period under review
Diary of Devereux Edgar, a Suffolk magistrate, early eighteenth century

IPSWICH: Public Library
Extracts transcribed from the Ipswich Sessions books by V.B. Redstone
Typescript of diary of Devereux Edgar, a Suffolk magistrate early eighteenth century

LEWES: East Sussex Record Office
QS rolls 1614-1754
Wage rate rolls 1755-87

LINCOLN: Lincolnshire Record Office
Holland and QS minutes 1673 onwards
Sessions rolls sampled
Lindsey QS minutes 1665-78, 1704-12 and 1738 onwards
Sessions rolls sampled

LINCOLN: Sir Francis Hill
Transcript of Lincoln QS minutes 1657-62 and 1668

LONDON: Greater London Record Office
Middlesex QS records

LONDON: Public Record Office
Privy Council Register

MAIDSTONE: Kent Record Office
QS records 1669-1752
New Romney borough records: Proclamations

MASHAM (West Riding): Parish Chest
Masham Churchwardens' accounts 1542-1678

MILLINGTON (East Riding): Parish Chest
Millington constables' accounts 1700 onwards

NEWPORT (Mon): County Record Office
QS records

NORTHAMPTON: Northamptonshire Record Office
QS records 1630, 1657 onwards

NORWICH: Norfolk and Norwich Record Office
Norfolk QS books of proceedings 1639-44, 1649-54, 1661-76 and 1683 onwards
Norfolk QS order books 1650 onwards
Norwich Sessions books covering practically the whole of the period under review
Sessions rolls sampled

NOTTINGHAM: County Record Office
QS records

OXFORD: Town Clerk
QS records 1687-1730

PONTEFRACT: Town Clerk
QS records

SCARBOROUGH: Town Clerk
Miscellaneous Scarborough Sessions papers seventeenth and eighteenth centuries
Miscellaneous Scarborough Corporation accounts

STAFFORD: Clerk of the Peace for Staffordshire
Staffordshire Sessions books 1619-30, 1640-67 and 1687 onwards
Sessions rolls sampled

TAUNTON: Somerset Record Office
QS records 1604-1727

THETFORD (Norfolk): Town Clerk
Thetford Sessions books 1570-90, 1610-29, 1623-9 and 1751 onwards

TOPCLIFFE (West Riding): Parish Chest
Topcliffe churchwardens' accounts 1690 onwards

TROWBRIDGE: Wiltshire County Record Office
QS records

WAKEFIELD: Clerk of the Peace for the West Riding
West Riding Sessions books sampled

WARWICK: County Record Office
QS records

II Printed material

i Sources

Acts of the Privy Council of England (1890-)

Anon, 'Sixteenth century wages' [Chester, 1575], *The Cheshire Sheaf,* 3rd series, LVIII (1963), 21-2

John C. Atkinson, ed *North Riding Quarter Sessions records, 1605-1786* (North Riding Record Society, old series, I-IX, 1884-92)

Ernest Axon, ed *Manchester Sessions, I. 1616 - 1622-23* (Lancashire and Cheshire Record Society, XLII, 1901)

W.T. Baker, ed *Records of the borough of Nottingham, being a series of extracts from the archives of the corporation of Nottingham, V* (London and Nottingham, 1900)

Thomas Barker, 'The rates of wages of servants, labourers and artificers, set down and assessed at Oakham, within the county of Rutland by the justices of peace there, the 28th day of April, Anno Domini 1610', *Archaeologia,* XI (1794), 200-7

Mary Bateson, ed *Records of the borough of Leicester* (London, 1899-1923)

Bedfordshire county records, II. Notes and extracts from the county records, being a calendar of volume 1 of the Sessions minute books, 1651 to 1660 (Bedford, 1909)

W.G. Benham, 'Essex wages in Cromwell's time' [1651], *Essex Review,* XLIII (1934), 10-11

William Blackstone, *Commentaries on the laws of England,* 4 vols. (Oxford: Clarendon P, 1765-9)

A.E. Bland, P.A. Brown and R.H. Tawney, *English economic history: select documents* (Bell, 1914)

Edward Boswell, *The civil division of the county of Dorset* (Sherborne, 1795)

John W.W. Bund, ed *Worcestershire county records: calendar of the Quarter Sessions papers,* 2 vols (Worcester Historical Society, 1899-1900)

Richard Burn, *The justice of the peace and the parish officer* (London, 2nd ed 2 vols 1756, 10th ed 2 vols 1766)

Sambrooke A.H. Burne, ed *The Staffordshire Quarter Sessions rolls,* I-IV (Kendal: William Salt Archaeological Library, 1931-6), V (Kendal: Staffordshire Record Society, 1940)

Civis (William Welfitt), *Minutes, collected from the ancient records and accounts in the Chamber of Canterbury, of transactions in that city* (Canterbury, 1800-1)

Roger Coke, *A discourse of trade* (London, 1670)

Henry Hampton Copnall, ed *Nottinghamshire county records: notes and extracts from the Nottinghamshire county records of the 17th century* (Nottingham, 1915)

J. Cowell, *The interpreter, or a booke containing the signification of words* (London, 1658)

John C. Cox, *Three centuries of Derbyshire annals as illustrated by the records of the Quarter Sessions of the county of Derby from Queen Elizabeth to Queen Victoria.* 2 vols (London and Derby, 1890)

Benjamin H. Cunnington, ed *Records of the county of Wilts: being extracts from the Quarter Sessions great rolls of the seventeenth century* (Devizes: G. Simpson, 1932)

Michael Dalton, *The countrey justice* (London, 1697)

Walter Davies, *General view of the agriculture and domestic economy of north Wales* (London, 1813)

Discourse of the common weal of this realm of England, ed Elizabeth Lamond (Cambridge UP, 1893)

Humphrey Dyson, *A booke containing all such proclamations as were published during the raigne of the late Queen Elizabeth* (London, 1618)

Robert East, ed *Extracts from records in the possession of the municipal corporation of the borough of Portsmouth and from other documents relating thereto* (Portsmouth, 1891)

Frederick M. Eden, *The state of the poor, or an history of the labouring classes of England from the conquest to the present period,* 3 vols (London, 1797)

Sir Anthony Fitzherbert, *The boke longyng to a justice of the peace* (London, 1538)

Arthur E. Gibbs, ed *The corporation records of St Albans* (St Albans, 1890)

Alexander H.A. Hamilton, *Quarter Sessions from Queen Elizabeth to Queen Anne* (Sampson Low, 1878)

Edward H.B. Harbin and M.C.B. Dawes, ed *Somerset Quarter Sessions records* (Somerset Record Society, XXIII, XXIV, XXVIII, XXXIV, 1907-19)

William J. Hardy, ed *Calendar to the records of the borough of Doncaster* (Doncaster, 1899-1903)

William J. Hardy, ed *Hertford county records: notes and extracts from the Sessions rolls, 1581-1850* (Hertford, 1905)

William J. Hardy, ed *Middlesex county records: calendar of the Sessions books, 1689 to 1709* (London, 1905)

Mary D. Harris, ed *The Coventry leet book or mayor's register* (Early English Text Society, 1907-13)

Historical Manuscripts Commission Reports (London, 1874-)

William Hudson and John C. Tingey, ed *Records of the city of Norwich,* 2 vols (Norwich: Jarrolds, 1910)

John C. Jeaffreson, ed *Middlesex county records: calendar of the sessions* County Records Society, 1886-92)

Justice's case-law (1731)

Thomas Kemp, ed *The book of John Fisher, town clerk and deputy recorder of Warwick,* 1580-88 (Warwick, 1900)

R.L. Kenyon, ed *Shropshire county records: orders of Shropshire Quarter Sessions*

William Lambard, *Eirenarcha or the offices of the justices of peace* (London, 1582)

Joseph Lee, *A vindication of a regulated enclosure* (London, 1656)

William Le Hardy, ed *Buckinghamshire Sessions records, I. 1678-1694* (Aylesbury, 1933)

William Le Hardy, ed *Hertford county records, V-VIII. 1619-1799* (Hertford, 1928-35)

William Le Hardy, ed *Calendar to the [Middlesex] Sessions records,* new series, I. 1612-14 (London, 1935)

John Lister, ed *West Riding Sessions rolls, 1597-1602* (Yorkshire Archaeological Society, Records series, III, 1888)

John Lister, ed *West Riding Sessions records, 1611-42* (Yorkshire Archaeological Society, Records series, LIV, 1915)

Gamaliel Lloyd, 'Wages of workmen in Lancashire, 1725', *Annals of Agriculture,* XXV (1796), 298-316

William O. Massingberd, ed *Court rolls of the manor of Ingoldmells in the county of Lincoln* (Spottiswoode, 1902)

Kenneth T. Meaby, *Nottinghamshire: extracts from the county records of the eighteenth century* (Nottingham: Thomas Forman, 1947)

Sir Thomas More, *Utopia* (Pitt Press Series, Cambridge UP, 1879)

Rupert H. Morris, *Chester in the Plantagenet and Tudor reigns* (Chester, 1893)

Thomas Parkyns, *A method proposed for the hiring and recording of servants in husbandry, arts, misteries etc* (Nottingham and Leicester, 1721)

Norman Penney, ed *Journal of George Fox ... eighth (bi-centenary) edition ... with revised and enlarged indexes* (Friends' Tract Association, 1901)

Sir William Petty, *A treatise of taxes and contributions* (London, 1662)

Sidney A. Peyton, ed *Minutes for proceedings in Quarter Sessions held for the parts of Kesteven in the county of Lincoln, 1674-1695* (Lincoln Record Society, XXV, XXVI, 1931)

James A. Picton, *Selections from the municipal archives and records from the 13th to the 17th century inclusive* (Liverpool, 1883-6)

Dorothy L. Powell and Hilary Jenkinson, ed *Surrey Quarter Sessions records: order book and sessions rolls, 1659-1663* (Surrey Record Society, XIII, XIV, 1934-5)

Pseudonismus, *Considerations concerning common field and enclosures* (London, 1654)

Pseudonismus, *A vindication of the considerations concerning common field and enclosures* (London, 1656)

Angelo Raine, *York civic records* (Yorkshire Archaeological Society, Record series, XCVIII, 1939-53)

Sidney C. Ratcliff and H.C. Johnson, ed *Warwick county records: Quarter Sessions order books, 1625-1674,* 5 vols (Warwick, 1935)

Conyers Read, ed *Bibliography of British history: the Tudor period, 1485-1603* (2nd ed Oxford UP, 1959)

Rural economy in York, being the farming books of H. Best, 1641 (Surtees Society, XXXIII, 1857)

William Salkeld, *Modern reports or select cases adjudged in the Courts of King's Bench, Chancery, Common Pleas and Exchequer* (London, 1700)

William Sheppard, *Whole office of the county justice of peace* (London, 1652)

Sir Thomas Smith, *De republica anglorum: the maner of gouernment or policie of the realm of England* (London, 1583)

Thomas Starkey, *A dialogue between Reginald Pole and Thomas Lupset,* ed Kathleen M. Burton (Chatto & Windus, 1948)

Robert R. Steele, ed *Tudor and Stuart proclamations, 1485-1714,* I (Oxford, 1910)

James Tait, ed *Lancashire Quarter Sessions records, I. Quarter Sessions rolls, 1590-1606* (Chetham Society, new series, LXXVII, 1917)

Richard H. Tawney and Eileen E. Power, ed *Tudor economic documents,* 3 vols (Longmans Green, 1924)

J.A. Twemlow, *Liverpool town books: proceedings of assemblies, common councils, portmoot courts &c, 1550-1862,* 2 vols (Liverpool UP, 1918-35

Joan Wake, ed *Quarter Sessions records of the county of Northampton: files for 6 Charles I and Commonwealth (AD 1630, 1657, 1657-8)* (Northamptonshire Record Society, I, 1924)

Arthur Young, ed *Annals of agriculture* (1784-1808)

ii Secondary

a books

Arthur W. Ashby, *One hundred years of poor law administration in a Warwickshire village* (Oxford: Clarendon P, 1912)

William J. Ashley, *An introduction to English economic history and theory, Part II. The end of the middle ages* (Longmans Green, 1906)

Tom Atkinson, *Elizabeth Winchester* (Faber & Faber, 1963)

Thomas G. Barnes, *Somerset 1625-1640: a county's government during the 'personal rule'* (Oxford UP, 1961)

Charles A. Beard, *Office of the justice of the peace in England* (New York: Columbia UP, 1904; Franklin, 1963)

Jonathan D. Chambers, *Nottinghamshire in the eighteenth century* (P.S. King, 1932)

George N. Clark, *The later Stuarts, 1660-1714* (Oxford: Clarendon P, 1934)

Robert Clutterbuck, *The history and antiquities of the county of Hertford compiled from parochial evidences and other authentic documents,* 3 vols (London, 1815-27)

Charles Creighton, *A history of epidemics in Britain from AD 664 to the extinction of plague,* 2 vols (Cambridge UP, 1891: Cass, 1969)

William Cunningham, *The growth of English industry and commerce* (Cambridge UP, 1882; 2nd ed in 2 vols 1907)

Godfrey Davies, *The early Stuarts, 1603-1660* (Oxford: Clarendon P, 1937)

Margaret G. Davies, *The enforcement of English apprenticeship: a study in applied mercantilism* (Cambridge, Mass: Harvard UP, 1956)

T.K. Derry, 'The enforcement of a seven years apprenticeship under the Statute of Artificers', DPhil thesis, University of Oxford, 1931

Eric G. Dowdell, *A hundred years of Quarter Sessions: the government of Middlesex from 1660 to 1760* (Cambridge UP, 1932)

Olive Jocelyn Dunlop, *English apprenticeship and child labour: a history with a supplementary section on the modern problem of juvenile labour* by O. Jocelyn Dunlop and Richard D. Denman (T. Fisher Unwin, 1912)

John S. Furley, *Quarter Sessions government in Hampshire in the seventeenth century* (Winchester: Warren, 1937)

Samuel R. Gardiner, *History of the Commonwealth and Protectorate, 1649-1660,* 3 vols (Longmans, 1894-1903)

Elizabeth W. Gilboy, *Wages in eighteenth century England* (Cambridge Mass: Harvard UP, 1934)

John H. Gleason, *The justices of the peace in England, 1558-1640: a later 'Eirenarcha'* (Oxford: Clarendon P, 1969)

May S. Gretton, *Oxfordshire justices of the peace in the seventeenth century* (Oxfordshire Record Society, XVI, 1934)

Ethel M. Hampson, *The treatment of poverty in Cambridgeshire, 1597-1834* (Cambridge UP, 1934)

Charles Hardwick, *History of the borough of Preston and its environs in the county of Lancaster* (Preston, 1857)

Herbert Heaton, *The Yorkshire woollen and worsted industries* (Oxford UP, 1920)

Eli Heckscher, *Mercantilism,* 2 vols (2nd ed Allen & Unwin, 1955)

William A.S. Hewins, *English trade and finance chiefly in the seventeenth century* (Methuen, 1892)

James W. Francis Hill, *Tudor and Stuart Lincoln* (Cambridge UP, 1956)

James W. Francis Hill, *Georgian Lincoln* (Cambridge UP, 1966)

Nora Hindmarsh, 'The assessment of wages by the justices of the peace, 1563-1700', PhD thesis, University of London, 1932

William S. Holdsworth, *A history of English law,* IV, VI, X, XI (Methuen, 1924, 1938)

William G. Hoskins, *Industry and trade in Exeter, 1688-1800* (Manchester UP, 1935; University of Exeter, 1968)

Paul L. Hughes and James F. Larkin, *Tudor royal proclamations,* 3 vols (New Haven, Conn: Yale UP, 1969)

Edward B. Jupp, *An historical account of the Worshipful Company of Carpenters of the city of London* (London, 1848)

Douglas Knoop and Gwilym P. Jones, *The medieval mason* (Manchester UP, 1933)

Douglas Knoop and Gwilym P. Jones, *The London mason in the seventeenth century* (Manchester UP, 1935)

Stella Kramer, *English craft gilds: studies in their progress and decline* (New York: Columbia UP, 1927)

Ellen M. Leonard, *The early history of English poor relief* (Cambridge UP, 1900)

Ephraim Lipson, *Economic history of England, III. The age of mercantilism* (3rd ed Black, 1943)

Dorothy Marshall, *The English poor in the eighteenth century: a study in social and administrative history* (Routledge, 1926, 1969)

Esther Moir, *The justice of the peace* (Penguin, 1969)

Bertha H. Putnam, *The enforcement of the statutes of labourers during the first decade after the Black Death, 1349-1359* (New York: Columbia UP, 1891)

Bertha H. Putnam, *Early treatises on the practice of the justices of the peace in the fifteenth and sixteenth centuries* (Oxford: Clarendon P, 1924

George Roberts, *The social history of the people of the southern counties of England in past centuries* (Longmans, 1856)

James E. Thorold Rogers, *A history of agriculture and prices in England* III-VII (Oxford: Clarendon P, 1882-1902)

James E. Thorold Rogers, *Six centuries of work and wages* (10th ed T. Fisher Unwin, 1909)

Gustaf F. Steffen, *Studien zur Geschichte der englischen Lohnarbeiter* 3 vols (Stuttgart, 1901-5)

Philip Styles, *Development of county administration in the late XVIIIth and early XIXth centuries, illustrated by the records of the Warwickshire Court of Quarter Sessions, 1773-1837* (Oxford: Dugdale Society, 1934)

Richard H. Tawney, *The agrarian problem in the sixteenth century* (Longmans, 1912; New York: Harper & Row, 1967)

Pishey Thompson, *The history and antiquities of Boston* (Boston, 1856)

Eleanor Trotter, *Seventeenth century life in the country parish, with special reference to local government* (Cambridge UP, 1919)

George Unwin, *Industrial organisation in the sixteenth and seventeenth centuries* (Oxford: Clarendon P, 1904)

Victoria histories of the counties of England (Institute of Historical Research, 1900-)

Sidney and Beatrice Webb, *English local government: the parish and the county* (Longmans, 1924)

Sidney and Beatrice Webb, *The history of trade unionism: revised edition extended to 1920* (Longmans Green, 1926)

b articles

William A.J. Archbold, 'An assessment of wages for 1630', *English Historical Review,* XII (1897), 307-11

Fairless Barber, 'The West Riding Sessions rolls', *Yorkshire Archaeological and Geographical Journal,* V (1877-8), 362-405

Philip S. Belasco, 'Note on the labour exchange idea in the seventeenth century', *Economic History,* I (1926-29), 275-9

Maurice W. Beresford, 'The common informer, the penal statutes and economic regulation', *Economic History Review,* 2nd series, X (1957), 221-39

William H. Beveridge, 'A seventeenth-century labour exchange', *Economic Journal,* XXIV (1914), 371-6

William H. Beveridge, 'Westminster wages in the manorial era', *Economic History Review,* 2nd series, VIII (1955), 18-35

Stanley T. Bindoff, 'The making of the Statute of Artificers' in Stanley T. Bindoff, Joel Hurstfield and C.H. Williams, ed *Elizabethan government and society: essays presented to Sir John Neale* (Athlone Press, 1961), pp 56-94

Ernest H. Phelps Brown and Sheila V. Hopkins, 'Seven centuries of building wages', *Economica,* new series, XXII (1955), 195-206

William Cunningham, 'Dr Cunningham and his critics', *Economic Journal,* IV (1894), 508-18

Marcus P. Dare, 'Old time law keepers, being a study of the constables of Ayleston, Co Leics and their accounts', *Associated Architectural Societies Reports,* XXXVIII (1926), 106-65

Geoffrey R. Elton, 'Informing for profit; a sidelight on Tudor methods of law enforcement', *Cambridge Historical Journal,* XI (1954), 149-67

Frederick J. Fisher, 'Commercial trends and policy in sixteenth-century England', *Economic History Review,* X (1940), 95-117 reprinted in Eleanora M. Carus-Wilson, ed *Essays in economic history,* I (Arnold, 1954), pp 152-72

Frederick J. Fisher, 'Influenza and inflation in Tudor England', *Economic History Review,* 2nd series, XVIII (1965), 120-9

Margaret R. Gay, 'Aspects of Elizabethan apprenticeship' in *Facts and factors in economic history* (Cambridge, Mass: Harvard UP, 1932), pp 134-63

Francis F. Giraud, 'Wages in AD 1621 and innkeepers' bills in AD 1668', *Archaeologia Cantiana,* XVI (1886), 270-4

Theodore E. Gregory, 'The economics of employment in England 1660-1713', *Economica,* I (1921), 37-51

Herbert Heaton, 'The assessment of wages in the West Riding of Yorkshire in the seventeenth and eighteenth centuries', *Economic Journal,* XXIV (1914), 218-35

William A.S. Hewins, 'The regulation of wages by the justices of the peace', *Economic Journal,* VIII (1898), 340-6

B.L. Hutchins, 'The regulation of wages by gilds and town authorities', *Economic Journal,* X (1900), 404-11

Roger K. Kelsall, 'Two East Yorkshire wage assessments 1669, 1679', *English Historical Review,* LII

Douglas Knoop and Gwilym P. Jones, 'Overtime in the age of Henry VIII', *Economic History,* IV (1938), 13-20

Ellen M. Leonard, 'The relief of the poor by the state regulation of wages', *English Historical Review,* XIII (1898), 91-3

Ellen M. McArthur, 'The boke longyng to a justice of the peace and the assessment of wages', *English Historical Review,* IX (1894), 305-14, 554

Ellen M. McArthur, 'A fifteenth-century assessment of wages', *English Historical Review,* XIII (1898), 299-302

Ellen M. McArthur, 'The regulation of wages in the sixteenth century', *English Historical Review,* XV (1900), 445-55

Thomas C. Mendenhall, 'A Merioneth wage assessment of 1601', *Journal of the Merioneth Historical Record Society,* II (1955), 204-8

Walter E. Minchinton, 'The beginnings of trade unionism in the Gloucestershire woollen industry', *Transactions of the Bristol and Gloucestershire Archaeological Society,* LXX (1951), 126-41

Walter E. Minchinton, 'The petitions of the weavers and clothiers of Gloucestershire in 1756', *Transactions of the Bristol and Gloucestershire Archaeological Society,* LXXIII (1954), 216-27

Frank A. Norman and L. Gordon Lee, 'A further note on labour exchanges in the seventeenth century', *Economic History,* I (1926-29), 399-404

Bertha H. Putnam, 'Lambard's "Eirenarcha" and a Kent wage assessment of 1563', *English Historical Review,* XLI (1926), 260-73

Bertha H. Putnam, 'Northamptonshire wage assessments of 1560 and

1667', *Economic History Review,* I (1927-8), 124-34

Michael Reed, 'Early seventeenth century wage assessments for the borough of Shrewsbury', *Transactions of the Salop Archaeological Society,* LVII (1956), 136-42

Richard A. Roberts, 'The borough business of a Suffolk town (Orford) 1559-1660', *Royal Historical Society Transactions,* 4th series, XIV (1931), 95-102

Daphne Simon, 'Master and servant' in John Saville, ed *Democracy and the labour movement: essays in honour of Dona Torr* (Lawrence & Wishart, 1954), pp 160-200

John C. Tingey, 'An assessment of wages for the county of Norfolk in 1610', *English Historical Review,* XIII (1898), 522-7

Thomas S. Willan, 'A Bedfordshire wage assessment of 1684', *Bedfordshire Historical Record Society Publications, XXV. Miscellaneous records* (1947), 129-37

Elizabeth L. Waterman, 'Some new evidence on wage assessments in the eighteenth century', *English Historical Review,* XLIII (1927), 398-408

Charles Eveleigh Woodruff, 'Wages paid at Maidstone in Queen Elizabeth's reign', *Archaeologia Cantiana,* XXII (1897), 316-19

Donald M. Woodward, 'The assessment of wages by justices of the peace, 1563-1814', *The Local Historian,* VIII (1969), 293-9

Index